The Story of a

Anna Howard Shaw and
Elizabeth Garver Jordan

Alpha Editions

This edition published in 2024

ISBN : 9789362921499

Design and Setting By
Alpha Editions
www.alphaedis.com
Email - info@alphaedis.com

Contents

I. FIRST MEMORIES

My father's ancestors were the Shaws of Rothiemurchus, in Scotland, and the ruins of their castle may still be seen on the island of Loch-an-Eilan, in the northern Highlands. It was never the picturesque castle of song and story, this home of the fighting Shaws, but an austere fortress, probably built in Roman times; and even to-day the crumbling walls which alone are left of it show traces of the relentless assaults upon them. Of these the last and the most successful were made in the seventeenth century by the Grants and Rob Roy; and it was into the hands of the Grants that the Shaw fortress finally fell, about 1700, after almost a hundred years of ceaseless warfare.

It gives me no pleasure to read the grisly details of their struggles, but I confess to a certain satisfaction in the knowledge that my ancestors made a good showing in the defense of what was theirs. Beyond doubt they were brave fighters and strong men. There were other sides to their natures, however, which the high lights of history throw up less appealingly. As an instance, we have in the family chronicles the blood-stained page of Allen Shaw, the oldest son of the last Lady Shaw who lived in the fortress. It appears that when the father of this young man died, about 1560, his mother married again, to the intense disapproval of her son. For some time after the marriage he made no open revolt against the new-comer in the domestic circle; but finally, on the pretext that his dog had been attacked by his stepfather, he forced a quarrel with the older man and the two fought a duel with swords, after which the victorious Allen showed a sad lack of chivalry. He not only killed his stepfather, but he cut off that gentleman's head and bore it to his mother in her bedchamber—an action which was considered, even in that tolerant age, to be carrying filial resentment too far.

Probably Allen regretted it. Certainly he paid a high penalty for it, and his clan suffered with him. He was outlawed and fled, only to be hunted down for months, and finally captured and executed by one of the Grants, who, in further virtuous disapproval of Allen's act, seized and held the Shaw stronghold. The other Shaws of the clan fought long and ably for its recovery, but though they were helped by their kinsmen, the Mackintoshes, and though good Scotch blood dyed the gray walls of the fortress for many generations, the castle never again came into the hands of the Shaws. It still entails certain obligations for the Grants, however, and one of these is to give the King of England a snowball whenever he visits Loch-an-Eilan!

As the years passed the Shaw clan scattered. Many Shaws are still to be found in the Mackintosh country and throughout southern Scotland.

Others went to England, and it was from this latter branch that my father sprang. His name was Thomas Shaw, and he was the younger son of a gentleman—a word which in those days seemed to define a man who devoted his time largely to gambling and horse-racing. My grandfather, like his father before him, was true to the traditions of his time and class. Quite naturally and simply he squandered all he had, and died abruptly, leaving his wife and two sons penniless. They were not, however, a helpless band. They, too, had their traditions, handed down by the fighting Shaws. Peter, the older son, became a soldier, and died bravely in the Crimean War. My father, through some outside influence, turned his attention to trade, learning to stain and emboss wallpaper by hand, and developing this work until he became the recognized expert in his field. Indeed, he progressed until he himself checked his rise by inventing a machine that made his handwork unnecessary. His employer at once claimed and utilized this invention, to which, by the laws of those days, he was entitled, and thus the cornerstone on which my father had expected to build a fortune proved the rock on which his career was wrecked. But that was years later, in America, and many other things had happened first.

For one, he had temporarily dropped his trade and gone into the flour-and-grain business; and, for another, he had married my mother. She was the daughter of a Scotch couple who had come to England and settled in Alnwick, in Northumberland County. Her father, James Stott, was the driver of the royal-mail stage between Alnwick and Newcastle, and his accidental death while he was still a young man left my grandmother and her eight children almost destitute. She was immediately given a position in the castle of the Duke of Northumberland, and her sons were educated in the duke's school, while her daughters were entered in the school of the duchess.

My thoughts dwell lovingly on this grandmother, Nicolas Grant Stott, for she was a remarkable woman, with a dauntless soul and progressive ideas far in advance of her time. She was one of the first Unitarians in England, and years before any thought of woman suffrage entered the minds of her country-women she refused to pay tithes to the support of the Church of England—an action which precipitated a long-drawn-out conflict between her and the law. In those days it was customary to assess tithes on every pane of glass in a window, and a portion of the money thus collected went to the support of the Church. Year after year my intrepid grandmother refused to pay these assessments, and year after year she sat pensively upon her door-step, watching articles of her furniture being sold for money to pay her tithes. It must have been an impressive picture, and it was one with which the community became thoroughly familiar, as the determined old lady never won her fight and never abandoned it. She had at least the comfort of public sympathy, for she was by far the most popular woman in the countryside. Her neighbors admired her courage; perhaps they appreciated still more what she did for them, for she spent all her leisure in the homes of the very poor, mending their clothing and teaching them to sew. Also, she left behind her a path of cleanliness as definite as the line of foam that follows a ship; for it soon became known among her protegees that Nicolas Stott was as much opposed to dirt as she was to the payment of tithes.

She kept her children in the schools of the duke and duchess until they had completed the entire course open to them. A hundred times, and among many new scenes and strange people, I have heard my mother describe her own experiences as a pupil. All the children of the dependents of the castle were expected to leave school at fourteen years of age. During their course they were not allowed to study geography, because, in the sage opinion of their elders, knowledge of foreign lands might make them discontented and inclined to wander. Neither was composition encouraged—that might lead to the writing of love-notes! But they were permitted to absorb all the reading and arithmetic their little brains could hold, while the art of sewing was not only encouraged, but proficiency in it was stimulated by the award of prizes. My mother, being a rather precocious young person, graduated at thirteen and carried off the first prize. The garment she made was a linen chemise for the duchess, and the little needlewoman had embroidered on it, with her own hair, the august lady's coat of arms. The offering must have been appreciated, for my mother's story always ended with the same words, uttered with the same air of gentle pride, "And the duchess gave me with her own hands my Bible and my mug of beer!" She never saw anything amusing in this association of gifts, and I always stood behind her when she told the incident, that she might not see the disrespectful mirth it aroused in me.

My father and mother met in Alnwick, and were married in February, 1835. Ten years after his marriage father was forced into bankruptcy by the passage of the corn law, and to meet the obligations attending his failure he and my mother sold practically everything they possessed—their home, even their furniture. Their little sons, who were away at school, were brought home, and the family expenses were cut down to the barest margin; but all these sacrifices paid only part of the debts. My mother, finding that her early gift had a market value, took in sewing. Father went to work on a small salary, and both my parents saved every penny they could lay aside, with the desperate determination to pay their remaining debts. It was a long struggle and a painful one, but they finally won it. Before they had done so, however, and during their bleakest days, their baby died, and my mother, like her mother before her, paid the penalty of being outside the fold of the Church of England. She, too, was a Unitarian, and her baby, therefore, could not be laid in any consecrated burial-ground in her neighborhood. She had either to bury it in the Potter's Field, with criminals, suicides, and paupers, or to take it by stage-coach to Alnwick, twenty miles away, and leave it in the little Unitarian churchyard where, after her strenuous life, Nicolas Stott now lay in peace. She made the dreary journey alone, with the dear burden across her lap.

In 1846, my parents went to London. There they did not linger long, for the big, indifferent city had nothing to offer them. They moved to Newcastle-on-Tyne, and here I was born, on the fourteenth day of February, in 1847. Three boys and two girls had preceded me in the family circle, and when I was two years old my younger sister came. We were little better off in Newcastle than in London, and now my father began to dream the great dream of those days. He would go to America. Surely, he felt, in that land of infinite promise all would be well with him and his. He waited for the final payment of his debts and for my younger sister's birth. Then he bade us good-by and sailed away to make an American home for us; and in the spring of 1851 my mother followed him with her six children, starting from Liverpool in a sailing-vessel, the John Jacob Westervelt.

I was then little more than four years old, and the first vivid memory I have is that of being on shipboard and having a mighty wave roll over me. I was lying on what seemed to be an enormous red box under a hatchway, and the water poured from above, almost drowning me. This was the beginning of a storm which raged for days, and I still have of it a confused memory, a sort of nightmare, in which strange horrors figure, and which to this day haunts me at intervals when I am on the sea. The thing that stands out most strongly during that period is the white face of my mother, ill in her berth. We were with five hundred emigrants on the lowest deck of the ship but one, and as the storm grew wilder an unreasoning terror filled our fellow-passengers. Too ill to protect her helpless brood, my mother saw us carried away from her for hours at a time, on the crests of waves of panic that sometimes approached her and sometimes receded, as they swept through the black hole in which we found ourselves when the hatches were nailed down. No madhouse, I am sure, could throw more hideous pictures on the screen of life than those which met our childish eyes during the appalling three days of the storm. Our one comfort was the knowledge that our mother was not afraid. She was desperately ill, but when we were able to reach her, to cling close to her for a blessed interval, she was still the sure refuge she had always been.

On the second day the masts went down, and on the third day the disabled ship, which now had sprung a leak and was rolling helplessly in the trough of the sea, was rescued by another ship and towed back to Queenstown, the nearest port. The passengers, relieved of their anxieties, went from their extreme of fear to an equal extreme of drunken celebration. They laughed, sang, and danced, but when we reached the shore many of them returned to the homes they had left, declaring that they had had enough of the ocean. We, however, remained on the ship until she was repaired, and then sailed on her again. We were too poor to return home; indeed, we had no home to which we could return. We were even too poor to live ashore. But we made some penny excursions in the little boats that plied back and forth, and to us children at least the weeks of waiting were not without interest. Among other places we visited Spike Island, where the convicts were, and for hours we watched the dreary shuttle of labor swing back and forth as the convicts carried pails of water from one side of the island, only to empty them into the sea at the other side. It was merely "busy work," to keep them occupied at hard labor; but even then I must have felt some dim sense of the irony of it, for I have remembered it vividly all these years.

Our second voyage on the John Jacob Westervelt was a very different experience from the first. By day a glorious sun shone overhead; by night we had the moon and stars, as well as the racing waves we never wearied of watching. For some reason, probably because of my intense admiration for them, which I showed with unmaidenly frankness, I became the special pet of the sailors. They taught me to sing their songs as they hauled on their ropes, and I recall, as if I had learned it yesterday, one pleasing ditty:

Haul on the bow-line,

Kitty is my darling,

Haul on the bow-line,

The bow-line—HAUL!

When I sang "haul" all the sailors pulled their hardest, and I had an exhilarating sense of sharing in their labors. As a return for my service of song the men kept my little apron full of ship sugar—very black stuff and probably very bad for me; but I ate an astonishing amount of it during that voyage, and, so far as I remember, felt no ill effects.

The next thing I recall is being seriously scalded. I was at the foot of a ladder up which a sailor was carrying a great pot of hot coffee. He slipped, and the boiling liquid poured down on me. I must have had some bad days after that, for I was terribly burned, but they are mercifully vague. My next vivid impression is of seeing land, which we sighted at sunset, and I remember very distinctly just how it looked. It has never looked the same since. The western sky was a mass of crimson and gold clouds, which took on the shapes of strange and beautiful things. To me it seemed that we were entering heaven. I remember also the doctors coming on board to examine us, and I can still see a line of big Irishmen standing very straight and holding out their tongues for inspection. To a little girl only four years old their huge, open mouths looked appalling.

On landing a grievous disappointment awaited us; my father did not meet us. He was in New Bedford, Massachusetts, nursing his grief and preparing to return to England, for he had been told that the John Jacob Westervelt had been lost at sea with every soul on board. One of the missionaries who met the ship took us under his wing and conducted us to a little hotel, where we remained until father had received his incredible news and rushed to New York. He could hardly believe that we were really restored to him; and even now, through the mists of more than half a century, I can still see the expression in his wet eyes as he picked me up and tossed me into the air.

I can see, too, the toys he brought me—a little saw and a hatchet, which became the dearest treasures of my childish days. They were fatidical gifts, that saw and hatchet; in the years ahead of me I was to use tools as well as my brothers did, as I proved when I helped to build our frontier home.

We went to New Bedford with father, who had found work there at his old trade; and here I laid the foundations of my first childhood friendship, not with another child, but with my next-door neighbor, a ship-builder. Morning after morning this man swung me on his big shoulder and took me to his shipyard, where my hatchet and saw had violent exercise as I imitated the workers around me. Discovering that my tiny petticoats were in my way, my new friend had a little boy's suit made for me; and thus emancipated, at this tender age, I worked unwearyingly at his side all day long and day after day. No doubt it was due to him that I did not casually saw off a few of my toes and fingers. Certainly I smashed them often enough with blows of my dull but active hatchet. I was very, very busy; and I have always maintained that I began to earn my share of the family's living at the age of five—for in return for the delights of my society, which seemed never to pall upon him, my new friend allowed my brothers to carry home from the shipyard all the wood my mother could use.

We remained in New Bedford less than a year, for in the spring of 1852 my father made another change, taking his family to Lawrence, Massachusetts, where we lived until 1859. The years in Lawrence were interesting and formative ones. At the tender age of nine and ten I became interested in the Abolition movement. We were Unitarians, and General Oliver and many of the prominent citizens of Lawrence belonged to the Unitarian Church. We knew Robert Shaw, who led the first negro regiment, and Judge Storrow, one of the leading New England judges of his time, as well as the Cabots and George A. Walton, who was the author of Walton's Arithmetic and head of the Lawrence schools. Outbursts of war talk thrilled me, and occasionally I had a little adventure of my own, as when one day, in visiting our cellar, I heard a noise in the coal-bin. I investigated and discovered a negro woman concealed there. I had been reading Uncle Tom's Cabin, as well as listening to the conversation of my elders, so I was vastly stirred over the negro question. I raced up-stairs in a condition of awe-struck and quivering excitement, which my mother promptly suppressed by sending me to bed. No doubt she questioned my youthful discretion, for she almost convinced me that I had seen nothing at all—almost, but not quite; and she wisely kept me close to her for several days, until the escaped slave my father was hiding was safely out of the house and away. Discovery of this serious offense might have borne grave results for him.

It was in Lawrence, too, that I received and spent my first twenty-five cents. I used an entire day in doing this, and the occasion was one of the most delightful and memorable of my life. It was the Fourth of July, and I was dressed in white and rode in a procession. My sister Mary, who also graced the procession, had also been given twenty-five cents; and during the parade, when, for obvious reasons, we were unable to break ranks and spend our wealth, the consciousness of it lay heavily upon us. When we finally began our shopping the first place we visited was a candy store, and I recall distinctly that we forced the weary proprietor to take down and show us every jar in the place before we spent one penny. The first banana I ever ate was purchased that day, and I hesitated over it a long time. Its cost was five cents, and in view of that large expenditure, the eating of the fruit, I was afraid, would be too brief a joy. I bought it, however, and the experience developed into a tragedy, for, not knowing enough to peel the banana, I bit through skin and pulp alike, as if I were eating an apple, and then burst into ears of disappointment. The beautiful conduct of my sister Mary shines down through the years. She, wise child, had taken no chances with the unknown; but now, moved by my despair, she bought half of my banana, and we divided the fruit, the loss, and the lesson. Fate, moreover, had another turn of the screw for us, for, after Mary had taken a bite of it, we gave what was left of the banana to a boy who stood near us and who knew how to eat it; and not even the large amount of candy in our sticky hands enabled us to regard with calmness the subsequent happiness of that little boy.

Another experience with fruit in Lawrence illustrates the ideas of my mother and the character of the training she gave her children. Our neighbors, the Cabots, were one day giving a great garden party, and my sister was helping to pick strawberries for the occasion. When I was going home from school I passed the berry-patches and stopped to speak to my sister, who at once presented me with two strawberries. She said Mrs.

Cabot had told her to eat all she wanted, but that she would eat two less than she wanted and give those two to me. To my mind, the suggestion was generous and proper; in my life strawberries were rare. I ate one berry, and then, overcome by an ambition to be generous also, took the other berry home to my mother, telling her how I had got it. To my chagrin, mother was deeply shocked. She told me that the transaction was all wrong, and she made me take back the berry and explain the matter to Mrs. Cabot. By the time I reached that generous lady the berry was the worse for its journey, and so was I. I was only nine years old and very sensitive. It was clear to me that I could hardly live through the humiliation of the confession, and it was indeed a bitter experience the worst, I think, in my young life, though Mrs. Cabot was both sympathetic and understanding. She kissed me, and sent a quart of strawberries to my mother; but for a long time afterward I could not meet her kind eyes, for I believed that in her heart she thought me a thief.

My second friendship, and one which had a strong influence on my after-life, was formed in Lawrence. I was not more than ten years old when I met this new friend, but the memory of her in after-years, and the impression she had made on my susceptible young mind, led me first into the ministry, next into medicine, and finally into suffrage-work. Living next door to us, on Prospect Hill, was a beautiful and mysterious woman. All we children knew of her was that she was a vivid and romantic figure, who seemed to have no friends and of whom our elders spoke in whispers or not at all. To me she was a princess in a fairy-tale, for she rode a white horse and wore a blue velvet riding-habit with a blue velvet hat and a picturesquely drooping white plume. I soon learned at what hours she went forth to ride, and I used to hover around our gate for the joy of seeing her mount and gallop away. I realized that there was something unusual about her house, and I had an idea that the prince was waiting for her somewhere in the far distance, and that for the time at least she had escaped the ogre in the castle she left behind. I was wrong about the prince, but right about the ogre. It was only when my unhappy lady left her castle that she was free.

Very soon she noticed me. Possibly she saw the adoration in my childish eyes. She began to nod and smile at me, and then to speak to me, but at first I was almost afraid to answer her. There were stories now among the children that the house was haunted, and that by night a ghost walked there and in the grounds. I felt an extraordinary interest in the ghost, and I spent hours peering through our picket fence, trying to catch a glimpse of it; but I hesitated to be on terms of neighborly intimacy with one who dwelt with ghosts.

One day the mysterious lady bent and kissed me. Then, straightening up, she looked at me queerly and said: "Go and tell your mother I did that."

There was something very compelling in her manner. I knew at once that I must tell my mother what she had done, and I ran into our house and did so. While my mother was considering the problem the situation presented, for she knew the character of the house next door, a note was handed in to her—a very pathetic little note from my mysterious lady, asking my mother to let me come and see her. Long afterward mother showed it to me. It ended with the words: "She will see no one but me. No harm shall come to her. Trust me."

That night my parents talked the matter over and decided to let me go. Probably they felt that the slave next door was as much to be pitied as the escaped-negro slaves they so often harbored in our home. I made my visit, which was the first of many, and a strange friendship began and developed between the woman of the town and the little girl she loved. Some of those visits I remember as vividly as if I had made them yesterday. There was never the slightest suggestion during any of them of things I should not see or hear, for while I was with her my hostess became a child again, and we played together like children. She had wonderful toys for me, and pictures and books; but the thing I loved best of all and played with for hours was a little stuffed hen which she told me had been her dearest treasure when she was a child at home. She had also a stuffed puppy, and she once mentioned that those two things alone were left of her life as a little girl. Besides the toys and books and pictures, she gave me ice-cream and cake, and told me fairy-tales. She had a wonderful understanding of what a child likes. There were half a dozen women in the house with her, but I saw none of them nor any of the men who came.

Once, when we had become very good friends indeed and my early shyness had departed, I found courage to ask her where the ghost was—the ghost that haunted her house. I can still see the look in her eyes as they met mine. She told me the ghost lived in her heart, and that she did not like to talk about it, and that we must not speak of it again. After that I never mentioned it, but I was more deeply interested than ever, for a ghost that lived in a heart was a new kind of ghost to me at that time, though I have met many of them since then. During all our intercourse my mother never entered the house next door, nor did my mysterious lady enter our home; but she constantly sent my mother secret gifts for the poor and the sick of the neighborhood, and she was always the first to offer help for those who were in trouble. Many years afterward mother told me she was the most generous woman she had ever known, and that she had a rarely beautiful nature. Our departure for Michigan broke up the friendship, but I have never forgotten her; and whenever, in my later work as minister, physician, and suffragist, I have been able to help women of the class to which she belonged, I have mentally offered that help for credit in the tragic ledger of her life, in which the clean and the blotted pages were so strange a contrast.

One more incident of Lawrence I must describe before I leave that city behind me, as we left it for ever in 1859. While we were still there a number of Lawrence men decided to go West, and amid great public excitement they departed in a body for Kansas, where they founded the town of Lawrence in that state. I recall distinctly the public interest which attended their going, and the feeling every one seemed to have that they were passing forever out of the civilized world. Their farewells to their friends were eternal; no one expected to see them again, and my small brain grew dizzy as I tried to imagine a place so remote as their destination. It was, I finally decided, at the uttermost ends of the earth, and it seemed quite possible that the brave adventurers who reached it might then drop off into space. Fifty years later I was talking to a California girl who complained lightly of the monotony of a climate where the sun shone and the flowers bloomed all the year around. "But I had a delightful change last year," she added, with animation. "I went East for the winter."

"To New York?" I asked.

"No," corrected the California girl, easily, "to Lawrence, Kansas."

Nothing, I think, has ever made me feel quite so old as that remark. That in my life, not yet, to me at least, a long one, I should see such an arc described seemed actually oppressive until I realized that, after all, the arc was merely a rainbow of time showing how gloriously realized were the hopes of the Lawrence pioneers.

The move to Michigan meant a complete upheaval in our lives. In Lawrence we had around us the fine flower of New England civilization. We children went to school; our parents, though they were in very humble circumstances, were associated with the leading spirits and the big movements of the day. When we went to Michigan we went to the wilderness, to the wild pioneer life of those times, and we were all old enough to keenly feel the change.

My father was one of a number of Englishmen who took up tracts in the northern forests of Michigan, with the old dream of establishing a colony there. None of these men had the least practical knowledge of farming. They were city men or followers of trades which had no connection with farm life. They went straight into the thick timber-land, instead of going to the rich and waiting prairies, and they crowned this initial mistake by cutting down the splendid timber instead of letting it stand. Thus bird's-eye maple and other beautiful woods were used as fire-wood and in the construction of rude cabins, and the greatest asset of the pioneers was ignored.

Father preceded us to the Michigan woods, and there, with his oldest son, James, took up a claim. They cleared a space in the wilderness just large enough for a log cabin, and put up the bare walls of the cabin itself. Then father returned to Lawrence and his work, leaving James behind. A few months later (this was in 1859), my mother, my two sisters, Eleanor and Mary, my youngest brother, Henry, eight years of age, and I, then twelve, went to Michigan to work on and hold down the claim while father, for eighteen months longer, stayed on in Lawrence, sending us such remittances as he could. His second and third sons, John and Thomas, remained in the East with him.

Every detail of our journey through the wilderness is clear in my mind. At that time the railroad terminated at Grand Rapids, Michigan, and we covered the remaining distance—about one hundred miles—by wagon, riding through a dense and often trackless forest. My brother James met us at Grand Rapids with what, in those days, was called a lumber-wagon, but which had a horrible resemblance to a vehicle from the health department. My sisters and I gave it one cold look and turned from it; we were so pained by its appearance that we refused to ride in it through the town. Instead, we started off on foot, trying to look as if we had no association with it, and we climbed into the unwieldy vehicle only when the city streets were far behind us. Every available inch of space in the wagon was filled with bedding and provisions. As yet we had no furniture; we were to make that for ourselves when we reached our cabin; and there was so little room for us to ride that we children walked by turns, while James, from the beginning of the journey to its end, seven days later, led our weary horses.

To my mother, who was never strong, the whole experience must have been a nightmare of suffering and stoical endurance. For us children there were compensations. The expedition took on the character of a high adventure, in which we sometimes had shelter and sometimes failed to find it, sometimes were fed, but often went hungry. We forded innumerable streams, the wheels of the heavy wagon sinking so deeply into the stream-beds that we often had to empty our load before we could get them out again. Fallen trees lay across our paths, rivers caused long detours, while again and again we lost our way or were turned aside by impenetrable forest tangles.

Our first day's journey covered less than eight miles, and that night we stopped at a farm-house which was the last bit of civilization we saw. Early the next morning we were off again, making the slow progress due to the rough roads and our heavy load. At night we stopped at a place called

Thomas's Inn, only to be told by the woman who kept it that there was nothing in the house to eat. Her husband, she said, had gone "outside" (to Grand Rapids) to get some flour, and had not returned—but she added that we could spend the night, if we chose, and enjoy shelter, if not food. We had provisions in our wagon, so we wearily entered, after my brother had got out some of our pork and opened a barrel of flour. With this help the woman made some biscuits, which were so green that my poor mother could not eat them. She had admitted to us that the one thing she had in the house was saleratus, and she had used this ingredient with an unsparing hand. When the meal was eaten she broke the further news that there were no beds.

"The old woman can sleep with me," she suggested, "and the girls can sleep on the floor. The boys will have to go to the barn." She and her bed were not especially attractive, and mother decided to lie on the floor with us. We had taken our bedding from the wagon, and we slept very well; but though she was usually superior to small annoyances, I think my mother resented being called an "old woman." She must have felt like one that night, but she was only about forty-eight years of age.

At dawn the next morning we resumed our journey, and every day after that we were able to cover the distance demanded by the schedule arranged before we started. This meant that some sort of shelter usually awaited us at night. But one day we knew there would be no houses between the place we left in the morning and that where we were to sleep. The distance was about twenty miles, and when twilight fell we had not made it. In the back of the wagon my mother had a box of little pigs, and during the afternoon these had broken loose and escaped into the woods. We had lost much time in finding them, and we were so exhausted that when we came to a hut made of twigs and boughs we decided to camp in it for the night, though we knew nothing about it. My brother had unharnessed the horses, and my mother and sister were cooking dough-god—a mixture of flour, water, and soda, fried in a pan-when two men rode up on horseback and called my brother to one side. Immediately after the talk which followed James harnessed his horses again and forced us to go on, though by that time darkness had fallen. He told mother, but did not tell us children until long afterward, that a man had been murdered in the hut only the night before. The murderer was still at large in the woods, and the new-comers were members of a posse who were searching for him. My brother needed no urging to put as many miles as he could between us and the sinister spot.

In that fashion we made our way to our new home. The last day, like the first, we traveled only eight miles, but we spent the night in a house I shall never forget. It was beautifully clean, and for our evening meal its mistress brought out loaves of bread which were the largest we had ever seen. She cut great slices of this bread for us and spread maple sugar on them, and it seemed to us that never before had anything tasted so good.

The next morning we made the last stage of our journey, our hearts filled with the joy of nearing our new home. We all had an idea that we were going to a farm, and we expected some resemblance at least to the prosperous farms we had seen in New England. My mother's mental picture was, naturally, of an English farm. Possibly she had visions of red barns and deep meadows, sunny skies and daisies. What we found awaiting us were the four walls and the roof of a good-sized log-house, standing in a small cleared strip of the wilderness, its doors and windows represented by square holes, its floor also a thing of the future, its whole effect achingly forlorn and desolate. It was late in the afternoon when we drove up to the opening that was its front entrance, and I shall never forget the look my mother turned upon the place. Without a word she crossed its threshold, and, standing very still, looked slowly around her. Then something within her seemed to give way, and she sank upon the ground. She could not realize even then, I think, that this was really the place father had prepared for us, that here he expected us to live. When she finally took it in she buried her face in her hands, and in that way she sat for hours without moving or speaking. For the first time in her life she had forgotten us; and we, for our part, dared not speak to her. We stood around her in a frightened group, talking to one another in whispers. Our little world had crumbled under our feet. Never before had we seen our mother give way to despair.

Night began to fall. The woods became alive with night creatures, and the most harmless made the most noise. The owls began to hoot, and soon we heard the wildcat, whose cry—a screech like that of a lost and panic-stricken child—is one of the most appalling sounds of the forest. Later the wolves added their howls to the uproar, but though darkness came and we children whimpered around her, our mother still sat in her strange lethargy.

At last my brother brought the horses close to the cabin and built fires to protect them and us. He was only twenty, but he showed himself a man during those early pioneer days. While he was picketing the horses and building his protecting fires my mother came to herself, but her face when she raised it was worse than her silence had been. She seemed to have died and to have returned to us from the grave, and I am sure she felt that she had done so. From that moment she took up again the burden of her life, a burden she did not lay down until she passed away; but her face never lost the deep lines those first hours of her pioneer life had cut upon it.

That night we slept on boughs spread on the earth inside the cabin walls, and we put blankets before the holes which represented our doors and windows, and kept our watch-fires burning. Soon the other children fell asleep, but there was no sleep for me. I was only twelve years old, but my mind was full of fancies. Behind our blankets, swaying in the night wind, I thought I saw the heads and pushing shoulders of animals and heard their padded footfalls. Later years brought familiarity with wild things, and with worse things than they. But to-night that which I most feared was within, not outside of, the cabin. In some way which I did not understand the one sure refuge in our new world had been taken from us. I hardly knew the silent woman who lay near me, tossing from side to side and staring into the darkness; I felt that we had lost our mother.

II. IN THE WILDERNESS

Like most men, my dear father should never have married. Though his nature was one of the sweetest I have ever known, and though he would at any call give his time to or risk his life for others, in practical matters he remained to the end of his days as irresponsible as a child. If his mind turned to practical details at all, it was solely in their bearing toward great developments of the future. To him an acorn was not an acorn, but a forest of young oaks.

Thus, when he took up his claim of three hundred and sixty acres of land in the wilderness of northern Michigan, and sent my mother and five young children to live there alone until he could join us eighteen months later, he gave no thought to the manner in which we were to make the struggle and survive the hardships before us. He had furnished us with land and the four walls of a log cabin. Some day, he reasoned, the place would be a fine estate, which his sons would inherit and in the course of time pass on to their sons—always an Englishman's most iridescent dream. That for the present we were one hundred miles from a railroad, forty miles from the nearest post-office, and half a dozen miles from any neighbors save Indians, wolves, and wildcats; that we were wholly unlearned in the ways of the woods as well as in the most primitive methods of farming; that we lacked not only every comfort, but even the bare necessities of life; and that we must begin, single-handed and untaught, a struggle for existence in which some of the severest forces of nature would be arrayed against us—these facts had no weight in my father's mind. Even if he had witnessed my mother's despair on the night of our arrival in our new home, he would not have understood it. From his viewpoint, he was doing a man's duty. He was working steadily in Lawrence, and, incidentally, giving much time to the Abolition cause and to other big public movements of his day which had his interest and sympathy. He wrote to us regularly and sent us occasional remittances, as well as a generous supply of improving literature for our minds. It remained for us to strengthen our bodies, to meet the conditions in which he had placed us, and to survive if we could.

We faced our situation with clear and unalarmed eyes the morning after our arrival. The problem of food, we knew, was at least temporarily solved. We had brought with us enough coffee, pork, and flour to last for several weeks; and the one necessity father had put inside the cabin walls was a great fireplace, made of mud and stones, in which our food could be cooked. The problem of our water-supply was less simple, but my brother James solved it for the time by showing us a creek a long distance from the house; and for months we carried from this creek, in pails, every drop of water we used, save that which we caught in troughs when the rain fell.

We held a family council after breakfast, and in this, though I was only twelve, I took an eager and determined part. I loved work—it has always been my favorite form of recreation—and my spirit rose to the opportunities of it which smiled on us from every side. Obviously the first thing to do was to put doors and windows into the yawning holes father had left for them, and to lay a board flooring over the earth inside our cabin walls, and these duties we accomplished before we had occupied our new home a fortnight. There was a small saw-mill nine miles from our cabin, on the spot that is now Big Rapids, and there we bought our lumber. The labor we supplied ourselves, and though we put our hearts into it and the results at the time seemed beautiful to our partial eyes, I am forced to admit, in looking back upon them, that they halted this side of perfection. We began by making three windows and two doors; then, inspired by these achievements, we ambitiously constructed an attic and divided the ground floor with partitions, which gave us four rooms.

The general effect was temperamental and sketchy. The boards which formed the floor were never even nailed down; they were fine, wide planks without a knot in them, and they looked so well that we merely fitted them together as closely as we could and lightheartedly let them go at that. Neither did we properly chink the house. Nothing is more comfortable than a log cabin which has been carefully built and finished; but for some reason—probably because there seemed always a more urgent duty calling to us around the corner—we never plastered our house at all. The result was that on many future winter mornings we awoke to find ourselves chastely blanketed by snow, while the only warm spot in our living-room was that directly in front of the fireplace, where great logs burned all day. Even there our faces scorched while our spines slowly congealed, until we learned to revolve before the fire like a bird upon a spit. No doubt we would have worked more thoroughly if my brother James, who was twenty years old and our tower of strength, had remained with us; but when we had been in our new home only a few months he fell and was forced to go East for an operation. He was never able to return to us, and thus my mother, we three young girls, and my youngest brother—Harry, who was only eight years old—made our fight alone until father came to us, more than a year later.

Mother was practically an invalid. She had a nervous affection which made it impossible for her to stand without the support of a chair. But she sewed with unusual skill, and it was due to her that our clothes, notwithstanding the strain to which we subjected them, were always in good condition. She sewed for hours every day, and she was able to move about the house, after a fashion, by pushing herself around on a stool which James made for her as soon as we arrived. He also built for her a more comfortable chair with a high back.

The division of labor planned at the first council was that mother should do our sewing, and my older sisters, Eleanor and Mary, the housework, which was far from taxing, for of course we lived in the simplest manner. My brothers and I were to do the work out of doors, an arrangement that suited me very well, though at first, owing to our lack of experience, our activities were somewhat curtailed. It was too late in the season for plowing or planting, even if we had possessed anything with which to plow, and, moreover, our so-called "cleared" land was thick with sturdy tree-stumps. Even during the second summer plowing was impossible; we could only plant potatoes and corn, and follow the most primitive method in doing even this. We took an ax, chopped up the sod, put the seed under it, and let the seed grow. The seed did grow, too—in the most gratifying and encouraging manner. Our green corn and potatoes were the best I have ever eaten. But for the present we lacked these luxuries.

We had, however, in their place, large quantities of wild fruit— gooseberries, raspberries, and plums—which Harry and I gathered on the banks of our creek. Harry also became an expert fisherman. We had no hooks or lines, but he took wires from our hoop-skirts and made snares at the ends of poles. My part of this work was to stand on a log and frighten the fish out of their holes by making horrible sounds, which I did with impassioned earnestness. When the fish hurried to the surface of the water to investigate the appalling noises they had heard, they were easily snared by our small boy, who was very proud of his ability to contribute in this way to the family table.

During our first winter we lived largely on cornmeal, making a little journey of twenty miles to the nearest mill to buy it; but even at that we were better off than our neighbors, for I remember one family in our region who for an entire winter lived solely on coarse-grained yellow turnips, gratefully changing their diet to leeks when these came in the spring.

Such furniture as we had we made ourselves. In addition to my mother's two chairs and the bunks which took the place of beds, James made a settle for the living-room, as well as a table and several stools. At first we had our tree-cutting done for us, but we soon became expert in this gentle art, and I developed such skill that in later years, after father came, I used to stand with him and "heart" a log.

On every side, and at every hour of the day, we came up against the relentless limitations of pioneer life. There was not a team of horses in our entire region. The team with which my brother had driven us through the wilderness had been hired at Grand Rapids for that occasion, and, of course, immediately returned. Our lumber was delivered by ox-teams, and the absolutely essential purchases we made "outside" (at the nearest shops, forty miles away) were carried through the forest on the backs of men. Our mail was delivered once a month by a carrier who made the journey in alternate stages of horseback riding and canoeing. But we had health, youth, enthusiasm, good appetites, and the wherewithal to satisfy them, and at night in our primitive bunks we sank into abysses of dreamless slumber such as I have never known since. Indeed, looking back upon them, those first months seem to have been a long-drawn-out and glorious picnic, interrupted only by occasional hours of pain or panic, when we were hurt or frightened.

Naturally, our two greatest menaces were wild animals and Indians, but as the days passed the first of these lost the early terrors with which we had associated them. We grew indifferent to the sounds that had made our first night a horror to us all—there was even a certain homeliness in them— while we regarded with accustomed, almost blase eyes the various furred creatures of which we caught distant glimpses as they slunk through the forest. Their experience with other settlers had taught them caution; it soon became clear that they were as eager to avoid us as we were to shun them, and by common consent we gave each other ample elbow-room. But the Indians were all around us, and every settler had a collection of hair-raising tales to tell of them. It was generally agreed that they were dangerous only when they were drunk; but as they were drunk whenever they could get whisky, and as whisky was constantly given them in exchange for pelts and game, there was a harrowing doubt in our minds whenever they approached us.

In my first encounter with them I was alone in the woods at sunset with my small brother Harry. We were hunting a cow James had bought, and our young eyes were peering eagerly among the trees, on the alert for any moving object. Suddenly, at a little distance, and coming directly toward us, we saw a party of Indians. There were five of them, all men, walking in single file, as noiselessly as ghosts, their moccasined feet causing not even a rustle among the dry leaves that carpeted the woods. All the horrible stories we had heard of Indian cruelty flashed into our minds, and for a moment we were dumb with terror. Then I remembered having been told that the one thing one must not do before them is to show fear. Harry was carrying a rope with which we had expected to lead home our reluctant cow, and I seized one end of it and whispered to him that we would "play horse," pretending he was driving me. We pranced toward the Indians on feet that felt like lead, and with eyes so glazed by terror that we could see nothing save a line of moving figures; but as we passed them they did not give to our little impersonation of care-free children even the tribute of a side-glance. They were, we realized, headed straight for our home; and after a few moments we doubled on our tracks and, keeping at a safe distance from them among the trees, ran back to warn our mother that they were coming.

As it happened, James was away, and mother had to meet her unwelcome guests supported only by her young children. She at once prepared a meal, however, and when they arrived she welcomed them calmly and gave them the best she had. After they had eaten they began to point at and demand objects they fancied in the room—my brother's pipe, some tobacco, a bowl, and such trifles—and my mother, who was afraid to annoy them by refusal, gave them what they asked. They were quite sober, and though they left without expressing any appreciation of her hospitality, they made her a second visit a few months later, bringing a large quantity of venison and a bag of cranberries as a graceful return. These Indians were Ottawas; and later we became very friendly with them and their tribe, even to the degree of attending one of their dances, which I shall describe later.

Our second encounter with Indians was a less agreeable experience. There were seven "Marquette warriors" in the next group of callers, and they were all intoxicated. Moreover, they had brought with them several jugs of bad whisky—the raw and craze-provoking product supplied them by the fur-dealers—and it was clear that our cabin was to be the scene of an orgy. Fortunately, my brother James was at home on this occasion, and as the evening grew old and the Indians, grouped together around the fire, became more and more irresponsible, he devised a plan for our safety. Our attic was finished, and its sole entrance was by a ladder through a trap-door. At James's whispered command my sister Eleanor slipped up into the attic, and from the back window let down a rope, to which he tied all the weapons we had—his gun and several axes. These Eleanor drew up and concealed in one of the bunks. My brother then directed that as quietly as possible, and at long intervals, one member of the family after another was to slip up the ladder and into the attic, going quite casually, that the Indians might not realize what we were doing. Once there, with the ladder drawn up after us and the trap-door closed, we would be reasonably safe, unless our guests decided to burn the cabin.

The evening seemed endless, and was certainly nerve-racking. The Indians ate everything in the house, and from my seat in a dim corner I watched them while my sisters waited on them. I can still see the tableau they made in the firelit room and hear the unfamiliar accents of their speech as they talked together. Occasionally one of them would pull a hair from his head, seize his scalping-knife; and cut the hair with it—a most unpleasant sight! When either of my sisters approached them some of the Indians would make gestures, as if capturing and scalping her. Through it all, however, the whisky held their close attention, and it was due to this that we succeeded in reaching the attic unobserved, James coming last of all and drawing the ladder after him. Mother and the children were then put to bed; but through that interminable night James and Eleanor lay flat upon the floor, watching through the cracks between the boards the revels of the drunken Indians, which grew wilder with every hour that crawled toward sunrise. There was no knowing when they would miss us or how soon their mood might change. At any moment they might make an attack upon us or set fire to the cabin. By dawn, however, their whisky was all gone, and they were in so deep a stupor that, one after the other, the seven fell from their chairs to the floor, where they sprawled unconscious. When they awoke they left quietly and without trouble of any kind. They seemed a strangely subdued and chastened band; probably they were wretchedly ill after their debauch on the adulterated whisky the traders had given them.

That autumn the Ottawa tribe had a great corn celebration, to which we and the other settlers were invited. James and my older sisters attended it, and I went with them, by my own urgent invitation. It seemed to me that as I was sharing the work and the perils of our new environment, I might as well share its joys; and I finally succeeded in making my family see the logic of this position. The central feature of the festivity was a huge kettle, many feet in circumference, into which the Indians dropped the most extraordinary variety of food we had ever seen combined. Deer heads went into it whole, as well as every kind of meat and vegetable the members of the tribe could procure. We all ate some of this agreeable mixture, and later, with one another, and even with the Indians, we danced gaily to the music of a tom-tom and a drum. The affair was extremely interesting until the whisky entered and did its unpleasant work. When our hosts began to fall over in the dance and slumber where they lay, and when the squaws began to show the same ill effects of their refreshments, we unostentatiously slipped away.

During the winter life offered us few diversions and many hardships. Our creek froze over, and the water problem became a serious one, which we met with increasing difficulty as the temperature steadily fell. We melted snow and ice, and existed through the frozen months, but with an amount of discomfort which made us unwilling to repeat at least that special phase of our experience. In the spring, therefore, I made a well. Long before this, James had gone, and Harry and I were now the only outdoor members of our working-force. Harry was still too small to help with the well; but a young man, who had formed the neighborly habit of riding eighteen miles to call on us, gave me much friendly aid. We located the well with a switch, and when we had dug as far as we could reach with our spades, my assistant descended into the hole and threw the earth up to the edge, from which I in turn removed it. As the well grew deeper we made a half-way shelf, on which I stood, he throwing the earth on the shelf, and I shoveling it up from that point. Later, as he descended still farther into the hole we were making, he shoveled the earth into buckets and passed them up to me, I passing them on to my sister, who was now pressed into service. When the excavation was deep enough we made the wall of slabs of wood, roughly joined together. I recall that well with calm content. It was not a thing of beauty, but it was a thoroughly practical well, and it remained the only one we had during the twelve years the family occupied the cabin.

During our first year there was no school within ten miles of us, but this lack failed to sadden Harry or me. We had brought with us from Lawrence a box of books, in which, in winter months, when our outdoor work was restricted, we found much comfort. They were the only books in that part of the country, and we read them until we knew them all by heart. Moreover, father sent us regularly the New York Independent, and with this admirable literature, after reading it, we papered our walls. Thus, on stormy days, we could lie on the settle or the floor and read the Independent over again with increased interest and pleasure.

Occasionally father sent us the Ledger, but here mother drew a definite line. She had a special dislike for that periodical, and her severest comment on any woman was that she was the type who would "keep a dog, make saleratus biscuit, and read the New York Ledger in the daytime." Our modest library also contained several histories of Greece and Rome, which must have been good ones, for years later, when I entered college, I passed my examination in ancient history with no other preparation than this reading. There were also a few arithmetics and algebras, a historical novel or two, and the inevitable copy of Uncle Tom's Cabin, whose pages I had freely moistened with my tears.

When the advantages of public education were finally extended to me, at thirteen, by the opening of a school three miles from our home, I accepted them with growing reluctance. The teacher was a spinster forty-four years of age and the only genuine "old maid" I have ever met who was not a married woman or a man. She was the real thing, and her name, Prudence Duncan, seemed the fitting label for her rigidly uncompromising personality. I graced Prudence's school for three months, and then left it at her fervid request. I had walked six miles a day through trackless woods and Western blizzards to get what she could give me, but she had little to offer my awakened and critical mind. My reading and my Lawrence school-work had already taught me more than Prudence knew—a fact we both inwardly—admitted and fiercely resented from our different viewpoints. Beyond doubt I was a pert and trying young person. I lost no opportunity to lead Prudence beyond her intellectual depth and leave her there, and Prudence vented her chagrin not alone upon me, but upon my little brother. I became a thorn in her side, and one day, after an especially unpleasant episode in which Harry also figured, she plucked me out, as it were, and cast me for ever from her. From that time I studied at home, where I was a much more valuable economic factor than I had been in school.

The second spring after our arrival Harry and I extended our operations by tapping the sugar-bushes, collecting all the sap, and carrying it home in pails slung from our yoke-laden shoulders. Together we made one hundred and fifty pounds of sugar and a barrel of syrup, but here again, as always, we worked in primitive ways. To get the sap we chopped a gash in the tree and drove in a spile. Then we dug out a trough to catch the sap. It was no light task to lift these troughs full of sap and empty the sap into buckets, but we did it successfully, and afterward built fires and boiled it down. By this time we had also cleared some of our ground, and during the spring we were able to plow, dividing the work in a way that seemed fair to us both. These were strenuous occupations for a boy of nine and a girl of thirteen, but, though we were not inordinately good children, we never complained; we found them very satisfactory substitutes for more normal bucolic joys. Inevitably, we had our little tragedies. Our cow died, and for an entire winter we went without milk. Our coffee soon gave out, and as a substitute we made and used a mixture of browned peas and burnt rye. In the winter we were always cold, and the water problem, until we had built our well, was ever with us.

Father joined us at the end of eighteen months, but though his presence gave us pleasure and moral support, he was not an addition to our executive staff. He brought with him a rocking-chair for mother and a new supply of books, on which I fell as a starving man falls upon food. Father read as eagerly as I, but much more steadily. His mind was always busy with problems, and if, while he was laboring in the field, a new problem presented itself to him, the imperishable curiosity that was in him made him scurry at once to the house to solve it. I have known him to spend a planting season in figuring on the production of a certain number of kernels of corn, instead of planting the corn and raising it. In the winter he was supposed to spend his time clearing land for orchards and the like, but instead he pored over his books and problems day after day and often half the night as well. It soon became known among our neighbors, who were rapidly increasing in number, that we had books and that father like to read aloud, and men walked ten miles or more to spend the night with us and listen to his reading. Often, as his fame grew, ten or twelve men would arrive at our cabin on Saturday and remain over Sunday. When my mother once tried to check this influx of guests by mildly pointing out, among other things, the waste of candles represented by frequent all-night readings, every man humbly appeared again on the following Saturday with a candle in each hand. They were not sensitive; and, as they had brought their candles, it seemed fitting to them and to father that we girls should cook for them and supply them with food.

Father's tolerance of idleness in others, however, did not extend to tolerance of idleness in us, and this led to my first rebellion, which occurred when I was fourteen. For once, I had been in the woods all day, buried in my books; and when I returned at night, still in the dream world these books had opened to me, father was awaiting my coming with a brow dark with disapproval. As it happened, mother had felt that day some special need of me, and father reproached me bitterly for being beyond reach—an idler who wasted time while mother labored. He ended a long arraignment by predicting gloomily that with such tendencies I would make nothing of my life.

The injustice of the criticism cut deep; I knew I had done and was doing my share for the family, and already, too, I had begun to feel the call of my career. For some reason I wanted to preach—to talk to people, to tell them things. Just why, just what, I did not yet know—but I had begun to preach in the silent woods, to stand up on stumps and address the unresponsive trees, to feel the stir of aspiration within me.

When my father had finished all he wished to say, I looked at him and answered, quietly, "Father, some day I am going to college."

I can still see his slight, ironical smile. It drove me to a second prediction. I was young enough to measure success by material results, so I added, recklessly:

"And before I die I shall be worth ten thousand dollars!"

The amount staggered me even as it dropped from my lips. It was the largest fortune my imagination could conceive, and in my heart I believed that no woman ever had possessed or would possess so much. So far as I knew, too, no woman had gone to college. But now that I had put my secret hopes into words, I was desperately determined to make those hopes come true. After I became a wage-earner I lost my desire to make a fortune, but the college dream grew with the years; and though my college career seemed as remote as the most distant star, I hitched my little wagon to that star and never afterward wholly lost sight of its friendly gleam.

When I was fifteen years old I was offered a situation as school-teacher. By this time the community was growing around us with the rapidity characteristic of these Western settlements, and we had nearer neighbors whose children needed instruction. I passed an examination before a schoolboard consisting of three nervous and self-conscious men whose certificate I still hold, and I at once began my professional career on the modest salary of two dollars a week and my board. The school was four miles from my home, so I "boarded round" with the families of my pupils, staying two weeks in each place, and often walking from three to six miles a day to and from my little log school-house in every kind of weather. During the first year I had about fourteen pupils, of varying ages, sizes, and temperaments, and there was hardly a book in the school-room except those I owned. One little girl, I remember, read from an almanac, while a second used a hymn-book.

In winter the school-house was heated by a woodstove, to which the teacher had to give close personal attention. I could not depend on my pupils to make the fires or carry in the fuel; and it was often necessary to fetch the wood myself, sometimes for long distances through the forest. Again and again, after miles of walking through winter storms, I reached the school-house with my clothing wet through, and in these soaked garments I taught during the day. In "boarding round" I often found myself in one-room cabins, with bunks at the end and the sole partition a sheet or a blanket, behind which I slept with one or two of the children. It was the custom on these occasions for the man of the house to delicately retire to the barn while we women got to bed, and to disappear again in the morning while we dressed. In some places the meals were so badly cooked that I could not eat them, and often the only food my poor little pupils brought to school for their noonday meal was a piece of bread or a bit of raw pork.

I earned my two dollars a week that year, but I had to wait for my wages until the dog tax was collected in the spring. When the money was thus raised, and the twenty-six dollars for my thirteen weeks of teaching were graciously put into my hands, I went "outside" to the nearest shop and joyously spent almost the entire amount for my first "party dress." The gown I bought was, I considered, a beautiful creation. In color it was a rich magenta, and the skirt was elaborately braided with black cable-cord. My admiration for it was justified, for it did all a young girl's eager heart could ask of any gown—it led to my first proposal.

The youth who sought my hand was about twenty years old, and by an unhappy chance he was also the least attractive young person in the countryside—the laughing-stock of the neighbors, the butt of his associates. The night he came to offer me his heart there were already two young men at our home calling on my sisters, and we were all sitting around the fire in the living-room when my suitor appeared. His costume, like himself, left much to be desired. He wore a blue flannel shirt and a pair of trousers made of flour-bags. Such trousers were not uncommon in our region, and the boy's mother, who had made them for him, had thoughtfully selected a nice clean pair of sacks. But on one leg was the name of the firm that made the flour—A. and G. W. Green—and by a charming coincidence A. and G. W. Green happened to be the two young men who were calling on my sisters! On the back of the bags, directly in the rear of the wearer, was the simple legend, "96 pounds"; and the striking effect of the young man's costume was completed by a bright yellow sash which held his trousers in place.

The vision fascinated my sisters and their two guests. They gave it their entire attention, and when the new-comer signified with an eloquent gesture that he was calling on me, and beckoned me into an inner room, the quartet arose as one person and followed us to the door. Then, as we inhospitably closed the door, they fastened their eyes to the cracks in the living-room wall, that they might miss none of the entertainment. When we were alone my guest and I sat down in facing chairs and in depressed silence. The young man was nervous, and I was both frightened and annoyed. I had heard suppressed giggles on the other side of the wall, and I realized, as my self-centered visitor failed to do, that we were not enjoying the privacy the situation seemed to demand. At last the youth informed me that his "dad" had just given him a cabin, a yoke of steers, a cow, and some hens. When this announcement had produced its full effect, he straightened up in his chair and asked, solemnly, "Will ye have me?"

An outburst of chortles from the other side of the wall greeted the proposal, but the ardent youth ignored it, if indeed he heard it. With eyes staring straight ahead, he sat rigid, waiting for my answer; and I, anxious only to get rid of him and to end the strain of the moment, said the first thing that came into my head. "I can't," I told him. "I'm sorry, but—but—I'm engaged."

He rose quickly, with the effect of a half-closed jack-knife that is suddenly opened, and for an instant stood looking down upon me. He was six feet two inches tall, and extremely thin. I am very short, and, as I looked up, his flour-bag trousers seemed to join his yellow sash somewhere near the ceiling of the room. He put both hands into his pockets and slowly delivered his valedictory. "That's darned disappointing to a fellow," he said, and left the house. After a moment devoted to regaining my maidenly composure I returned to the living-room, where I had the privilege of observing the enjoyment of my sisters and their visitors. Helpless with mirth and with tears of pleasure on their cheeks, the four rocked and shrieked as they recalled the picture my gallant had presented. For some time after that incident I felt a strong distaste for sentiment.

Clad royally in the new gown, I attended my first ball in November, going with a party of eight that included my two sisters, another girl, and four young men. The ball was at Big Rapids, which by this time had grown to be a thriving lumber town. It was impossible to get a team of horses or even a yoke of oxen for the journey, so we made a raft and went down the river on that, taking our party dresses with us in trunks. Unfortunately, the raft "hung up" in the stream, and the four young men had to get out into the icy water and work a long time before they could detach it from the rocks. Naturally, they were soaked and chilled through, but they all bore the experience with a gay philosophy.

When we reached Big Rapids we dressed for the ball, and, as in those days it was customary to change one's gown again at midnight, I had an opportunity to burst on the assemblage in two costumes—the second made of bedroom chintz, with a low neck and short sleeves. We danced the "money musk," and the "Virginia reel," "hoeing her down" (which means changing partners) in true pioneer style. I never missed a dance at this or any subsequent affair, and I was considered the gayest and the most tireless young person at our parties until I became a Methodist minister and dropped such worldly vanities. The first time I preached in my home region all my former partners came to hear me, and listened with wide, understanding, reminiscent smiles which made it very hard for me to keep soberly to my text.

In the near future I had reason to regret the extravagant expenditure of my first earnings. For my second year of teaching, in the same school, I was to receive five dollars a week and to pay my own board. I selected a place two miles and a half from the school-house, and was promptly asked by my host to pay my board in advance. This, he explained, was due to no lack of faith in me; the money would enable him to go "outside" to work, leaving his family well supplied with provisions. I allowed him to go to the school committee and collect my board in advance, at the rate of three dollars a week for the season. When I presented myself at my new boarding-place, however, two days later, I found the house nailed up and deserted; the man and his family had departed with my money, and I was left, as my committeemen sympathetically remarked, "high and dry." There were only two dollars a week coming to me after that, so I walked back and forth between my home and my school, almost four miles, twice a day; and during this enforced exercise there was ample opportunity to reflect on the fleeting joy of riches.

In the mean time war had been declared. When the news came that Fort Sumter had been fired on, and that Lincoln had called for troops, our men were threshing. There was only one threshing-machine in the region at that time, and it went from place to place, the farmers doing their threshing whenever they could get the machine. I remember seeing a man ride up on horseback, shouting out Lincoln's demand for troops and explaining that a regiment was being formed at Big Rapids. Before he had finished speaking the men on the machine had leaped to the ground and rushed off to enlist, my brother Jack, who had recently joined us, among them. In ten minutes not one man was left in the field. A few months later my brother Tom enlisted as a bugler—he was a mere boy at the time—and not long after that my father followed the example of his sons and served until the war was ended. He had entered on the twenty-ninth of August, 1862, as an army steward; he came back to us with the rank of lieutenant and assistant surgeon of field and staff.

Between those years I was the principal support of our family, and life became a strenuous and tragic affair. For months at a time we had no news from the front. The work in our community, if it was done at all, was done by despairing women whose hearts were with their men. When care had become our constant guest, Death entered our home as well. My sister Eleanor had married, and died in childbirth, leaving her baby to me; and the blackest hours of those black years were the hours that saw her passing. I can see her still, lying in a stupor from which she roused herself at intervals to ask about her child. She insisted that our brother Tom should name the baby, but Tom was fighting for his country, unless he had already preceded Eleanor through the wide portal that was opening before her. I could only tell her that I had written to him; but before the assurance was an hour old she would climb up from the gulf of unconsciousness with infinite effort to ask if we had received his reply. At last, to calm her, I told her it had come, and that Tom had chosen for her little son the name of Arthur. She smiled at this and drew a deep breath; then, still smiling, she passed away. Her baby slipped into her vacant place and almost filled our heavy hearts, but only for a short time; for within a few months after his mother's death his father married again and took him from me, and it seemed that with his going we had lost all that made life worth while.

The problem of living grew harder with everyday. We eked out our little income in every way we could, taking as boarders the workers in the logging-camps, making quilts, which we sold, and losing no chance to earn a penny in any legitimate manner. Again my mother did such outside sewing as she could secure, yet with every month of our effort the gulf between our income and our expenses grew wider, and the price of the bare necessities of exisence{sic} climbed up and up. The largest amount I could earn at teaching was six dollars a week, and our school year included only two terms of thirteen weeks each. It was an incessant struggle to keep our land, to pay our taxes, and to live. Calico was selling at fifty cents a yard. Coffee was one dollar a pound. There were no men left to grind our corn, to get in our crops, or to care for our live stock; and all around us we saw our struggle reflected in the lives of our neighbors.

At long intervals word came to us of battles in which my father's regiment—the Tenth Michigan Cavalry Volunteers—or those of my brothers were engaged, and then longer intervals followed in which we heard no news. After Eleanor's death my brother Tom was wounded, and for months we lived in terror of worse tidings, but he finally recovered. I was walking seven and eight miles a day, and doing extra work before and after school hours, and my health began to fail. Those were years I do not like to look back upon—years in which life had degenerated into a treadmill whose monotony was broken only by the grim messages from the front. My sister Mary married and went to Big Rapids to live. I had no time to dream my dream, but the star of my one purpose still glowed in my dark horizon. It seemed that nothing short of a miracle could lift my feet from their plodding way and set them on the wider path toward which my eyes were turned, but I never lost faith that in some manner the miracle would come to pass. As certainly as I have ever known anything, I KNEW that I was going to college!

III. HIGH-SCHOOL AND COLLEGE DAYS

The end of the Civil War brought freedom to me, too. When peace was declared my father and brothers returned to the claim in the wilderness which we women of the family had labored so desperately to hold while they were gone. To us, as to others, the final years of the war had brought many changes. My sister Eleanor's place was empty. Mary, as I have said, had married and gone to live in Big Rapids, and my mother and I were alone with my brother Harry, now a boy of fourteen. After the return of our men it was no longer necessary to devote every penny of my earnings to the maintenance of our home. For the first time I could begin to save a portion of my income toward the fulfilment of my college dream, but even yet there was a long, arid stretch ahead of me before the college doors came even distantly into sight.

The largest salary I could earn by teaching in our Northern woods was one hundred and fifty-six dollars a year, for two terms of thirteen weeks each; and from this, of course, I had to deduct the cost of my board and clothing—the sole expenditure I allowed myself. The dollars for an education accumulated very, very slowly, until at last, in desperation, weary of seeing the years of my youth rush past, bearing my hopes with them, I took a sudden and radical step. I gave up teaching, left our cabin in the woods, and went to Big Rapids to live with my sister Mary, who had married a successful man and who generously offered me a home. There, I had decided, I would learn a trade of some kind, of any kind; it did not greatly matter what it was. The sole essential was that it should be a money-making trade, offering wages which would make it possible to add more rapidly to my savings. In those days, almost fifty years ago, and in a small pioneer town, the fields open to women were few and unfruitful. The needle at once presented itself, but at first I turned with loathing from it. I would have preferred the digging of ditches or the shoveling of coal; but the needle alone persistently pointed out my way, and I was finally forced to take it.

Fate, however, as if weary at last of seeing me between her paws, suddenly let me escape. Before I had been working a month at my uncongenial trade Big Rapids was favored by a visit from a Universalist woman minister, the Reverend Marianna Thompson, who came there to preach. Her sermon was delivered on Sunday morning, and I was, I think, almost the earliest arrival of the great congregation which filled the church. It was a wonderful moment when I saw my first woman minister enter her pulpit; and as I listened to her sermon, thrilled to the soul, all my early aspirations to become a minister myself stirred in me with cumulative force. After the services I hung for a time on the fringe of the group that surrounded her, and at last, when she was alone and about to leave, I found courage to introduce myself and pour forth the tale of my ambition. Her advice was as prompt as if she had studied my problem for years.

"My child," she said, "give up your foolish idea of learning a trade, and go to school. You can't do anything until you have an education. Get it, and get it NOW."

Her suggestion was much to my liking, and I paid her the compliment of acting on it promptly, for the next morning I entered the Big Rapids High School, which was also a preparatory school for college. There I would study, I determined, as long as my money held out, and with the optimism of youth I succeeded in confining my imagination to this side of that crisis. My home, thanks to Mary, was assured; the wardrobe I had brought from the woods covered me sufficiently; to one who had walked five and six miles a day for years, walking to school held no discomfort; and as for pleasure, I found it, like a heroine of fiction, in my studies. For the first time life was smiling at me, and with all my young heart I smiled back.

The preceptress of the high school was Lucy Foot, a college graduate and a remarkable woman. I had heard much of her sympathy and understanding; and on the evening following my first day in school I went to her and repeated the confidences I had reposed in the Reverend Marianna Thompson. My trust in her was justified. She took an immediate interest in me, and proved it at once by putting me into the speaking and debating classes, where I was given every opportunity to hold forth to helpless classmates when the spirit of eloquence moved me.

As an aid to public speaking I was taught to "elocute," and I remember in every mournful detail the occasion on which I gave my first recitation. We were having our monthly "public exhibition night," and the audience included not only my classmates, but their parents and friends as well. The selection I intended to recite was a poem entitled "No Sects in Heaven," but when I faced my audience I was so appalled by its size and by the sudden realization of my own temerity that I fainted during the delivery of the first verse. Sympathetic classmates carried me into an anteroom and revived me, after which they naturally assumed that the entertainment I furnished was over for the evening. I, however, felt that if I let that failure stand against me I could never afterward speak in public; and within ten minutes, notwithstanding the protests of my friends, I was back in the hall and beginning my recitation a second time. The audience gave me its eager attention. Possibly it hoped to see me topple off the platform again, but nothing of the sort occurred. I went through the recitation with self-possession and received some friendly applause at the end. Strangely enough, those first sensations of "stage fright" have been experienced, in a lesser degree, in connection with each of the thousands of public speeches I have made since that time. I have never again gone so far as to faint in the presence of an audience; but I have invariably walked out on the platform feeling the sinking sensation at the pit of the stomach, the weakness of the knees, that I felt in the hour of my debut. Now, however, the nervousness passes after a moment or two.

From that night Miss Foot lost no opportunity of putting me into the foreground of our school affairs. I took part in all our debates, recited yards of poetry to any audience we could attract, and even shone mildly in our amateur theatricals. It was probably owing to all this activity that I attracted the interest of the presiding elder of our district—Dr. Peck, a man of progressive ideas. There was at that time a movement on foot to license women to preach in the Methodist Church, and Dr. Peck was ambitious to be the first presiding elder to have a woman ordained for the Methodist ministry. He had urged Miss Foot to be this pioneer, but her ambitions did not turn in that direction. Though she was a very devout Methodist, she had no wish to be the shepherd of a religious flock. She loved her school-work, and asked nothing better than to remain in it. Gently but persistently she directed the attention of Dr. Peck to me, and immediately things began to happen.

Without telling me to what it might lead, Miss Foot finally arranged a meeting at her home by inviting Dr. Peck and me to dinner. Being unconscious of any significance in the occasion, I chatted light-heartedly about the large issues of life and probably settled most of them to my personal satisfaction. Dr. Peck drew me out and led me on, listened and smiled. When the evening was over and we rose to go, he turned to me with sudden seriousness:

"My quarterly meeting will be held at Ashton," he remarked, casually. "I would like you to preach the quarterly sermon."

For a moment the earth seemed to slip away from my feet. I stared at him in utter stupefaction. Then slowly I realized that, incredible as it seemed, the man was in earnest.

"Why," I stammered, "I can't preach a sermon!"

Dr. Peck smiled at me. "Have you ever tried?" he asked.

I started to assure him vehemently that I never had. Then, as if Time had thrown a picture on a screen before me, I saw myself as a little girl preaching alone in the forest, as I had so often preached to a congregation of listening trees. I qualified my answer.

"Never," I said, "to human beings."

Dr. Peck smiled again. "Well," he told me, "the door is open. Enter or not, as you wish."

He left the house, but I remained to discuss his overwhelming proposition with Miss Foot. A sudden sobering thought had come to me.

"But," I exclaimed, "I've never been converted. How can I preach to any one?"

We both had the old-time idea of conversion, which now seems so mistaken. We thought one had to struggle with sin and with the Lord until at last the heart opened, doubts were dispersed, and the light poured in. Miss Foot could only advise me to put the matter before the Lord, to wrestle and to pray; and thereafter, for hours at a time, she worked and prayed with me, alternately urging, pleading, instructing, and sending up petitions in my behalf. Our last session was a dramatic one, which took up the entire night. Long before it was over we were both worn out; but toward morning, either from exhaustion of body or exaltation of soul, I seemed to see the light, and it made me very happy. With all my heart I wanted to preach, and I believed that now at last I had my call. The following day we sent word to Dr. Peck that I would preach the sermon at Ashton as he had asked, but we urged him to say nothing of the matter for the present, and Miss Foot and I also kept the secret locked in our breasts. I knew only too well what view my family and my friends would take of such a step and of me. To them it would mean nothing short of personal disgrace and a blotted page in the Shaw record.

I had six weeks in which to prepare my sermon, and I gave it most of my waking hours as well as those in which I should have been asleep. I took for my text: "And as Moses lifted up the serpent in the wilderness, even so must the Son of Man be lifted up; that whosoever believeth in Him should not perish, but have eternal life."

It was not until three days before I preached the sermon that I found courage to confide my purpose to my sister Mary, and if I had confessed my intention to commit a capital crime she could not have been more disturbed. We two had always been very close, and the death of Eleanor, to whom we were both devoted, had drawn us even nearer to each other. Now Mary's tears and prayers wrung my heart and shook my resolution. But, after all, she was asking me to give up my whole future, to close my ears to my call, and I felt that I could not do it. My decision caused an estrangement between us which lasted for years. On the day preceding the delivery of my sermon I left for Ashton on the afternoon train; and in the same car, but as far away from me as she could get, Mary sat alone and wept throughout the journey. She was going to my mother, but she did not speak to me; and I, for my part, facing both alienation from her and the ordeal before me, found my one comfort in Lucy Foot's presence and understanding sympathy.

There was no church in Ashton, so I preached my sermon in its one little school-house, which was filled with a curious crowd, eager to look at and hear the girl who was defying all conventions by getting out of the pew and into the pulpit. There was much whispering and suppressed excitement before I began, but when I gave out my text silence fell upon the room, and from that moment until I had finished my hearers listened quietly. A kerosene-lamp stood on a stand at my elbow, and as I preached I trembled so violently that the oil shook in its glass globe; but I finished without breaking down, and at the end Dr. Peck, who had his own reasons for nervousness, handsomely assured me that my first sermon was better than his maiden effort had been. It was evidently not a failure, for the next day he invited me to follow him around in his circuit, which included thirty-six appointments; he wished me to preach in each of the thirty-six places, as it was desirable to let the various ministers hear and know me before I applied for my license as a local preacher.

The sermon also had another result, less gratifying. It brought out, on the following morning, the first notice of me ever printed in a newspaper. This was instigated by my brother-in-law, and it was brief but pointed. It read:

A young girl named Anna Shaw, seventeen years old, 1 preached at Ashton yesterday. Her real friends deprecate the course she is pursuing.

1   (return)
[A misstatement by the brother-in-law. Dr. Shaw was at this time twenty-three years old.—E. J.]

The little notice had something of the effect of a lighted match applied to gunpowder. An explosion of public sentiment followed it, the entire community arose in consternation, and I became a bone of contention over which friends and strangers alike wrangled until they wore themselves out. The members of my family, meeting in solemn council, sent for me, and I responded. They had a proposition to make, and they lost no time in putting it before me. If I gave up my preaching they would send me to college and pay for my entire course. They suggested Ann Arbor, and Ann Arbor tempted me sorely; but to descend from the pulpit I had at last entered—the pulpit I had visualized in all my childish dreams—was not to be considered. We had a long evening together, and it was a very unhappy one. At the end of it I was given twenty-four hours in which to decide whether I would choose my people and college, or my pulpit and the arctic loneliness of a life that held no family-circle. It did not require twenty-four hours of reflection to convince me that I must go my solitary way.

That year I preached thirty-six times, at each of the presiding elder's appointments; and the following spring, at the annual Methodist Conference of our district, held at Big Rapids, my name was presented to the assembled ministers as that of a candidate for a license to preach. There was unusual interest in the result, and my father was among those who came to the Conference to see the vote taken. During these Conferences a minister voted affirmatively on a question by holding up his hand, and negatively by failing to do so. When the question of my license came up the majority of the ministers voted by raising both hands, and in the pleasant excitement which followed my father slipped away. Those who saw him told me he looked pleased; but he sent me no message showing a change of viewpoint, and the gulf between the family and its black sheep remained unbridged. Though the warmth of Mary's love for me had become a memory, the warmth of her hearthstone was still offered me. I accepted it, perforce, and we lived together like shadows of what we had been. Two friends alone of all I had made stood by me without qualification—Miss Foot and Clara Osborn, the latter my "chum" at Big Rapids and a dweller in my heart to this day.

In the mean time my preaching had not interfered with my studies. I was working day and night, but life was very difficult; for among my schoolmates, too, there were doubts and much head-shaking over this choice of a career. I needed the sound of friendly voices, for I was very lonely; and suddenly, when the pressure from all sides was strongest and I was going down physically under it, a voice was raised that I had never dared to dream would speak for me. Mary A. Livermore came to Big Rapids, and as she was then at the height of her career, the entire countryside poured in to hear her. Far back in the crowded hall I sat alone and listened to her, thrilled by the lecture and tremulous with the hope of meeting the lecturer. When she had finished speaking I joined the throng that surged forward from the body of the hall, and as I reached her and felt the grasp of her friendly hand I had a sudden conviction that the meeting was an epoch in my life. I was right. Some one in the circle around us told her that I wanted to preach, and that I was meeting tremendous opposition. She was interested at once. She looked at me with quickening sympathy, and then, suddenly putting an arm around me, drew me close to her side.

"My dear," she said, quietly, "if you want to preach, go on and preach. Don't let anybody stop you. No matter what people say, don't let them stop you!"

For a moment I was too overcome to answer her. These were almost my first encouraging words, and the morning stars singing together could not have made sweeter music for my ears. Before I could recover a woman within hearing spoke up.

"Oh, Mrs. Livermore," she exclaimed, "don't say that to her! We're all trying to stop her. Her people are wretched over the whole thing. And don't you see how ill she is? She has one foot in the grave and the other almost there!"

Mrs. Livermore turned upon me a long and deeply thoughtful look. "Yes," she said at last, "I see she has. But it is better that she should die doing the thing she wants to do than that she should die because she can't do it."

Her words were a tonic which restored my voice. "So they think I'm going to die!" I cried. "Well, I'm not! I'm going to live and preach!"

I have always felt since then that without the inspiration of Mrs. Livermore's encouragement I might not have continued my fight. Her sanction was a shield, however, from which the criticisms of the world fell back. Fate's more friendly interest in my affairs that year was shown by the fact that she sent Mrs. Livermore into my life before I had met Anna Dickinson. Miss Dickinson came to us toward spring and lectured on Joan of Arc. Never before or since have I been more deeply moved by a speaker. When she had finished her address I made my happy way to the front of the hall with the others who wished to meet the distinguished guest. It was our local manager who introduced me, and he said, "This is our Anna Shaw. She is going to be a lecturer, too."

I looked up at the brilliant Miss Dickinson with the trustfulness of youth in my eyes. I remembered Mrs. Livermore and I thought all great women were like her, but I was now to experience a bitter disillusionment. Miss Dickinson barely touched the tips of my fingers as she looked indifferently past the side of my face. "Ah," she said, icily, and turned away. In later years I learned how impossible it is for a public speaker to leave a gracious impression on every life that for a moment touches her own; but I have never ceased to be thankful that I met Mrs. Livermore before I met Miss Dickinson at the crisis in my career.

In the autumn of 1873 I entered Albion College, in Albion, Michigan. I was twenty-five years of age, but I looked much younger—probably not more than eighteen to the casual glance. Though I had made every effort to save money, I had not been successful, for my expenses constantly outran my little income, and my position as preacher made it necessary for me to have a suitable wardrobe. When the time came to enter college I had exactly eighteen dollars in the world, and I started for Albion with this amount in my purse and without the slightest notion of how I was to add to it. The money problem so pressed upon me, in fact, that when I reached my destination at midnight and discovered that it would cost fifty cents to ride from the station to the college, I saved that amount by walking the entire distance on the railroad tracks, while my imagination busied itself pleasantly with pictures of the engine that might be thundering upon me in the rear. I had chosen Albion because Miss Foot had been educated there, and I was encouraged by an incident that happened the morning after my arrival. I was on the campus, walking toward the main building, when I saw a big copper penny lying on the ground, and, on picking it up, I discovered that it bore the year of my birth. That seemed a good omen, and it was emphatically underlined by the finding of two exactly similar pennies within a week. Though there have been days since then when I was sorely tempted to spend them, I have those three pennies still, and I confess to a certain comfort in their possession!

As I had not completed my high-school course, my first days at Albion were spent in strenuous preparation for the entrance examinations; and one morning, as I was crossing the campus with a History of the United States tucked coyly under my arm, I met the president of the college, Dr. Josclyn. He stopped for a word of greeting, during which I betrayed the fact that I had never studied United States history. Dr. Josclyn at once invited me into his office with, I am quite sure, the purpose of explaining as kindly as he could that my preparation for college was insufficient. As an opening to the subject he began to talk of history, and we talked and talked on, while unheeded hours were born and died. We discussed the history of the United States, the governments of the world, the causes which led to the influence of one nation on another, the philosophical basis of the different national movements westward, and the like. It was the longest and by far the most interesting talk I have ever had with a highly educated man, and during it I could actually feel my brain expand. When I rose to go President Josclyn stopped me.

"I have something to give you," he said, and he wrote a few words on a slip of paper and handed the slip to me. When, on reaching the dormitory, I opened it, I found that the president had passed me in the history of the entire college course! This, moreover, was not the only pleasant result of our interview, for within a few weeks President and Mrs. Josclyn, whose daughter had recently died, invited me to board with them, and I made my home with them during my first year at Albion.

My triumph in history was followed by the swift and chastening discovery that I was behind my associates in several other branches. Owing to my father's early help, I was well up in mathematics, but I had much to learn of philosophy and the languages, and to these I devoted many midnight candles.

Naturally, I soon plunged into speaking, and my first public speech at college was a defense of Xantippe. I have always felt that the poor lady was greatly abused, and that Socrates deserved all he received from her, and more. I was glad to put myself on record as her champion, and my fellow-students must soon have felt that my admiration for Xantippe was based on similarities of temperament, for within a few months I was leading the first college revolt against the authority of the men students.

Albion was a coeducational institution, and the brightest jewels in its crown were its three literary societies—the first composed of men alone, the second of women alone, and the third of men and women together. Each of the societies made friendly advances to new students, and for some time I hesitated on the brink of the new joys they offered, uncertain which to choose. A representative of the mixed society, who was putting its claims before me, unconsciously helped me to make up my mind.

"Women," he pompously assured me, "need to be associated with men, because they don't know how to manage meetings."

On the instant the needle of decision swung around to the women's society and remained there, fixed.

"If they don't," I told the pompous young man, "it's high time they learned. I shall join the women, and we'll master the art."

I did join the women's society, and I had not been a member very long before I discovered that when there was an advantage of any kind to be secured the men invariably got it. While I was brooding somberly upon this wrong an opportunity came to make a formal and effective protest against the men's high-handed methods. The Quinquennial reunion of all the societies was about to be held, and the special feature of this festivity was always an oration. The simple method of selecting the orator which had formerly prevailed had been for the young men to decide upon the speaker and then announce his name to the women, who humbly confirmed it. On this occasion, however, when the name came in to us, I sent a message to our brother society to the effect that we, too, intended to make a nomination and to send in a name.

At such unprecedented behavior the entire student body arose in excitement, which, among the girls, was combined with equal parts of exhilaration and awe. The men refused to consider our nominee, and as a friendly compromise we suggested that we have a joint meeting of all the societies and elect the speaker at this gathering; but this plan also the men at first refused, giving in only after weeks of argument, during which no one had time for the calmer pleasures of study. When the joint meeting was finally held, nothing was accomplished; we girls had one more member than the boys had, and we promptly re-elected our candidate, who was as promptly declined by the boys. Two of our girls were engaged to two of the boys, and it was secretly planned by our brother society that during a second joint meeting these two men should take the girls out for a drive and then slip back to vote, leaving the girls at some point sufficiently remote from college. We discovered the plot, however, in time to thwart it, and at last, when nothing but the unprecedented tie-up had been discussed for months, the boys suddenly gave up their candidate and nominated me for orator.

This was not at all what I wanted, and I immediately declined to serve. We girls then nominated the young man who had been first choice of our brother society, but he haughtily refused to accept the compliment. The reunion was only a fortnight away, and the programme had not been printed, so now the president took the situation in hand and peremptorily ordered me to accept the nomination or be suspended. This was a wholly unexpected boomerang. I had wished to make a good fight for equal rights for the girls, and to impress the boys with the fact of our existence as a society; but I had not desired to set the entire student body by the ears nor to be forced to prepare and deliver an oration at the eleventh hour. Moreover, I had no suitable gown to wear on so important an occasion. One of my classmates, however, secretly wrote to my sister, describing my blushing honors and explaining my need, and my family rallied to the call. My father bought the material, and my mother and Mary paid for the making of the gown. It was a white alpaca creation, trimmed with satin, and the consciousness that it was extremely becoming sustained me greatly during the mental agony of preparing and delivering my oration. To my family that oration was the redeeming episode of my early career. For the moment it almost made them forget my crime of preaching.

My original fund of eighteen dollars was now supplemented by the proceeds of a series of lectures I gave on temperance. The temperance women were not yet organized, but they had their speakers, and I was occasionally paid five dollars to hold forth for an hour or two in the little country school-houses of our region. As a licensed preacher I had no tuition fees to pay at college; but my board, in the home of the president and his wife, was costing me four dollars a week, and this was the limit of my expenses, as I did my own laundry-work. During my first college year the amount I paid for amusement was exactly fifty cents; that went for a lecture. The mental strain of the whole experience was rather severe, for I never knew how much I would be able to earn; and I was beginning to feel the effects of this when Christmas came and brought with it a gift of ninety-two dollars, which Miss Foot had collected among my Big Rapids friends. That, with what I could earn, carried me through the year.

The following spring our brother James, who was now living in St. Johnsbury, Vermont, invited my sister Mary and me to spend the summer with him, and Mary and I finally dug a grave for our little hatchet and went East together with something of our old-time joy in each other's society. We reached St. Johnsbury one Saturday, and within an hour of our arrival learned that my brother had arranged for me to preach in a local church the following day. That threatened to spoil the visit for Mary and even to disinter the hatchet! At first she positively refused to go to hear me, but after a few hours of reflection she announced gloomily that if she did not go I would not have my hair arranged properly or get my hat on straight. Moved by this conviction, she joined the family parade to the church, and later, in the sacristy, she pulled me about and pinned me up to her heart's content. Then, reluctantly, she went into the church and heard me preach. She offered no tributes after our return to the house, but her protests ceased from that time, and we gave each other the love and understanding which had marked our girlhood days. The change made me very happy; for Mary was the salt of the earth, and next only to my longing for my mother, I had longed for her in the years of our estrangement.

Every Sunday that summer I preached in or near St. Johnsbury, and toward autumn we had a big meeting which the ministers of all the surrounding churches attended. I was asked to preach the sermon—a high compliment—and I chose that important day to make a mistake in quoting a passage from Scripture. I asked, "Can the Ethiopian change his spots or the leopard his skin?" I realized at once that I had transposed the words, and no doubt a look of horror dawned in my eyes; but I went on without correcting myself and without the slightest pause. Later, one of the ministers congratulated me on this presence of mind.

"If you had corrected yourself," he said, "all the young people would have been giggling yet over the spotted nigger. Keep to your rule of going right ahead!"

At the end of the summer the various churches in which I had preached gave me a beautiful gold watch and one hundred dollars in money, and with an exceedingly light heart I went back to college to begin my second year of work.

From that time life was less complex. I had enough temperance-work and preaching in the country school-houses and churches to pay my college expenses, and, now that my financial anxieties were relieved, my health steadily improved. Several times I preached to the Indians, and these occasions were among the most interesting of my experiences. The squaws invariably brought their babies with them, but they had a simple and effective method of relieving themselves of the care of the infants as soon as they reached the church. The papooses, who were strapped to their boards, were hung like a garment on the back wall of the building by a hole in the top of the board, which projected above their heads. Each papoose usually had a bit of fat pork tied to the end of a string fastened to its wrist, and with these sources of nourishment the infants occupied themselves pleasantly while the sermon was in progress. Frequently the pork slipped down the throat of the papoose, but the struggle of the child and the jerking of its hands in the strangulation that followed pulled the piece safely out again. As I faced the congregation I also faced the papooses, to whom the indifferent backs of their mothers were presented; it seemed to me there was never a time when some papoose was not choking, but no matter how much excitement or discomfort was going on among the babies, not one squaw turned her head to look back at them. In that assemblage the emotions were not allowed to interrupt the calm intellectual enjoyment of the sermon.

My most dramatic experience during this period occurred in the summer of 1874, when I went to a Northern lumber-camp to preach in the pulpit of a minister who was away on his honeymoon. The stage took me within twenty-two miles of my destination, to a place called Seberwing. To my dismay, however, when I arrived at Seberwing, Saturday evening, I found that the rest of the journey lay through a dense woods, and that I could reach my pulpit in time the next morning only by having some one drive me through the woods that night. It was not a pleasant prospect, for I had heard appalling tales of the stockades in this region and of the women who were kept prisoners there. But to miss the engagement was not to be thought of, and when, after I had made several vain efforts to find a driver, a man appeared in a two-seated wagon and offered to take me to my destination, I felt that I had to go with him, though I did not like his appearance. He was a huge, muscular person, with a protruding jaw and a singularly evasive eye; but I reflected that his forbidding expression might be due, in part at least, to the prospect of the long night drive through the woods, to which possibly he objected as much as I did.

It was already growing dark when we started, and within a few moments we were out of the little settlement and entering the woods. With me I had a revolver I had long since learned to use, but which I very rarely carried. I had hesitated to bring it now—had even left home without it; and then, impelled by some impulse I never afterward ceased to bless, had returned for it and dropped it into my hand-bag.

I sat on the back seat of the wagon, directly behind the driver, and for a time, as we entered the darkening woods, his great shoulders blotted out all perspective as he drove on in stolid silence. Then, little by little, they disappeared like a rapidly fading negative. The woods were filled with Norway pines, hemlocks, spruce, and tamaracks-great, somber trees that must have shut out the light even on the brightest days. To-night the heavens held no lamps aloft to guide us, and soon the darkness folded around us like a garment. I could see neither the driver nor his horses. I could hear only the sibilant whisper of the trees and the creak of our slow wheels in the rough forest road.

Suddenly the driver began to talk, and at first I was glad to hear the reassuring human tones, for the experience had begun to seem like a bad dream. I replied readily, and at once regretted that I had done so, for the man's choice of topics was most unpleasant. He began to tell me stories of the stockades—grim stories with horrible details, repeated so fully and with such gusto that I soon realized he was deliberately affronting my ears. I checked him and told him I could not listen to such talk.

He replied with a series of oaths and shocking vulgarities, stopping his horses that he might turn and fling the words into my face. He ended by snarling that I must think him a fool to imagine he did not know the kind of woman I was. What was I doing in that rough country, he demanded, and why was I alone with him in those black woods at night?

Though my heart missed a beat just then, I tried to answer him calmly.

"You know perfectly well who I am," I reminded him. "And you understand that I am making this journey to-night because I am to preach to-morrow morning and there is no other way to keep my appointment."

He uttered a laugh which was a most unpleasant sound.

"Well," he said, coolly, "I'm damned if I'll take you. I've got you here, and I'm going to keep you here!"

I slipped my hand into the satchel in my lap, and it touched my revolver. No touch of human fingers ever brought such comfort. With a deep breath of thanksgiving I drew it out and cocked it, and as I did so he recognized the sudden click.

"Here! What have you got there?" he snapped.

"I have a revolver," I replied, as steadily as I could. "And it is cocked and aimed straight at your back. Now drive on. If you stop again, or speak, I'll shoot you."

For an instant or two he blustered.

"By God," he cried, "you wouldn't dare."

"Wouldn't I?" I asked. "Try me by speaking just once more."

Even as I spoke I felt my hair rise on my scalp with the horror of the moment, which seemed worse than any nightmare a woman could experience. But the man was conquered by the knowledge of the waiting, willing weapon just behind him. He laid his whip savagely on the backs of his horses and they responded with a leap that almost knocked me out of the wagon.

The rest of the night was a black terror I shall never forget. He did not speak again, nor stop, but I dared not relax my caution for an instant. Hour after hour crawled toward day, and still I sat in the unpierced darkness, the revolver ready. I knew he was inwardly raging, and that at any instant he might make a sudden jump and try to get the revolver away from me. I decided that at his slightest movement I must shoot. But dawn came at last, and just as its bluish light touched the dark tips of the pines we drove up to the log hotel in the settlement that was our destination. Here my driver spoke. "Get down," he said, gruffly. "This is the place."

I sat still. Even yet I dared not trust him. Moreover, I was so stiff after my vigil that I was not sure I could move. "You get down," I directed, "and wake up the landlord. Bring him out here." He sullenly obeyed and aroused the hotel-owner, and when the latter appeared I climbed out of the wagon with some effort but without explanation. That morning I preached in my friend's pulpit as I had promised to do, and the rough building was packed to its doors with lumbermen who had come in from the neighboring camp. Their appearance caused great surprise, as they had never attended a service before. They formed a most picturesque congregation, for they all wore brilliant lumber-camp clothing—blue or red shirts with yellow scarfs twisted around their waists, and gay-colored jackets and logging-caps. There were forty or fifty of them, and when we took up our collection they responded with much liberality and cheerful shouts to one another.

"Put in fifty cents!" they yelled across the church. "Give her a dollar!"

The collection was the largest that had been taken up in the history of the settlement, but I soon learned that it was not the spiritual comfort I offered which had appealed to the lumber-men. My driver of the night before, who was one of their number, had told his pals of his experience, and the whole camp had poured into town to see the woman minister who carried a revolver. "Her sermon?" said one of them to my landlord, after the meeting. "Huh! I dunno what she preached. But, say, don't make no mistake about one thing: the little preacher has sure got grit!"

IV. THE WOLF AT THE DOOR

When I returned to Albion College in the autumn of 1875 I brought with me a problem which tormented me during my waking hours and chattered on my pillow at night. Should I devote two more years of my vanishing youth to the completion of my college course, or, instead, go at once to Boston University, enter upon my theological studies, take my degree, and be about my Father's business?

I was now twenty-seven years old, and I had been a licensed preacher for three years. My reputation in the Northwest was growing, and by sermons and lectures I could certainly earn enough to pay the expenses of the full college course. On the other hand, Boston was a new world. There I would be alone and practically penniless, and the opportunities for work might be limited. Quite possibly in my final two years at Albion I could even save enough money to make the experience in Boston less difficult, and the clear common sense I had inherited from my mother reminded me that in this course lay wisdom. Possibly it was some inheritance from my visionary father which made me, at the end of three months, waive these sage reflections, pack my few possessions, and start for Boston, where I entered the theological school of the university in February, 1876.

It was an instance of stepping off a solid plank and into space; and though there is exhilaration in the sensation, as I discovered then and at later crises in life when I did the same thing, there was also an amount of subsequent discomfort for which even my lively imagination had not prepared me. I went through some grim months in Boston—months during which I learned what it was to go to bed cold and hungry, to wake up cold and hungry, and to have no knowledge of how long these conditions might continue. But not more than once or twice during the struggle there, and then only for an hour or two in the physical and mental depression attending malnutrition, did I regret coming. At that period of my life I believed that the Lord had my small personal affairs very much on His mind. If I starved and froze it was His test of my worthiness for the ministry, and if He had really chosen me for one of His servants, He would see me through. The faith that sustained me then has still a place in my life, and existence without it would be an infinitely more dreary affair than it is. But I admit that I now call upon the Lord less often and less imperatively than I did before the stern years taught me my unimportance in the great scheme of things.

My class at the theological school was composed of forty-two young men and my unworthy self, and before I had been a member of it an hour I realized that women theologians paid heavily for the privilege of being women. The young men of my class who were licensed preachers were given free accommodations in the dormitory, and their board, at a club formed for their assistance, cost each of them only one dollar and twenty-five cents a week. For me no such kindly provision was made. I was not allowed a place in the dormitory, but instead was given two dollars a week to pay the rent of a room outside. Neither was I admitted to the economical comforts of the club, but fed myself according to my income, a plan which worked admirably when there was an income, but left an obvious void when there was not.

With characteristic optimism, however, I hired a little attic room on Tremont Street and established myself therein. In lieu of a window the room offered a pale skylight to the February storms, and there was neither heat in it nor running water; but its possession gave me a pleasant sense of proprietorship, and the whole experience seemed a high adventure. I at once sought opportunities to preach and lecture, but these were even rarer than firelight and food. In Albion I had been practically the only licensed preacher available for substitute and special work. In Boston University's three theological classes there were a hundred men, each snatching eagerly at the slightest possibility of employment; and when, despite this competition, I received and responded to an invitation to preach, I never knew whether I was to be paid for my services in cash or in compliments. If, by a happy chance, the compensation came in cash, the amount was rarely more than five dollars, and never more than ten. There was no help in sight from my family, whose early opposition to my career as a minister had hotly flamed forth again when I started East. I lived, therefore, on milk and crackers, and for weeks at a time my hunger was never wholly satisfied. In my home in the wilderness I had often heard the wolves prowling around our door at night. Now, in Boston, I heard them even at high noon.

There is a special and almost indescribable depression attending such conditions. No one who has not experienced the combination of continued cold, hunger, and loneliness in a great, strange, indifferent city can realize how it undermines the victim's nerves and even tears at the moral fiber. The self-humiliation I experienced was also intense. I had worked my way in the Northwest; why could I not work my way in Boston? Was there, perhaps, some lack in me and in my courage? Again and again these questions rose in my mind and poisoned my self-confidence. The one comfort I had in those black days was the knowledge that no one suspected the depth of the abyss in which I dwelt. We were all struggling; to the indifferent glance—and all glances were indifferent—my struggle was no worse than that of my classmates whose rooms and frugal meals were given them.

After a few months of this existence I was almost ready to believe that the Lord's work for me lay outside of the ministry, and while this fear was gripping me a serious crisis came in my financial affairs. The day dawned when I had not a cent, nor any prospect of earning one. My stock of provisions consisted of a box of biscuit, and my courage was flowing from me like blood from an opened vein. Then came one of the quick turns of the wheel of chance which make for optimism. Late in the afternoon I was asked to do a week of revival work with a minister in a local church, and when I accepted his invitation I mentally resolved to let that week decide my fate. My shoes had burst open at the sides; for lack of car-fare I had to walk to and from the scene of my meetings, though I had barely strength for the effort. If my week of work brought me enough to buy a pair of cheap shoes and feed me for a few days I would, I decided, continue my theological course. If it did not, I would give up the fight.

Never have I worked harder or better than during those seven days, when I put into the effort not only my heart and soul, but the last flame of my dying vitality, We had a rousing revival—one of the good old-time affairs when the mourners' benches were constantly filled and the air resounded with alleluias. The excitement and our success, mildly aided by the box of biscuit, sustained me through the week, and not until the last night did I realize how much of me had gone into this final desperate charge of mine. Then, the service over and the people departed, I sank, weak and trembling, into a chair, trying to pull myself together before hearing my fate in the good-night words of the minister I had assisted. When he came to me and began to compliment me on the work I had done, I could not rise. I sat still and listened with downcast eyes, afraid to lift them lest he read in them something of my need and panic in this moment when my whole future seemed at stake.

At first his words rolled around the empty church as if they were trying to get away from me, but at last I began to catch them. I was, it seemed, a most desirable helper. It had been a privilege and a pleasure to be associated with me. Beyond doubt, I would go far in my career. He heartily wished that he could reward me adequately. I deserved fifty dollars.

My tired heart fluttered at this. Probably my empty stomach fluttered, too; but in the next moment something seemed to catch my throat and stop my breath. For it appeared that, notwithstanding the enthusiasm and the spiritual uplift of the week, the collections had been very disappointing and the expenses unusually heavy. He could not give me fifty dollars. He could not give me anything at all. He thanked me warmly and wished me good night.

I managed to answer him and to get to my feet, but that journey down the aisle from my chair to the church door was the longest journey I have ever made. During it I felt not only the heart-sick disappointment of the moment, but the cumulative unhappiness of the years to come. I was friendless, penniless, and starving, but it was not of these conditions that I thought then. The one overwhelming fact was that I had been weighed and found wanting. I was not worthy.

I stumbled along, passing blindly a woman who stood on the street near the church entrance. She stopped me, timidly, and held out her hand. Then suddenly she put her arms around me and wept. She was an old lady, and I did not know her, but it seemed fitting that she should cry just then, as it would have seemed fitting to me if at that black moment all the people on the earth had broken into sudden wailing.

"Oh, Miss Shaw," she said, "I'm the happiest woman in the world, and I owe my happiness to you. To-night you have converted my grandson. He's all I have left, but he has been a wild boy, and I've prayed over him for years. Hereafter he is going to lead a different life. He has just given me his promise on his knees."

Her hand fumbled in her purse.

"I am a poor woman," she went on, "but I have enough, and I want to make you a little present. I know how hard life is for you young students."

She pressed a bill into my fingers. "It's very little," she said, humbly; "it is only five dollars."

I laughed, and in that exultant moment I seemed to hear life laughing with me. With the passing of the bill from her hand to mine existence had become a new experience, wonderful and beautiful.

"It's the biggest gift I have ever had," I told her. "This little bill is big enough to carry my future on its back!"

I had a good meal that night, and I bought the shoes the next morning. Infinitely more sustaining than the food, however, was the conviction that the Lord was with me and had given me a sign of His approval. The experience was the turning-point of my theological career. When the money was gone I succeeded in obtaining more work from time to time—and though the grind was still cruelly hard, I never again lost hope. The theological school was on Bromfield Street, and we students climbed three flights of stairs to reach our class-rooms. Through lack of proper food I had become too weak to ascend these stairs without sitting down once or twice to rest, and within a month after my experience with the appreciative grandmother I was discovered during one of these resting periods by Mrs.

Barrett, the superintendent of the Woman's Foreign Missionary Society, which had offices in our building. She stopped, looked me over, and then invited me into her room, where she asked me if I felt ill. I assured her that I did not. She asked a great many additional questions and, little by little, under the womanly sympathy of them, my reserve broke down and she finally got at the truth, which until that hour I had succeeded in concealing. She let me leave without much comment, but the next day she again invited me into her office and came directly to the purpose of the interview.

"Miss Shaw," she said, "I have been talking to a friend of mine about you, and she would like to make a bargain with you. She thinks you are working too hard. She will pay you three dollars and a half a week for the rest of this school year if you will promise to give up your preaching. She wants you to rest, study, and take care of your health."

I asked the name of my unknown friend, but Mrs. Barrett said that was to remain a secret. She had been given a check for seventy-eight dollars, and from this, she explained, my allowance would be paid in weekly instalments. I took the money very gratefully, and a few years later I returned the amount to the Missionary Society; but I never learned the identity of my benefactor. Her three dollars and a half a week, added to the weekly two dollars I was allowed for room rent, at once solved the problem of living; and now that meal-hours had a meaning in my life, my health improved and my horizon brightened. I spent most of my evenings in study, and my Sundays in the churches of Phillips Brooks and James Freeman Clark, my favorite ministers. Also, I joined the university's praying-band of students, and took part in the missionary-work among the women of the streets. I had never forgotten my early friend in Lawrence, the beautiful "mysterious lady" who had loved me as a child, and, in memory of her, I set earnestly about the effort to help unfortunates of her class. I went into the homes of these women, followed them to the streets and the dance-halls, talked to them, prayed with them, and made friends among them. Some of them I was able to help, but many were beyond help; and I soon learned that the effective work in that field is the work which is done for women before, not after, they have fallen.

During my vacation in the summer of 1876 I went to Cape Cod and earned my expenses by substituting in local pulpits. Here, at East Dennis, I formed the friendship which brought me at once the greatest happiness and the deepest sorrow of that period of my life. My new friend was a widow whose name was Persis Addy, and she was also the daughter of Captain Prince Crowell, then the most prominent man in the Cape Cod community—a bank president, a railroad director, and a citizen of wealth, as wealth was rated in those days. When I returned to the theological school in the autumn Mrs. Addy came to Boston with me, and from that time until her death, two years later, we lived together. She was immensely interested in my work, and the friendly part she took in it diverted her mind from the bereavement over which she had brooded for years, while to me her coming opened windows into a new world. I was no longer lonely; and though in my life with her I paid my way to the extent of my small income, she gave me my first experience of an existence in which comfort and culture, recreation, and leisurely reading were cheerful commonplaces. For the first time I had some one to come home to, some one to confide in, some one to talk to, listen to, and love. We read together and went to concerts together; and it was during this winter that I attended my first theatrical performance. The star was Mary Anderson, in "Pygmalion and Galatea," and play and player charmed me so utterly that I saw them every night that week, sitting high in the gallery and enjoying to the utmost the unfolding of this new delight. It was so glowing a pleasure that I longed to make some return to the giver of it; but not until many years afterward, when I met Madame Navarro in London, was I able to tell her what the experience had been and to thank her for it.

I did not long enjoy the glimpses into my new world, for soon, and most tragically, it was closed to me. In the spring following our first Boston winter together Mrs. Addy and I went to Hingham, Massachusetts, where I had been appointed temporary pastor of the Methodist Church. There Mrs. Addy was taken ill, and as she grew steadily worse we returned to Boston to live near the best available physicians, who for months theorized over her malady without being able to diagnose it. At last her father, Captain Crowell, sent to Paris for Dr. Brown-Sequard, then the most distinguished specialist of his day, and Dr. Brown-Sequard, when he arrived and examined his patient, discovered that she had a tumor on the brain. She had had a great shock in her life—the tragic death of her husband at sea during their wedding tour around the world—and it was believed that her disease dated from that time. Nothing could be done for her, and she failed daily during our second year together, and died in March, 1878, just before I finished my theological course and while I was still temporary pastor of the church at Hingham. Every moment I could take from my parish and my studies I spent with her, and those were sorrowful months. In her poor, tortured brain the idea formed that I, not she, was the sick person in our family of two, and when we were at home together she insisted that I must lie down and let her nurse me; then for hours she brooded over me, trying to relieve the agony she believed I was experiencing. When at last she was at peace her father and I took her home to Cape Cod and laid her in the graveyard of the little church where we had met at the beginning of our brief and beautiful friendship; and the subsequent loneliness I felt was far greater than any I had ever suffered in the past, for now I had learned the meaning of companionship.

Three months after Mrs. Addy's death I graduated. She had planned to take me abroad, and during our first winter together we had spent countless hours talking and dreaming of our European wanderings. When she found that she must die she made her will and left me fifteen hundred dollars for the visit to Europe, insisting that I must carry out the plan we had made; and during her conscious periods she constantly talked of this and made me promise that I would go. After her death it seemed to me that to go without her was impossible. Everything of beauty I looked upon would hold memories of her, keeping fresh my sorrow and emphasizing my loneliness; but it was her last expressed desire that I should go, and I went.

First, however, I had graduated—clad in a brandnew black silk gown, and with five dollars in my pocket, which I kept there during the graduation exercises. I felt a special satisfaction in the possession of that money, for, notwithstanding the handicap of being a woman, I was said to be the only member of my class who had worked during the entire course, graduated free from debt, and had a new outfit as well as a few dollars in cash.

I graduated without any special honors. Possibly I might have won some if I had made the effort, but my graduation year, as I have just explained, had been very difficult. As it was, I was merely a good average student, feeling my isolation as the only woman in my class, but certainly not spurring on my men associates by the display of any brilliant gifts. Naturally, I missed a great deal of class fellowship and class support, and throughout my entire course I rarely entered my class-room without the abysmal conviction that I was not really wanted there. But some of the men were goodhumoredly cordial, and several of them are among my friends to-day. Between myself and my family there still existed the breach I had created when I began to preach. With the exception of Mary and James, my people openly regarded me, during my theological course, as a dweller in outer darkness, and even my mother's love was clouded by what she felt to be my deliberate and persistent flouting of her wishes.

Toward the end of my university experience, however, an incident occurred which apparently changed my mother's viewpoint. She was now living with my sister Mary, in Big Rapids, Michigan, and, on the occasion of one of my rare and brief visits to them I was invited to preach in the local church. Here, for the first time, my mother heard me. Dutifully escorted by one of my brothers, she attended church that morning in a state of shivering nervousness. I do not know what she expected me to do or say, but toward the end of the sermon it became clear that I had not justified her fears. The look of intense apprehension left her eyes, her features relaxed into placidity, and later in the day she paid me the highest compliment I had yet received from a member of my family.

"I liked the sermon very much," she peacefully told my brother. "Anna didn't say anything about hell, or about anything else!"

When we laughed at this handsome tribute, she hastened to qualify it.

"What I mean," she explained, "is that Anna didn't say anything objectionable in the pulpit!" And with this recognition I was content.

Between the death of my friend and my departure for Europe I buried myself in the work of the university and of my little church; and as if in answer to the call of my need, Mary E. Livermore, who had given me the first professional encouragement I had ever received, re-entered my life. Her husband, like myself, was pastor of a church in Hingham, and whenever his finances grew low, or there was need of a fund for some special purpose—conditions that usually exist in a small church—his brilliant wife came to his assistance and raised the money, while her husband retired modestly to the background and regarded her with adoring eyes. On one of these occasions, I remember, when she entered the pulpit to preach her sermon, she dropped her bonnet and coat on an unoccupied chair. A little later there was need of this chair, and Mr. Livermore, who sat under the pulpit, leaned forward, picked up the garments, and, without the least trace of selfconsciousness, held them in his lap throughout the sermon. One of the members of the church, who appeared to be irritated by the incident, later spoke of it to him and added, sardonically, "How does it feel to be merely 'Mrs. Livermore's husband'?"

In reply Mr. Livermore flashed on him one of his charming smiles. "Why, I'm very proud of it," he said, with the utmost cheerfulness. "You see, I'm the only man in the world who has that distinction."

They were a charming couple, the Livermores, and they deserved far more than they received from a world to which they gave so freely and so richly. To me, as to others, they were more than kind; and I never recall them without a deep feeling of gratitude and an equally deep sense of loss in their passing.

It was during this period, also, that I met Frances E. Willard. There was a great Moody revival in progress in Boston, and Miss Willard was the righthand assistant of Mr. Moody. To her that revival must have been marked with a star, for during it she met for the first time Miss Anna Gordon, who became her life-long friend and her biographer. The meetings also laid the foundation of our friendship, and for many years Miss Willard and I were closely associated in work and affection.

On the second or third night of the revival, during one of the "mixed meetings," attended by both women and men, Mr. Moody invited those who were willing to talk to sinners to come to the front. I went down the aisle with others, and found a seat near Miss Willard, to whom I was then introduced by some one who knew us both. I wore my hair short in those days, and I had a little fur cap on my head. Though I had been preaching for several years, I looked absurdly young—far too young, it soon became evident, to interest Mr. Moody. He was already moving about among the men and women who had responded to his invitation, and one by one he invited them to speak, passing me each time until at last I was left alone. Then he took pity on me and came to my side to whisper kindly that I had misunderstood his invitation. He did not want young girls to talk to his people, he said, but mature women with worldly experience. He advised me to go home to my mother, adding, to soften the blow, that some time in the future when there were young girls at the meeting I could come and talk to them.

I made no explanations to him, but started to leave, and Miss Willard, who saw me departing, followed and stopped me. She asked why I was going, and I told her that Mr. Moody had sent me home to grow. Frances Willard had a keen sense of humor, and she enjoyed the joke so thoroughly that she finally convinced me it was amusing, though at first the humor of it had escaped me. She took me back to Mr. Moody and explained the situation to him, and he apologized and put me to work. He said he had thought I was about sixteen. After that I occasionally helped him in the intervals of my other work.

The time had come to follow Mrs. Addy's wishes and go to Europe, and I sailed in the month of June following my graduation, and traveled for three months with a party of tourists under the direction of Eben Tourgee, of the Boston Conservatory of Music. We landed in Glasgow, and from there went to England, Belgium, Holland, Germany, France, and last of all to Italy. Our company included many clergymen and a never-to-be-forgotten widow whose light-hearted attitude toward the memory of her departed spouse furnished the comedy of our first voyage. It became a pet diversion to ask her if her husband still lived, for she always answered the question in the same mournful words, and with the same manner of irrepressible gaiety.

"Oh no!" she would chirp. "My dear departed has been in our Heavenly Father's house for the past eight years!"

At its best, the vacation without my friend was tragically incomplete, and only a few of its incidents stand out with clearness across the forty-six years that have passed since then. One morning, I remember, I preached an impromptu sermon in the Castle of Heidelberg before a large gathering; and a little later, in Genoa, I preached a very different sermon to a wholly different congregation. There was a gospel-ship in the harbor, and one Saturday the pastor of it came ashore to ask if some American clergyman in our party would preach on his ship the next morning. He was an old-time, orthodox Presbyterian, and from the tips of his broad-soled shoes to the severe part in the hair above his sanctimonious brow he looked the type. I was not present when he called at our hotel, and my absence gave my fellow-clergymen an opportunity to play a joke on the gentleman from the gospel-ship. They assured him that "Dr. Shaw" would preach for him, and the pastor returned to his post greatly pleased. When they told me of his invitation, however, they did not add that they had neglected to tell him Dr. Shaw was a woman, and I was greatly elated by the compliment I thought had been paid me.

Our entire party of thirty went out to the gospelship the next morning, and when the pastor came to meet us, lank and forbidding, his austere lips vainly trying to curve into a smile of welcome, they introduced me to him as the minister who was to deliver the sermon. He had just taken my hand; he dropped it as if it had burned his own. For a moment he had no words to meet the crisis. Then he stuttered something to the effect that the situation was impossible that his men would not listen to a woman, that they would mob her, that it would be blasphemous for a woman to preach. My associates, who had so light-heartedly let me in for this unpleasant experience, now realized that they must see me through it. They persuaded him to allow me to preach the sermon.

With deep reluctance the pastor finally accepted me and the situation; but when the moment came to introduce me, he devoted most of his time to heartfelt apologies for my presence. He explained to the sailors that I was a woman, and fervidly assured them that he himself was not responsible for my appearance there. With every word he uttered he put a brick in the wall he was building between me and the crew, until at last I felt that I could never get past it. I was very unhappy, very lonely, very homesick; and suddenly the thought came to me that these men, notwithstanding their sullen eyes and forbidding faces, might be lonely and homesick, too. I decided to talk to them as a woman and not as a minister, and I came down from the pulpit and faced them on their own level, looking them over and mentally selecting the hardest specimens of the lot as the special objects of my appeal. One old fellow, who looked like a pirate with his red-rimmed eyes, weather-beaten skin, and fimbriated face, grinned up at me in such sardonic challenge that I walked directly in front of him and began to speak. I said:

"My friends, I hope you will forget everything Dr. Blank has just said. It is true that I am a minister, and that I came here to preach. But now I do not intend to preach—only to have a friendly talk, on a text which is not in the Bible. I am very far from home, and I feel as homesick as some of you men look. So my text is, 'Blessed are the homesick, for they shall go home.'"

In my summers at Cape Cod I had learned something about sailors. I knew that in the inprepossessing congregation before me there were many boys who had run away from home, and men who had left home because of family troubles. I talked to the young men first, to those who had forgotten their mothers and thought their mothers had forgotten them, and I told of my experiences with waiting, heavy-hearted mothers who had sons at sea. Some heads went down at that, and here and there I saw a boy gulp, but the old fellow I was particularly anxious to move still grinned up at me like a malicious monkey. Then I talked of the sailor's wife, and of her double burden of homemaking and anxiety, and soon I could pick out some of the husbands by their softened faces. But still my old man grinned and squinted. Last of all I described the whalers who were absent from home for years, and who came back to find their children and their grandchildren waiting for them. I told how I had seen them, in our New England coast towns, covered, as a ship is covered with barnacles, by grandchildren who rode on their shoulders and sat astride of their necks as they walked down the village streets. And now at last the sneer left my old man's loose lips. He had grandchildren somewhere. He twisted uneasily in his seat, coughed, and finally took out a big red handkerchief and wiped his eyes. The episode encouraged me.

"When I came here," I added, "I intended to preach a sermon on 'The Heavenly Vision.' Now I want to give you a glimpse of that in addition to the vision we have had of home."

I ended with a bit of the sermon and a prayer, and when I raised my head the old man of the sardonic grin was standing before me.

"Missus," he said in a husky whisper, "I'd like to shake your hand."

I took his hard old fist, and then, seeing that many of the other sailors were beginning to move hospitably but shyly toward me, I said:

"I would like to shake hands with every man here."

At the words they surged forward, and the affair became a reception, during which I shook hands with every sailor of my congregation. The next day my hand was swollen out of shape, for the sailors had gripped it as if they were hauling on a hawser; but the experience was worth the discomfort. The best moment of the morning came, however, when the pastor of the ship faced me, goggle-eyed and marveling.

"I wouldn't have believed it," was all he could say. "I thought the men would mob you."

"Why should they mob me?" I wanted to know.

"Why," he stammered, "because the thing is so—so—unnatural."

"Well," I said, "if it is unnatural for women to talk to men, we have been living in an unnatural world for a long time. Moreover, if it is unnatural, why did Jesus send a woman out as the first preacher?"

He waived a discussion of that question by inviting us all to his cabin to drink wine with him—and as we were "total abstainers," it seemed as unnatural to us to have him offer us wine as a woman's preaching had seemed to him.

The next European incident on which memory throws a high-light was our audience with Pope Leo XIII. As there were several distinguished Americans in our party, a private audience was arranged for us, and for days before the time appointed we nervously rehearsed the etiquette of the occasion. When we reached the Vatican we were marched between rows of Swiss Guards to the Throne Room, only to learn there that we were to be received in the Tapestry Room. Here we found a very impressive assemblage of cardinals and Vatican officials, and while we were still lost in the beauty of the picture they made against the room's superb background, the approach of the Pope was announced. Every one immediately knelt, except a few persons who tried to show their democracy by standing; but I am sure that even these individuals felt a thrill when the slight, exquisite figure appeared at the door and gave us a general benediction. Then the Pope passed slowly down the line, offering his hand to each of us, and radiating a charm so gracious and so human that few failed to respond to the appeal of his engaging personality. There was nothing fleshly about Leo XIII. His body was so frail, so wraithlike, that one almost expected to see through it the magnificent tapestries on the walls. But from the moment he appeared every eye clung to him, every thought was concentrated upon him. This effect I think he would have produced even if he had come among us unrecognized, for through the thin shell that housed it shone the steady flame of a wonderful spirit.

I had previously remarked to my friends that kissing the Pope's ring after so many other lips had touched it did not appeal to me as hygienic, and that I intended to kiss his hand instead. When my opportunity came I kept my word; but after I had kissed the venerable hand I remained kneeling for an instant with bowed head, a little aghast at my daring. The gentle Father thought, however, that I was waiting for a special blessing. He gave it to me gravely and passed on, and I devoted the next few hours to ungodly crowing over the associates who had received no such individual attention.

In Venice we attended the great fete celebrating the first visit of King Humbert and Queen Margherita. It was also the first time Venice had entertained a queen since the Italian union, and the sea-queen of the Adriatic outdid herself in the gorgeousness and the beauty of her preparations. The Grand Canal was like a flowing rainbow, reflecting the brilliant decorations on every side, and at night the moonlight, the music, the chiming church-bells, the colored lanterns, the gay voices, the lapping waters against the sides of countless gondolas made the experience seem like a dream of a new and unbelievably beautiful world. Forty thousand persons were gathered in the Square of St. Mark and in front of the Palace, and I recall a pretty incident in which the gracious Queen and a little street urchin figured. The small, ragged boy had crept as close to the royal balcony as he dared, and then, unobserved, had climbed up one of its pillars. At the moment when a sudden hush had fallen on the crowd this infant, overcome by patriotism and a glimpse of the royal lady on the balcony above him, suddenly piped up shrilly in the silence. "Long live the Queen!" he cried. "Long live the Queen!"

The gracious Margherita heard the childish voice, and, amused and interested, leaned over the balcony to see where it came from. What she saw doubtless touched the mother-heart in her. She caught the eye of the tattered urchin clinging to the pillar, and radiantly smiled on him. Then, probably thinking that the King was absorbing the attention of the great assemblage, she indulged in a little diversion. Leaning far forward, she kissed the tip of her lace handkerchief and swept it caressingly across the boy's brown cheek, smiling down at him as unconsciously as if she and the enraptured youngster were alone together in the world. The next instant she had straightened up and flushed, for the watchful crowd had seen the episode and was wild with enthusiasm. For ten minutes the people cheered the Queen without ceasing, and for the next few days they talked of little but the spontaneous, girlish action which had delighted them all.

One more sentimental record, and I shall have reached another mile-stone. As I have said, my friend Mrs. Addy left me in her will fifteen hundred dollars for my visit to Europe, and before I sailed her father, who was one of the best friends I have ever had, made a characteristically kind proposition in connection with the little fund. Instead of giving me the money, he gave me two railroad bonds, one for one thousand dollars, the other for five hundred dollars, and each drawing seven per cent. interest. He suggested that I deposit these bonds in the bank of which he was president, and borrow from the bank the money to go abroad. Then, when I returned and went into my new parish, I could use some of my salary every month toward repaying the loan. These monthly payments, he explained, could be as small as I wished, but each month the interest on the amount I paid would cease. I gladly took his advice and borrowed seven hundred dollars. After I returned from Europe I repaid the loan in monthly instalments, and eventually got my bonds, which I still own. They will mature in 1916. I have had one hundred and five dollars a year from them, in interest, ever since I received them in 1878—more than twice as much interest as their face value—and every time I have gone abroad I have used this interest toward paying my passage. Thus my friend has had a share in each of the many visits I have made to Europe, and in all of them her memory has been vividly with me.

With my return from Europe my real career as a minister began. The year in the pulpit at Hingham had been merely tentative, and though I had succeeded in building up the church membership to four times what it had been when I took charge, I was not reappointed. I had paid off a small church debt, and had had the building repaired, painted, and carpeted. Now that it was out of its difficulties it offered some advantages to the occupant of its pulpit, and of these my successor, a man, received the benefit. I, however, had small ground for complaint, for I was at once offered and accepted the pastorate of a church at East Dennis, Cape Cod. Here I went in October, 1878, and here I spent seven of the most interesting years of my life.

V. SHEPHERD OF A DIVIDED FLOCK

On my return from Europe, as I have said, I took up immediately and most buoyantly the work of my new parish. My previous occupation of various pulpits, whether long or short, had always been in the role of a substitute. Now, for the first time, I had a church of my own, and was to stand or fall by the record made in it. The ink was barely dry on my diploma from the Boston Theological School, and, as it happened, the little church to which I was called was in the hands of two warring factions, whose battles furnished the most fervid interest of the Cape Cod community. But my inexperience disturbed me not at all, and I was blissfully ignorant of the division in the congregation. So I entered my new field as trustfully as a child enters a garden; and though I was in trouble from the beginning, and resigned three times in startling succession, I ended by remaining seven years.

My appointment did not cause even a lull in the warfare among my parishioners. Before I had crossed the threshold of my church I was made to realize that I was shepherd of a divided flock. Exactly what had caused the original breach I never learned; but it had widened with time, until it seemed that no peacemaker could build a bridge large enough to span it. As soon as I arrived in East Dennis each faction tried to pour into my ears its bitter criticisms of the other, but I made and consistently followed the safe rule of refusing to listen to either side, I announced publicly that I would hear no verbal charges whatever, but that if my two flocks would state their troubles in writing I would call a board meeting to discuss and pass upon them. This they both resolutely refused to do (it was apparently the first time they had ever agreed on any point); and as I steadily declined to listen to complaints, they devised an original method of putting them before me.

During the regular Thursday-night prayer-meeting, held about two weeks after my arrival, and at which, of course, I presided, they voiced their difficulties in public prayer, loudly and urgently calling upon the Lord to pardon such and such a liar, mentioning the gentleman by name, and such and such a slanderer, whose name was also submitted. By the time the prayers were ended there were few untarnished reputations in the congregation, and I knew, perforce, what both sides had to say.

The following Thursday night they did the same thing, filling their prayers with intimate and surprising details of one another's history, and I endured the situation solely because I did not know how to meet it. I was still young, and my theological course had set no guide-posts on roads as new as these. To interfere with souls in their communion with God seemed impossible;

to let them continue to utter personal attacks in church, under cover of prayer, was equally impossible. Any course I could follow seemed to lead away from my new parish, yet both duty and pride made prompt action necessary. By the time we gathered for the third prayermeeting I had decided what to do, and before the services began I rose and addressed my erring children. I explained that the character of the prayers at our recent meetings was making us the laughingstock of the community, that unbelievers were ridiculing our religion, and that the discipline of the church was being wrecked; and I ended with these words, each of which I had carefully weighed:

"Now one of two things must happen. Either you will stop this kind of praying, or you will remain away from our meetings. We will hold prayermeetings on another night, and I shall refuse admission to any among you who bring personal criticisms into your public prayers."

As I had expected it to do, the announcement created an immediate uproar. Both factions sprang to their feet, trying to talk at once. The storm raged until I dismissed the congregation, telling the members that their conduct was an insult to the Lord, and that I would not listen to either their protests or their prayers. They went unwillingly, but they went; and the excitement the next day raised the sick from their beds to talk of it, and swept the length and breadth of Cape Cod. The following Sunday the little church held the largest attendance in its history. Seemingly, every man and woman in town had come to hear what more I would say about the trouble, but I ignored the whole matter. I preached the sermon I had prepared, the subject of which was as remote from church quarrels as our atmosphere was remote from peace, and my congregation dispersed with expressions of such artless disappointment that it was all I could do to preserve a dignified gravity.

That night, however, the war was brought into my camp. At the evening meeting the leader of one of the factions rose to his feet with the obvious purpose of starting trouble. He was a retired sea-captain, of the ruthless type that knocks a man down with a belaying-pin, and he made his attack on me in a characteristically "straight from the shoulder" fashion. He began with the proposition that my morning sermon had been "entirely contrary to the Scriptures," and for ten minutes he quoted and misquoted me, hammering in his points. I let him go on without interruption. Then he added:

"And this gal comes to this church and undertakes to tell us how we shall pray. That's a highhanded measure, and I, for one, ain't goin' to stand it. I want to say right here that I shall pray as I like, when I like, and where I like. I have prayed in this heavenly way for fifty years before that gal was born, and she can't dictate to me now!"

By this time the whole congregation was aroused, and cries of "Sit down!" "Sit down!" came from every side of the church. It was a hard moment, but I was able to rise with some show of dignity. I was hurt through and through, but my fighting blood was stirring.

"No," I said, "Captain Sears has the floor. Let him say now all he wishes to say, for it is the last time he will ever speak at one of our meetings."

Captain Sears, whose exertions had already made him apoplectic, turned a darker purple. "What's that?" he shouted. "What d'ye mean?"

"I mean," I replied, "that I do not intend to allow you or anybody else to interfere with my meetings. You are a sea-captain. What would you do to me if I came on board your ship and started a mutiny in your crew, or tried to give you orders?"

Captain Sears did not reply. He stood still, with his legs far apart and braced, as he always stood when talking, but his eyes shifted a little. I answered my own question.

"You would put me ashore or in irons," I reminded him. "Now, Captain Sears, I intend to put you ashore. I am the master of this ship. I have set my course, and I mean to follow it. If you rebel, either you will get out or I will. But until the board asks for my resignation, I am in command."

As it happened, I had put my ultimatum in the one form the old man could understand. He sat down without a word and stared at me. We sang the Doxology, and I dismissed the meeting. Again we had omitted prayers. The next day Captain Sears sent me a letter recalling his subscription toward the support of the church; and for weeks he remained away from our services, returning under conditions I will mention later. Even at the time, however, his attack helped rather than hurt me. At the regular meeting the following Thursday night no personal criticisms were included in the prayers, and eventually we had peace. But many battles were lost and won before that happy day arrived.

Captain Sears's vacant place among us was promptly taken by another captain in East Dennis, whose name was also Sears. A few days after my encounter with the first captain I met the second on the street. He had never come to church, and I stopped and invited him to do so. He replied with simple candor.

"I ain't comin'," he told me. "There ain't no gal that can teach me nothin'."

"Perhaps you are wrong, Captain Sears," I replied. "I might teach you something."

"What?" demanded the captain, with chilling distrust.

"Oh," I said, cheerfully, "let us say tolerance, for one thing."

"Humph!" muttered the old man. "The Lord don't want none of your tolerance, and neither do I."

I laughed. "He doesn't object to tolerance," I said. "Come to church. You can talk, too; and the Lord will listen to us both."

To my surprise, the captain came the following Sunday, and during the seven years I remained in the church he was one of my strongest supporters and friends. I needed friends, for my second battle was not slow in following my first. There was, indeed, barely time between in which to care for the wounded.

We had in East Dennis what was known as the "Free Religious Group," and when some of the members of my congregation were not wrangling among themselves, they were usually locking horns with this group. For years, I was told, one of the prime diversions of the "Free Religious" faction was to have a dance in our town hall on the night when we were using it for our annual church fair. The rules of the church positively prohibited dancing, so the worldly group took peculiar pleasure in attending the fair, and during the evening in getting up a dance and whirling about among us, to the horror of our members. Then they spent the remainder of the year boasting of the achievement. It came to my ears that they had decided to follow this pleasing programme at our Christmas church celebration, so I called the church trustees together and put the situation to them.

"We must either enforce our discipline," I said, "or give it up. Personally I do not object to dancing, but, as the church has ruled against it, I intend to uphold the church. To allow these people to make us ridiculous year after year is impossible. Let us either tell them that they may dance or that they may not dance; but whatever we tell them, let us make them obey our ruling."

The trustees were shocked at the mere suggestion of letting them dance.

"Very well," I ended. "Then they shall not dance. That is understood."

Captain Crowell, the father of my dead friend Mrs. Addy, and himself my best man friend, was a strong supporter of the Free Religious Group. When its members raced to him with the news that I had said they could not dance at the church's Christmas party, Captain Crowell laughed goodhumoredly and told them to dance as much as they pleased, cheerfully adding that he would get them out of any trouble they got into. Knowing my friendship for him, and that I even owed my church appointment to him, the Free Religious people were certain that I would never take issue with him on dancing or on any other point. They made all their preparations for the dance, therefore, with entire confidence, and boasted that the affair would be the gayest they had ever arranged. My people began to look at me with sympathy, and for a time I felt very sorry for myself. It seemed sufficiently clear that "the gal" was to have more trouble.

On the night of the party things went badly from the first. There was an evident intention among the worst of the Free Religious Group to embarrass us at every turn. We opened the exercises with the Lord's Prayer, which this element loudly applauded. A live kitten was hung high on the Christmas tree, where it squalled mournfully beyond reach of rescue, and the young men of the outside group threw cake at one another across the hall. Finally tiring of these innocent diversions, they began to prepare for their dance, and I protested. The spokesman of the group waved me to one side.

"Captain Crowell said we could," he remarked, airily.

"Captain Crowell," I replied, "has no authority whatever in this matter. The church trustees have decided that you cannot dance here, and I intend to enforce their ruling."

It was interesting to observe how rapidly the men of my congregation disappeared from that hall. Like shadows they crept along the walls and vanished through the doors. But the preparations for the dance went merrily on. I walked to the middle of the room and raised my voice. I was always listened to, for my hearers always had the hope, usually realized, that I was about to get into more trouble.

"You are determined to dance," I began. "I cannot keep you from doing so. But I can and will make you regret that you have done so. The law of the State of Massachusetts is very definite in regard to religious meetings and religious gatherings. This hall was engaged and paid for by the Wesleyan Methodist Church, of which I am pastor, and we have full control of it to-night. Every man and woman who interrupts our exercises by attempting to dance, or by creating a disturbance of any kind, will be arrested to-morrow morning."

Surprise at first, then consternation, swept through the ranks of the Free Religious Group. They denied the existence of such a law as I had mentioned, and I promptly read it aloud to them. The leaders went off into a corner and consulted. By this time not one man in my parish was left in the hall. As a result of the consultation in the corner, a committee of the would-be dancers came to me and suggested a compromise.

"Will you agree to arrest the men only?" they wanted to know.

"No," I declared. "On the contrary, I shall have the women arrested first! For the women ought to be standing with me now in the support of law and order, instead of siding with the hoodlum element you represent."

That settled it. No girl or woman dared to go on the dancing-floor, and no man cared to revolve merrily by himself. A whisper went round, however, that the dance would begin when I had left. When the clock struck twelve, at which hour, according to the town rule, the hall had to be closed, I was the last person to leave it. Then I locked the door myself, and carried the key away with me. There had been no Free Religious dance that night.

On the following Sunday morning the attendance at my church broke all previous records. Every seat was occupied and every aisle was filled. Men and women came from surrounding towns, and strange horses were tied to all the fences in East Dennis. Every person in that church was looking for excitement, and this time my congregation got what it expected. Before I began my sermon I read my resignation, to take effect at the discretion of the trustees. Then, as it was presumably my last chance to tell the people and the place what I thought of them, I spent an hour and a half in fervidly doing so. In my study of English I had acquired a fairly large vocabulary. I think I used it all that morning—certainly I tried to. If ever an erring congregation and community saw themselves as they really were, mine did on that occasion. I was heartsick, discouraged, and full of resentment and indignation, which until then had been pent up. Under the arraignment my people writhed and squirmed. I ended:

"What I am saying hurts you, but in your hearts you know you deserve every word of it. It is high time you saw yourselves as you are—a disgrace to the religion you profess and to the community you live in."

I was not sure the congregation would let me finish, but it did. My hearers seemed torn by conflicting sentiments, in which anger and curiosity led opposing sides. Many of them left the church in a white fury, but others— more than I had expected—remained to speak to me and assure me of their sympathy. Once on the streets, different groups formed and mingled, and all day the little town rocked with arguments for and against "the gal."

Night brought another surprisingly large attendance. I expected more trouble, and I faced it with difficulty, for I was very tired. Just as I took my place in the pulpit, Captain Sears entered the church and walked down the aisle—the Captain Sears who had left us at my invitation some weeks before and had not since attended a church service. I was sure he was there to make another attack on me while I was down, and, expecting the worst, I wearily gave him his opportunity. The big old fellow stood up, braced himself on legs far apart, as if he were standing on a slippery deck during a high sea, and gave the congregation its biggest surprise of the year.

He said he had come to make a confession. He had been angry with "the gal" in the past, as they all knew. But he had heard about the sermon she had preached that morning, and this time she was right. It was high time quarreling and backbiting were stopped. They had been going on too long, and no good could come of them. Moreover, in all the years he had been a member of that congregation he had never until now seen the pulpit occupied by a minister with enough backbone to uphold the discipline of the church. "I've come here to say I'm with the gal," he ended. "Put me down for my original subscription and ten dollars extra!"

So we had the old man back again. He was a tower of strength, and he stood by me faithfully until he died. The trustees would not accept my resignation (indeed, they refused to consider it at all), and the congregation, when it had thought things over, apparently decided that there might be worse things in the pulpit than "the gal." It was even known to brag of what it called my "spunk," and perhaps it was this quality, rather than any other, which I most needed in that particular parish at that time. As for me, when the fight was over I dropped it from my mind, and it had not entered my thoughts for years, until I began to summon these memories.

At the end of my first six months in East Dennis I was asked to take on, also, the temporary charge of the Congregational Church at Dennis, two miles and a half away. I agreed to do this until a permanent pastor could be found, on condition that I should preach at Dennis on Sunday afternoons, using the same sermon I preached in my own pulpit in the morning. The arrangement worked so well that it lasted for six and a half years—until I resigned from my East Dennis church. During that period, moreover, I not only carried the two churches on my shoulders, holding three meetings each Sunday, but I entered upon and completed a course in the Boston Medical School, winning my M.D. in 1885, and I also lectured several times a month during the winter seasons. These were, therefore, among the most strenuous as well as the most interesting years of my existence, and I mention the strain of them only to prove my life-long contention, that congenial work, no matter how much there is of it, has never yet killed any one!

After my battle with the Free Religious Group things moved much more smoothly in the parish. Captain Crowell, instead of resenting my defiance of his ruling, helped to reconcile the divided factions in the church; and though, as I have said, twice afterward I submitted my resignation, in each case the fight I was making was for a cause which I firmly believed in and eventually won. My second resignation was brought about by the unwillingness of the church to have me exchange pulpits with the one minister on Cape Cod broad-minded enough to invite me to preach in his pulpit. I had done so, and had then sent him a return invitation. He was a gentleman and a scholar, but he was also a Unitarian; and though my people were willing to let me preach in his church, they were loath to let him preach in mine. After a surprising amount of discussion my resignation put a different aspect on the matter; it also led to the satisfactory ruling that I could exchange pulpits not only with this minister, but with any other in good standing in his own church.

My third resignation went before the trustees in consequence of my protest from the pulpit against a small drinking and gambling saloon in East Dennis; which was rapidly demoralizing our boys. Theoretically, only "soft drinks" were sold, but the gambling was open, and the resort was constantly filled with boys of all ages. There were influences back of this place which tried to protect it, and its owner was very popular in the town. After my first sermon I was waited upon by a committee, that warmly advised me to "let East Dennis alone" and confine my criticisms "to saloons in Boston and other big towns." As I had nothing to do with Boston, and much to do with East Dennis, I preached on that place three Sundays in succession, and feeling became so intense that I handed in my resignation and prepared to depart. Then my friends rallied and the resort was suppressed.

That was my last big struggle. During the remaining five years of my pastorate on Cape Cod the relations between my people and myself were wholly harmonious and beautiful. If I have seemed to dwell too much on these small victories, it must be remembered that I find in them such comfort as I can. I have not yet won the great and vital fight of my life, to which I have given myself, heart and soul, for the past thirty years—the campaign for woman suffrage. I have seen victories here and there, and shall see more. But when the ultimate triumph comes—when American women in every state cast their ballots as naturally as their husbands do—I may not be in this world to rejoice over it.

It is interesting to remember that during the strenuous period of the first few months in East Dennis, and notwithstanding the division in the congregation, we women of the church got together and repainted and refurnished the building, raising all the money and doing much of the work ourselves, as the expense of having it done was prohibitive. We painted the church, and even cut down and modernized the pulpit. The total cost of material and furniture was not half so great as the original estimate had indicated, and we had learned a valuable lesson. After this we spent very little money for labor, but did our own cleaning, carpet-laying, and the like;

and our little church, if I may be allowed to say so, was a model of neatness and good taste.

I have said that at the end of two years from the time of my appointment the long-continued warfare in the church was ended. I was not immediately allowed, however, to bask in an atmosphere of harmony, for in October, 1880, the celebrated contest over my ordination took place at the Methodist Protestant Conference in Tarrytown, New York; and for three days I was a storm-center around which a large number of truly good and wholly sincere men fought the fight of their religious lives. Many of them strongly believed that women were out of place in the ministry. I did not blame them for this conviction. But I was in the ministry, and I was greatly handicapped by the fact that, although I was a licensed preacher and a graduate of the Boston Theological School, I could not, until I had been regularly ordained, meet all the functions of my office. I could perform the marriage service, but I could not baptize. I could bury the dead, but I could not take members into my church. That had to be done by the presiding elder or by some other minister. I could not administer the sacraments. So at the New England Spring Conference of the Methodist Episcopal Church, held in Boston in 1880, I formally applied for ordination. At the same time application was made by another woman—Miss Anna Oliver—and as a preliminary step we were both examined by the Conference board, and were formally reported by that board as fitted for ordination. Our names were therefore presented at the Conference, over which Bishop Andrews presided, and he immediately refused to accept them. Miss Oliver and I were sitting together in the gallery of the church when the bishop announced his decision, and, while it staggered us, it did not really surprise us. We had been warned of this gentleman's deep-seated prejudice against women in the ministry.

After the services were over Miss Oliver and I called on him and asked him what we should do. He told us calmly that there was nothing for us to do but to get out of the Church. We reminded him of our years of study and probation, and that I had been for two years in charge of two churches. He set his thin lips and replied that there was no place for women in the ministry, and, as he then evidently considered the interview ended, we left him with heavy hearts. While we were walking slowly away, Miss Oliver confided to me that she did not intend to leave the Church. Instead, she told me, she would stay in and fight the matter of her ordination to a finish. I, however, felt differently. I had done considerable fighting during the past two years, and my heart and soul were weary. I said: "I shall get out, I am no better and no stronger than a man, and it is all a man can do to fight the world, the flesh, and the devil, without fighting his Church as well. I do not intend to fight my Church. But I am called to preach the gospel; and if I cannot preach it in my own Church, I will certainly preach it in some other Church!"

As if in response to this outburst, a young minister named Mark Trafton soon called to see me. He had been present at our Conference, he had seen my Church refuse to ordain me, and he had come to suggest that I apply for ordination in his Church—the Methodist Protestant. To leave my Church, even though urged to do so by its appointed spokesman, seemed a radical step. Before taking this I appealed from the decision of the Conference to the General Conference of the Methodist Episcopal Church, which held its session that year in Cincinnati, Ohio. Miss Oliver also appealed, and again we were both refused ordination, the General Conference voting to sustain Bishop Andrews in his decision. Not content with this achievement, the Conference even took a backward step. It deprived us of the right to be licensed as local preachers. After this blow I recalled with gratitude the Reverend Mark Trafton's excellent advice, and I immediately applied for ordination in the Methodist Protestant Church. My name was presented at the Conference held in Tarrytown in October, 1880, and the fight was on.

During these Conferences it is customary for each candidate to retire while the discussion of his individual fitness for ordination is in progress. When my name came up I was asked, as my predecessors had been, to leave the room for a few moments. I went into an anteroom and waited—a half-hour, an hour, all afternoon, all evening, and still the battle raged. I varied the monotony of sitting in the anteroom by strolls around Tarrytown, and I think I learned to know its every stone and turn. The next day passed in the same way. At last, late on Saturday night, it was suddenly announced by my opponents that I was not even a member of the Church in which I had applied for ordination. The statement created consternation among my friends. None of us had thought of that! The bomb, timed to explode at the very end of the session, threatened to destroy all my hopes. Of course, my opponents had reasoned, it would be too late for me to do anything, and my name would be dropped.

But it was not too late. Dr. Lyman Davis, the pastor of the Methodist Protestant Church in Tarrytown, was very friendly toward me and my ordination, and he proved his friendship in a singularly prompt and efficient fashion. Late as it was, he immediately called together the trustees of his church, and they responded. To them I made my application for church membership, which they accepted within five minutes. I was now a member of the Church, but it was too late to obtain any further action from the Conference. The next day, Sunday, all the men who had applied for ordination were ordained, and I was left out.

On Monday morning, however, when the Conference met in its final business session, my case was reopened, and I was eventually called before the members to answer questions. Some of these were extremely interesting, and several of the episodes that occurred were very amusing. One old gentleman I can see as I write. He was greatly excited, and he led the opposition by racing up and down the aisles, quoting from the Scriptures to prove his case against women ministers. As he ran about he had a trick of putting his arms under the back of his coat, making his coat-tails stand out like wings and incidentally revealing two long white tapestrings belonging to a flannel undergarment. Even in the painful stress of those hours I observed with interest how beautifully those tape-strings were ironed!

I was there to answer any questions that were asked of me, and the questions came like hailstones in a sudden summer storm.

"Paul said, 'Wives, obey your husbands,'" shouted my old man of the coat-tails. "Suppose your husband should refuse to allow you to preach? What then?"

"In the first place," I answered, "Paul did not say so, according to the Scriptures. But even if he did, it would not concern me, for I am a spinster."

The old man looked me over. "You might marry some day," he predicted, cautiously.

"Possibly," I admitted. "Wiser women than I am have married. But it is equally possible that I might marry a man who would command me to preach; and in that case I want to be all ready to obey him."

At this another man, a bachelor, also began to draw from the Scriptures. "An elder," he quoted, "shall be the husband of one wife." And he demanded, triumphantly, "How is it possible for you to be the husband of a wife?"

In response to that I quoted a bit myself. "Paul said, 'Anathema unto him who addeth to or taketh from the Scriptures,'" I reminded this gentleman; and added that a twisted interpretation of the Scriptures was as bad as adding to or taking from them, and that no one doubted that Paul was warning the elders against polygamy. Then I went a bit further, for by this time the absurd character of the questions was getting on my nerves.

"Even if my good brother's interpretation is correct," I said, "he has overlooked two important points. Though he is an elder, he is also a bachelor; so I am as much of a husband as he is!"

A good deal of that sort of thing went on. The most satisfactory episode of the session, to me, was the downfall of three pert young men who in turn tried to make it appear that as the duty of the Conference was to provide churches for all its pastors, I might become a burden to the Church if it proved impossible to provide a pastorate for me. At that, one of my friends in the council rose to his feet.

"I have had official occasion to examine into the matter of Miss Shaw's parish and salary," he said, "and I know what salaries the last three speakers are drawing. It may interest the Conference to know that Miss Shaw's present salary equals the combined salaries of the three young men who are so afraid she will be a burden to the Church. If, before being ordained, she can earn three times as much as they now earn after being ordained, it seems fairly clear that they will never have to support her. We can only hope that she will never have to support them."

The three young ministers subsided into their seats with painful abruptness, and from that time my opponents were more careful in their remarks. Still, many unpleasant things were said, and too much warmth was shown by both sides. We gained ground through the day, however, and at the end of the session the Conference, by a large majority, voted to ordain me.

The ordination service was fixed for the following evening, and even the gentlemen who had most vigorously opposed me were not averse to making the occasion a profitable one. The contention had already enormously advertised the Conference, and the members now helped the good work along by sending forth widespread announcements of the result. They also decided that, as the attendance at the service would be very large, they would take up a collection for the support of superannuated ministers. The three young men who had feared I would become a burden were especially active in the matter of this collection; and, as they had no sense of humor, it did not seem incongruous to them to use my ordination as a means of raising money for men who had already become burdens to the Church.

When the great night came (on October 12, 1880), the expected crowd came also. And to the credit of my opponents I must add that, having lost their fight, they took their defeat in good part and gracefully assisted in the services. Sitting in one of the front pews was Mrs. Stiles, the wife of Dr. Stiles, who was superintendent of the Conference. She was a dear little old lady of seventy, with a big, maternal heart; and when she saw me rise to walk up the aisle alone, she immediately rose, too, came to my side, offered me her arm, and led me to the altar.

The ordination service was very impressive and beautiful. Its peace and dignity, following the battle that had raged for days, moved me so deeply that I was nearly overcome. Indeed, I was on the verge of a breakdown when I was mercifully saved by the clause in the discipline calling for the pledge all ministers had to make—that I would not indulge in the use of tobacco. When this vow fell from my lips a perceptible ripple ran over the congregation.

I was homesick for my Cape Cod parish, and I returned to East Dennis immediately after my ordination, arriving there on Saturday night. I knew by the suppressed excitement of my friends that some surprise awaited me, but I did not learn what it was until I entered my dear little church the following morning. There I found the communion-table set forth with a beautiful new communion-service. This had been purchased during my absence, that I might dedicate it that day and for the first time administer the sacrament to my people.

VI. CAPE COD MEMORIES

Looking back now upon those days, I see my Cape Cod friends as clearly as if the intervening years had been wiped out and we were again together. Among those I most loved were two widely differing types—Captain Doane, a retired sea-captain, and Relief Paine, an invalid chained to her couch, but whose beautiful influence permeated the community like an atmosphere. Captain Doane was one of the finest men I have ever known—highminded, tolerant, sympathetic, and full of understanding, He was not only my friend, but my church barometer. He occupied a front pew, close to the pulpit; and when I was preaching without making much appeal he sat looking me straight in the face, listening courteously, but without interest. When I got into my subject, he would lean forward—the angle at which he sat indicating the degree of attention I had aroused—and when I was strongly holding my congregation Brother Doane would bend toward me, following every word I uttered with corresponding motions of his lips. When I resigned we parted with deep regret, but it was not until I visited the church several years afterward that he overcame his reserve enough to tell me how much he had felt my going.

"Oh, did you?" I asked, greatly touched. "You're not saying that merely to please me?"

The old man's hand fell on my shoulder. "I miss you," he said, simply. "I miss you all the time. You see, I love you." Then, with precipitate selfconsciousness, he closed the door of his New England heart, and from some remote corner of it sent out his cautious after-thought. "I love you," he repeated, primly, "as a sister in the Lord."

Relief Paine lived in Brewster. Her name seemed prophetic, and she once told me that she had always considered it so. Her brother-in-law was my Sunday-school superintendent, and her family belonged to my church. Very soon after my arrival in East Dennis I went to see her, and found her, as she always was, dressed in white and lying on a tiny white bed covered with pansies, in a room whose windows overlooked the sea. I shall never forget the picture she made. Over her shoulders was an exquisite white lace shawl brought from the other side of the world by some seafaring friend, and against her white pillow her hair seemed the blackest I had ever seen. When I entered she turned and looked toward me with wonderful dark eyes that were quite blind, and as she talked her hands played with the pansies around her. She loved pansies as she loved few human beings, and she knew their colors by touching them. She was then a little more than thirty years of age. At sixteen she had fallen downstairs in the dark, receiving an injury that paralyzed her, and for fifteen years she had lain on one side, perfectly still, the Stella Maris of the Cape. All who came to her, and they were many, went away the better for the visit, and the mere mention of her name along the coast softened eyes that had looked too bitterly on life.

Relief and I became close friends. I was greatly drawn to her, and deeply moved by the tragedy of her situation, as well as by the beautiful spirit with which she bore it. During my first visit I regaled her with stories of the community and of my own experiences, and when I was leaving it occurred to me that possibly I had been rather frivolous. So I said:

"I am coming to see you often, and when I come I want to do whatever will interest you most. Shall I bring some books and read to you?"

Relief smiled—the gay, mischievous little smile I was soon to know so well, but which at first seemed out of place on the tragic mask of her face.

"No, don't read to me," she decided. "There are enough ready to do that. Talk to me. Tell me about our life and our people here, as they strike you." And she added, slowly: "You are a queer minister. You have not offered to pray with me!"

"I feel," I told her, "more like asking you to pray for me."

Relief continued her analysis. "You have not told me that my affliction was a visitation from God," she added; "that it was discipline and well for me I had it."

"I don't believe it was from God," I said. "I don't believe God had anything to do with it. And I rejoice that you have not let it wreck your life."

She pressed my hand. "Thank you for saying that," she murmured. "If I thought God did it I could not love Him, and if I did not love Him I could not live. Please come and see me VERY often—and tell me stories!"

After that I collected stories for Relief. One of those which most amused her, I remember, was about my horse, and this encourages me to repeat it here. In my life in East Dennis I did not occupy the lonely little parsonage connected with my church, but instead boarded with a friend—a widow named Crowell. (There seemed only two names in Cape Cod: Sears and Crowell.) To keep in touch with my two churches, which were almost three miles apart, it became necessary to have a horse. As Mrs. Crowell needed one, too, we decided to buy the animal in partnership, and Miss Crowell, the daughter of the widow, who knew no more about horses than I did, undertook to lend me the support of her presence and advice during the purchase. We did not care to have the entire community take a passionate interest in the matter, as it would certainly have done if it had heard of our intention; so my friend and I departed somewhat stealthily for a neighboring town, where, we had heard, a very good horse was offered for sale. We saw the animal and liked it; but before closing the bargain we cannily asked the owner if the horse was perfectly sound, and if it was gentle with women. He assured us that it was both sound and gentle with women, and to prove the latter point he had his wife harness it to the buggy and drive it around the stable-yard. The animal behaved beautifully. After it had gone through its paces, Miss Crowell and I leaned confidingly against its side, patting it and praising its beauty, and the horse seemed to enjoy our attentions. We bought it then and there, drove it home, and put it in our barn; and the next morning we hired a man in the neighborhood to come over and take care of it.

He arrived. Five minutes later a frightful racket broke out in the barn— sounds of stamping, kicking, and plunging, mingled with loud shouts. We ran to the scene of the trouble, and found our "hired man" rushing breathlessly toward the house. When he was able to speak he informed us that we had "a devil in there," pointing back to the barn, and that the new horse's legs were in the air, all four of them at once, the minute he went near her. We insisted that he must have frightened or hurt her, but, solemnly and with anxious looks behind, he protested that he had not. Finally Miss Crowell and I went into the barn, and received a dignified welcome from the new horse, which seemed pleased by our visit. Together we harnessed her and, without the least difficulty, drove her out into the yard. As soon as our man took the reins, however, she reared, kicked, and smashed our brand-new buggy. We changed the man and had the buggy repaired, but by the end of the week the animal had smashed the buggy again. Then, with some natural resentment, we made a second visit to the man from whom we had bought her, and asked him why he had sold us such a horse.

He said he had told us the exact truth. The horse WAS sound and she WAS extremely gentle with women, but—and this point he had seen no reason to mention, as we had not asked about it—she would not let a man come near her. He firmly refused to take her back, and we had to make the best of the bargain. As it was impossible to take care of her ourselves, I gave some thought to the problem she presented, and finally devised a plan which worked very well. I hired a neighbor who was a small, slight man to take care of her, and made him wear his wife's sunbonnet and waterproof cloak whenever he approached the horse. The picture he presented in these garments still stands out pleasantly against the background of my Cape Cod memories. The horse, however, did not share our appreciation of it. She was suspicious, and for a time she shied whenever the man and his sunbonnet and cloak appeared; but we stood by until she grew accustomed to them and him; and as he was both patient and gentle, she finally allowed him to harness and unharness her. But no man could drive her, and when I drove to church I was forced to hitch and unhitch her myself. No one else could do it, though many a gallant and subsequently resentful man attempted the feat.

On one occasion a man I greatly disliked, and who I had reason to know disliked me, insisted that he could unhitch her, and started to do so, notwithstanding my protests and explanations. At his approach she rose on her hind-legs, and when he grasped her bridle she lifted him off his feet. His expression as he hung in mid-air was an extraordinary mixture of surprise and regret. The moment I touched her, however, she quieted down, and when I got into the buggy and gathered up the reins she walked off like a lamb, leaving the man staring after her with his eyes starting from his head.

The previous owner had called the horse Daisy, and we never changed the name, though it always seemed sadly inappropriate. Time proved, however, that there were advantages in the ownership of Daisy. No man would allow his wife or daughter to drive behind her, and no one wanted to borrow her. If she had been a different kind of animal she would have been used by the whole community, We kept Daisy for seven years, and our acquaintance ripened into a pleasant friendship.

Another Cape Cod resident to whose memory I must offer tribute in these pages was Polly Ann Sears—one of the dearest and best of my parishioners. She had six sons, and when five had gone to sea she insisted that the sixth must remain at home. In vain the boy begged her to let him follow his brothers. She stood firm. The sea, she said, should not swallow all her boys; she had given it five—she must keep one.

As it happened, the son she kept at home was the only one who was drowned. He was caught in a fish-net and dragged under the waters of the bay near his home; and when I went to see his mother to offer such comfort as I could, she showed that she had learned the big lesson of the experience.

"I tried to be a special Providence," she moaned, "and the one boy I kept home was the only boy I lost. I ain't a-goin' to be a Providence no more."

The number of funerals on Cape Cod was tragically large. I was in great demand on these occasions, and went all over the Cape, conducting funeral services—which seemed to be the one thing people thought I could do—and preaching funeral sermons. Besides the victims of the sea, many of the residents who had drifted away were brought back to sleep their last sleep within sound of the waves. Once I asked an old sea-captain why so many Cape Cod men and women who had been gone for years asked to be buried near their old homes, and his reply still lingers in my memory. He poked his toe in the sand for a moment and then said, slowly:

"Wal, I reckon it's because the Cape has such warm, comfortable sand to lie down in."

My friend Mrs. Addy lay in the Crowell family lot, and during my pastorate at East Dennis I preached the funeral sermon of her father, and later of her mother. Long after I had left Cape Cod I was frequently called back to say the last words over the coffins of my old friends, and the saddest of those journeys was the one I made in response to a telegram from the mother of Relief Paine. When I had arrived and we stood together beside the exquisite figure that seemed hardly more quiet in death than in life, Mrs. Paine voiced in her few words the feeling of the whole community—"Where shall we get our comfort and our inspiration, now that Relief is gone?"

The funeral which took all my courage from me, however, was that of my sister Mary. In its suddenness, Mary's death, in 1883, was as a thunderbolt from the blue; for she had been in perfect health three days before she passed away. I was still in charge of my two parishes in Cape Cod, but, as it mercifully happened, before she was stricken I had started West to visit Mary in her home at Big Rapids. When I arrived on the second day of her illness, knowing nothing of it until I reached her, I found her already past hope. Her disease was pneumonia, but she was conscious to the end, and her greatest desire seemed to be to see me christen her little daughter and her husband before she left them. This could not be realized, for my brotherin-law was absent on business, and with all his haste in returning did not reach his wife's side until after her death. As his one thought then was to carry out her last wishes, I christened him and his little girl just before the funeral; and during the ceremony we all experienced a deep conviction that Mary knew and was content.

She had become a power in her community, and was so dearly loved that on the day her body was borne to its last resting-place all the business houses in Big Rapids were closed, and the streets were filled with men who stood with bent, uncovered heads as the funeral procession went by. My father and mother, also, to whom she had given a home after they left the log-cabin where they had lived so long, had made many friends in their new environment and were affectionately known throughout the whole region as "Grandma and Grandpa Shaw."

When I returned to East Dennis I brought my mother and Mary's three children with me, and they remained throughout the spring and summer. I had hoped that they would remain permanently, and had rented and furnished a home for them with that end in view; but, though they enjoyed their visit, the prospect of the bleak winters of Cape Cod disturbed my mother, and they all returned to Big Rapids late in the autumn. Since entering upon my parish work it had been possible for me to help my father and mother financially; and from the time of Mary's death I had the privilege, a very precious one, of seeing that they were well cared for and contented. They were always appreciative, and as time passed they became more reconciled to the career I had chosen, and which in former days had filled them with such dire forebodings.

After I had been in East Dennis four years I began to feel that I was getting into a rut. It seemed to me that all I could do in that particular field had been done. My people wished me to remain, however, and so, partly as an outlet for my surplus energy, but more especially because I realized the splendid work women could do as physicians, I began to study medicine. The trustees gave me permission to go to Boston on certain days of each week, and we soon found that I could carry on my work as a medical student without in the least neglecting my duty toward my parish.

I entered the Boston Medical School in 1882, and obtained my diploma as a full-fledged physician in 1885. During this period I also began to lecture for the Massachusetts Woman Suffrage Association, of which Lucy Stone was president. Henry Blackwell was associated with her, and together they developed in me a vital interest in the suffrage cause, which grew steadily from that time until it became the dominating influence in my life. I preached it in the pulpit, talked it to those I met outside of the church, lectured on it whenever I had an opportunity, and carried it into my medical work in the Boston slums when I was trying my prentice hand on helpless pauper patients.

Here again, in my association with the women of the streets, I realized the limitations of my work in the ministry and in medicine. As minister to soul and body one could do little for these women. For such as them, one's efforts must begin at the very foundation of the social structure. Laws for them must be made and enforced, and some of those laws could only be made and enforced by women. So many great avenues of life were opening up before me that my Cape Cod environment seemed almost a prison where I was held with tender force. I loved my people and they loved me— but the big outer world was calling, and I could not close my ears to its summons. The suffrage lectures helped to keep me contented, however, and I was certainly busy enough to find happiness in my work.

I was in Boston three nights a week, and during these nights subject to sick calls at any hour. My favorite associates were Dr. Caroline Hastings, our professor of anatomy, and little Dr. Mary Safford, a mite of a woman with an indomitable soul. Dr. Safford was especially prominent in philanthropic work in Massachusetts, and it was said of her that at any hour of the day or night she could be found working in the slums of Boston. I, too, could frequently be found there—often, no doubt, to the disadvantage of my patients. I was quite famous in three Boston alleys—Maiden's Lane, Fellows Court, and Andrews Court. It most fortunately happened that I did not lose a case in those alleys, though I took all kinds, as I had to treat a certain number of surgical and obstetrical cases in my course. No doubt my patients and I had many narrow escapes of which we were blissfully ignorant, but I remember two which for a long time afterward continued to be features of my most troubled dreams.

The first was that of a big Irishman who had pneumonia. When I looked him over I was as much frightened as he was. I had got as far as pneumonia in my course, and I realized that here was a bad case of it. I knew what to do. The patient must be carefully packed in towels wrung out of cold water. When I called for towels I found that there was nothing in the place but a dish-towel, which I washed with portentous gravity. The man owned but one shirt, and, in deference to my visit, his wife had removed that to wash it. I packed the patient in the dish-towel, wrapped him in a piece of an old shawl, and left after instructing his wife to repeat the process. When I reached home I remembered that the patient must be packed "carefully," and I knew that his wife would do it carelessly. That meant great risk to the man's life. My impulse was to rush back to him at once, but this would never do. It would destroy all confidence in the doctor. I walked the floor for three hours, and then casually strolled in upon my patient, finding him, to my great relief, better than I had left him. As I was leaving, a child rushed into the room, begging me to come to an upper floor in the same building.

"The baby's got the croup," she gasped, "an' he's chokin' to death."

We had not reached croup in our course, and I had no idea what to do, but I valiantly accompanied the little girl. As we climbed the long flights of stairs to the top floor I remembered a conversation I had overheard between two medical students. One of them had said: "If the child is strangling when it inhales, as if it were breathing through a sponge, then give it spongia; but if it is strangling when it breathes out, give it aconite."

When I reached the baby I listened, but could not tell which way it was strangling. However, I happened to have both medicines with me, so I called for two glasses and mixed the two remedies, each in its own glass. I gave them both to the mother, and told her to use them alternately, every fifteen minutes, until the baby was better. The baby got well; but whether its recovery was due to the spongia or to the aconite I never knew.

In my senior year I fell in love with an infant of three, named Patsy. He was one of nine children when I was called to deliver his mother of her tenth child. She was drunk when I reached her, and so were two men who lay on the floor in the same room. I had them carried out, and after the mother and baby had been attended to I noticed Patsy. He was the most beautiful child I had ever seen—with eyes like Italian skies and yellow hair in tight curls over his adorable little head; but he was covered with filthy rags. I borrowed him, took him home with me, and fed and bathed him, and the next day fitted him out with new clothes. Every hour I had him tightened his hold on my heart-strings. I went to his mother and begged her to let me keep him, but she refused, and after a great deal of argument and entreaty I had to return him to her. When I went to see him a few days later I found him again in his horrible rags. His mother had pawned his new clothes for drink, and she was deeply under its influence. But no pressure I could exert then or later would make her part with Patsy. Finally, for my own peace of mind, I had to give up hope of getting him—but I have never ceased to regret the little adopted son I might have had.

VII. THE GREAT CAUSE

There is a theory that every seven years each human being undergoes a complete physical reconstruction, with corresponding changes in his mental and spiritual make-up. Possibly it was due to this reconstruction that, at the end of seven years on Cape Cod, my soul sent forth a sudden call to arms. I was, it reminded me, taking life too easily; I was in danger of settling into an agreeable routine. The work of my two churches made little drain on my superabundant vitality, and not even the winning of a medical degree and the increasing demands of my activities on the lecture platform wholly eased my conscience. I was happy, for I loved my people and they seemed to love me. It would have been pleasant to go on almost indefinitely, living the life of a country minister and telling myself that what I could give to my flock made such a life worth while.

But all the time, deep in my heart, I realized the needs of the outside world, and heard its prayer for workers. My theological and medical courses in Boston, with the experiences that accompanied them, had greatly widened my horizon. Moreover, at my invitation, many of the noble women of the day were coming to East Dennis to lecture, bringing with them the stirring atmosphere of the conflicts they were waging. One of the first of these was my friend Mary A. Livermore; and after her came Julia Ward Howe, Anna Garlin Spencer, Lucy Stone, Mary F. Eastman, and many others, each charged with inspiration for my people and with a special message for me, which she sent forth unknowingly and which I alone heard. They were fighting great battles, these women—for suffrage, for temperance, for social purity—and in every word they uttered I heard a rallying-cry. So it was that, in 1885, I suddenly pulled myself up to a radical decision and sent my resignation to the trustees of the two churches whose pastor I had been since 1878.

The action caused a demonstration of regret which made it hard to keep to my resolution and leave these men and women whose friendship was among the dearest of my possessions. But when we had all talked things over, many of them saw the situation as I did. No doubt there were those, too, who felt that a change of ministry would be good for the churches. During the weeks that followed my resignation I received many odd tributes, and of these one of the most amusing came from a young girl in the parish, who broke into loud protests when she heard that I was going away. To comfort her I predicted that she would now have a man minister—doubtless a very nice man. But the young person continued to sniffle disconsolately.

"I don't want a man," she wailed. "I don't like to see men in pulpits. They look so awkward." Her grief culminated in a final outburst. "They're all arms and legs!" she sobbed.

When my resignation was finally accepted, and the time of my departure drew near, the men of the community spent much of their leisure in discussing it and me. The social center of East Dennis was a certain grocery, to which almost every man in town regularly wended his way, and from which all the gossip of the town emanated. Here the men sat for hours, tilted back in their chairs, whittling the rungs until they nearly cut the chairs from under them, and telling one another all they knew or had heard about their fellow-townsmen. Then, after each session, they would return home and repeat the gossip to their wives. I used to say that I would give a dollar to any woman in East Dennis who could quote a bit of gossip which did not come from the men at that grocery. Even my old friend Captain Doane, fine and high-minded citizen though he was, was not above enjoying the mild diversion of these social gatherings, and on one occasion at least he furnished the best part of the entertainment. The departing minister was, it seemed, the topic of the day's discussion, and, to tease Captain Doane one young man who knew the strength of his friendship for me suddenly began to speak, then pursed up his lips and looked eloquently mysterious. As he had expected, Captain Doane immediately pounced on him.

"What's the matter with you?" demanded the old man. "Hev you got anything agin Miss Shaw?"

The young man sighed and murmured that if he wished he could repeat a charge never before made against a Cape Cod minister, but—and he shut his lips more obviously. The other men, who were in the plot, grinned, and this added the last touch to Captain Doane's indignation. He sprang to his feet. One of his peculiarities was a constant misuse of words, and now, in his excitement, he outdid himself.

"You've made an incineration against Miss Shaw," he shouted. "Do you hear—AN INCINERATION! Take it back or take a lickin'!"

The young man decided that the joke had gone far enough, so he answered, mildly: "Well, it is said that all the women in town are in love with Miss Shaw. Has that been charged against any other minister here?"

The men roared with laughter, and Captain Doane sat down, looking sheepish.

"All I got to say is this," he muttered: "That gal has been in this community for seven years, and she 'ain't done a thing during the hull seven years that any one kin lay a finger on!"

The men shouted again at this back-handed tribute, and the old fellow left the grocery in a huff. Later I was told of the "incineration" and his eloquent defense of me, and I thanked him for it. But I added:

"I hear you said I haven't done a thing in seven years that any one can lay a finger on?"

"I said it," declared the Captain, "and I'll stand by it."

"Haven't I done any good?" I asked.

"Sartin you have," he assured me, heartily. "Lots of good."

"Well," I said, "can't you put your finger on that?"

The Captain looked startled. "Why—why—Sister Shaw," he stammered, "you know I didn't mean THAT! What I meant," he repeated, slowly and solemnly, "was that the hull time you been here you ain't done nothin' anybody could put a finger on!"

Captain Doane apparently shared my girl parishioner's prejudice against men in the pulpit, for long afterward, on one of my visits to Cape Cod, he admitted that he now went to church very rarely.

"When I heard you preach," he explained, "I gen'ally followed you through and I knowed where you was a-comin' out. But these young fellers that come from the theological school—why, Sister Shaw, the Lord Himself don't know where they're comin' out!"

For a moment he pondered. Then he uttered a valedictory which I have always been glad to recall as his last message, for I never saw him again.

"When you fust come to us," he said, "you had a lot of crooked places, an' we had a lot of crooked places; and we kind of run into each other, all of us. But before you left, Sister Shaw, why, all the crooked places was wore off and everything was as smooth as silk."

"Yes," I agreed, "and that was the time to leave—when everything was running smoothly."

All is changed on Cape Cod since those days, thirty years ago. The old families have died or moved away, and those who replaced them were of a different type. I am happy in having known and loved the Cape as it was, and in having gathered there a store of delightful memories. In later strenuous years it has rested me merely to think of the place, and long afterward I showed my continued love of it by building a home there, which I still possess. But I had little time to rest in this or in my Moylan home, of which I shall write later, for now I was back in Boston, living my new life, and each crowded hour brought me more to do.

We were entering upon a deeply significant period. For the first time women were going into industrial competition with men, and already men were intensely resenting their presence. Around me I saw women overworked and underpaid, doing men's work at half men's wages, not because their work was inferior, but because they were women. Again, too, I studied the obtrusive problems of the poor and of the women of the streets; and, looking at the whole social situation from every angle, I could find but one solution for women—the removal of the stigma of disfranchisement. As man's equal before the law, woman could demand her rights, asking favors from no one. With all my heart I joined in the crusade of the men and women who were fighting for her. My real work had begun.

Naturally, at this period, I frequently met the members of Boston's most inspiring group—the Emersons and John Greenleaf Whittier, James Freeman Clark, Reverend Minot Savage, Bronson Alcott and his daughter Louisa, Wendell Phillips, William Lloyd Garrison, Stephen Foster, Theodore Weld, and the rest. Of them all, my favorite was Whittier. He had been present at my graduation from the theological school, and now he often attended our suffrage meetings. He was already an old man, nearing the end of his life; and I recall him as singularly tall and thin, almost gaunt, bending forward as he talked, and wearing an expression of great serenity and benignity. I once told Susan B. Anthony that if I needed help in a crowd of strangers that included her, I would immediately turn to her, knowing from her face that, whatever I had done, she would understand and assist me. I could have offered the same tribute to Whittier. At our meetings he was like a vesper-bell chiming above a battle-field. Garrison always became excited during our discussions, and the others frequently did; but Whittier, in whose big heart the love of his fellow-man burned as unquenchably as in any heart there, always preserved his exquisite tranquillity.

Once, I remember, Stephen Foster insisted on having the word "tyranny" put into a resolution, stating that women were deprived of suffrage by the TYRANNY of men. Mr. Garrison objected, and the debate that followed was the most exciting I have ever heard. The combatants actually had to adjourn before they could calm down sufficiently to go on with their meeting. Knowing the stimulating atmosphere to which he had grown accustomed, I was not surprised to have Theodore Weld explain to me; long afterward, why he no longer attended suffrage meetings.

"Oh," he said, "why should I go? There hasn't been any one mobbed in twenty years!"

The Ralph Waldo Emersons occasionally attended our meetings, and Mr. Emerson, at first opposed to woman suffrage, became a convert to it during the last years of his life—a fact his son and daughter omitted to mention in his biography. After his death I gave two suffrage lectures in Concord, and each time Mrs. Emerson paid for the hall. At these lectures Louisa M. Alcott graced the assembly with her splendid, wholesome presence, and on both occasions she was surrounded by a group of boys. She frankly cared much more for boys than for girls, and boys inevitably gravitated to her whenever she entered a place where they were. When women were given school suffrage in Massachusetts, Miss Alcott was the first woman to vote in Concord, and she went to the polls accompanied by a group of her boys, all ardently "for the Cause." My general impression of her was that of a fresh breeze blowing over wide moors. She was as different as possible from exquisite little Mrs. Emerson, who, in her daintiness and quiet charm, suggested an old New England garden.

Of Abby May and Edna Cheney I retain a general impression of "bagginess"—of loose jackets over loose waistbands, of escaping locks of hair, of bodies seemingly one size from the neck down. Both women were utterly indifferent to the details of their appearance, but they were splendid workers and leading spirits in the New England Woman's Club. It was said to be the trouble between Abby May and Kate Gannett Wells, both of whom stood for the presidency of the club, that led to the beginning of the anti-suffrage movement in Boston. Abby May was elected president, and all the suffragists voted for her. Subsequently Kate Gannett Wells began her anti-suffrage campaign. Mrs. Wells was the first anti-suffragist I ever knew in this country. Before her there had been Mrs. Dahlgren, wife of Admiral Dahlgren, and Mrs. William Tecumseh Sherman. On one occasion Elizabeth Cady Stanton challenged Mrs. Dahlgren to a debate on woman suffrage, and in the light of later events Mrs. Dahlgren's reply is amusing. She declined the challenge, explaining that for anti-suffragists to appear upon a public platform would be a direct violation of the principle for which they stood—which was the protection of female modesty! Recalling this, and the present hectic activity of the anti-suffragists, one must feel that they have either abandoned their principle or widened their views. For Julia Ward Howe I had an immense admiration; but, though from first to last I saw much of her, I never felt that I really knew her. She was a woman of the widest culture, interested in every progressive movement. With all her big heart she tried to be a democrat, but she was an aristocrat to the very core of her, and, despite her wonderful work for others, she lived in a splendid isolation. Once when I called on her I found her resting her mind by reading Greek, and she laughingly admitted that she was using a Latin pony, adding that she was growing "rusty." She seemed a little embarrassed by being caught with the pony, but she must have been reassured by my cheerful confession that if I tried to read either Latin or Greek I should need an English pony.

Of Frances E. Willard, who frequently came to Boston, I saw a great deal, and we soon became closely associated in our work. Early in our friendship, and at Miss Willard's suggestion, we made a compact that once a week each of us would point out to the other her most serious faults, and thereby help her to remedy them; but we were both too sane to do anything of the kind, and the project soon died a natural death. The nearest I ever came to carrying it out was in warning Miss Willard that she was constantly defying all the laws of personal hygiene. She never rested, rarely seemed to sleep, and had to be reminded at the table that she was there for the purpose of eating food. She was always absorbed in some great interest, and oblivious to anything else, I never knew a woman who could grip an audience and carry it with her as she could. She was intensely emotional, and swayed others by their emotions rather than by logic; yet she was the least conscious of her physical existence of any one I ever knew, with the exception of Susan B. Anthony. Like "Aunt Susan," Miss Willard paid no heed to cold or heat or hunger, to privation or fatigue. In their relations to such trifles both women were disembodied spirits.

Another woman doing wonderful work at this time was Mrs. Quincy Shaw, who had recently started her day nurseries for the care of tenement children whose mothers labored by the day. These nurseries were new in Boston, as was the kindergarten system she also established. I saw the effect of her work in the lives of the people, and it strengthened my growing conviction that little could be done for the poor in a spiritual or educational way until they were given a certain amount of physical comfort, and until more time was devoted to the problem of prevention. Indeed, the more I studied economic issues, the more strongly I felt that the position of most philanthropists is that of men who stand at the bottom of a precipice gathering up and trying to heal those who fall into it, instead of guarding the top and preventing them from going over.

Of course I had to earn my living; but, though I had taken my medical degree only a few months before leaving Cape Cod, I had no intention of practising medicine. I had merely wished to add a certain amount of medical knowledge to my mental equipment. The Massachusetts Woman Suffrage Association, of which Lucy Stone was president, had frequently employed me as a lecturer during the last two years of my pastorate. Now it offered me a salary of one hundred dollars a month as a lecturer and organizer. Though I may not have seemed so in these reminiscences, in which I have written as freely of my small victories as of my struggles and failures, I was a modest young person. The amount seemed too large, and I told Mrs. Stone as much, after which I humbly fixed my salary at fifty dollars a month. At the end of a year of work I felt that I had "made good";

then I asked for and received the one hundred dollars a month originally offered me.

During my second year Miss Cora Scott Pond and I organized and carried through in Boston a great suffrage bazaar, clearing six thousand dollars for the association—a large amount in those days. Elated by my share in this success, I asked that my salary should be increased to one hundred and twenty-five dollars a month—but this was not done. Instead, I received a valuable lesson. It was freely admitted that my work was worth one hundred and twenty-five dollars, but I was told that one hundred was the limit which could be paid, and I was reminded that this was a good salary for a woman.

The time seemed to have come to make a practical stand in defense of my principles, and I did so by resigning and arranging an independent lecture tour. The first month after my resignation I earned three hundred dollars. Later I frequently earned more than that, and very rarely less. Eventually I lectured under the direction of the Slaton Lecture Bureau of Chicago, and later still for the Redpath Bureau of Boston. My experience with the Redpath people was especially gratifying. Mrs. Livermore, who was their only woman lecturer, was growing old and anxious to resign her work. She saw in me a possible successor, and asked them to take me on their list. They promptly refused, explaining that I must "make a reputation" before they could even consider me. A year later they wrote me, making a very good offer, which I accepted. It may be worth while to mention here that through my lecture-work at this period I earned all the money I have ever saved. I lectured night after night, week after week, month after month, in "Chautauquas" in the summer, all over the country in the winter, earning a large income and putting aside at that time the small surplus I still hold in preparation for the "rainy day" every working-woman inwardly fears.

I gave the public at least a fair equivalent for what it gave me, for I put into my lectures all my vitality, and I rarely missed an engagement, though again and again I risked my life to keep one. My special subjects, of course, were the two I had most at heart-suffrage and temperance. For Frances Willard, then President of the Woman's Christian Temperance Union, had persuaded me to head the Franchise Department of that organization, succeeding Ziralda Wallace, the mother of Gen. Lew Wallace; and Miss Susan B. Anthony, who was beginning to study me closely, soon swung me into active work with her, of which, later, I shall have much to say. But before taking up a subject as absorbing to me as my friendship for and association with the most wonderful woman I have ever known, it may be interesting to record a few of my pioneer experiences in the lecture-field.

In those days—thirty years ago—the lecture bureaus were wholly regardless of the comfort of their lecturers. They arranged a schedule of engagements with exactly one idea in mind—to get the lecturer from one lecture-point to the next, utterly regardless of whether she had time between for rest or food or sleep. So it happened that all-night journeys in freight-cars, engines, and cabooses were casual commonplaces, while thirty and forty mile drives across the country in blizzards and bitter cold were equally inevitable. Usually these things did not trouble me. They were high adventures which I enjoyed at the time and afterward loved to recall. But there was an occasional hiatus in my optimism.

One night, for example, after lecturing in a town in Ohio, it was necessary to drive eight miles across country to a tiny railroad station at which a train, passing about two o'clock in the morning, was to be flagged for me. When we reached the station it was closed, but my driver deposited me on the platform and drove away, leaving me alone. The night was cold and very dark. All day I had been feeling ill and in the evening had suffered so much pain that I had finished my lecture with great difficulty. Now toward midnight, in this desolate spot, miles from any house, I grew alarmingly worse. I am not easily frightened, but that time I was sure I was going to die. Off in the darkness, very far away, as it seemed, I saw a faint light, and with infinite effort I dragged myself toward it. To walk, even to stand, was impossible; I crawled along the railroad track, collapsing, resting, going on again, whipping my will power to the task of keeping my brain clear, until after a nightmare that seemed to last through centuries I lay across the door of the switch-tower in which the light was burning. The switchman stationed there heard the cry I was able to utter, and came to my assistance. He carried me up to his signal-room and laid me on the floor by the stove; he had nothing to give me except warmth and shelter; but these were now all I asked. I sank into a comatose condition shot through with pain. Toward two o'clock in the morning he waked me and told me my train was coming, asking if I felt able to take it. I decided to make the effort. He dared not leave his post to help me, but he signaled to the train, and I began my progress back to the station. I never clearly remembered how I got there; but I arrived and was helped into a car by a brakeman. About four o'clock in the morning I had to change again, but this time I was left at the station of a town, and was there met by a man whose wife had offered me hospitality. He drove me to their home, and I was cared for. What I had, it developed, was a severe case of ptomaine poisoning, and I soon recovered; but even after all these years I do not like to recall that night.

To be "snowed in" was a frequent experience. Once, in Minnesota, I was one of a dozen travelers who were driven in an omnibus from a country hotel to the nearest railroad station, about two miles away. It was snowing hard, and the driver left us on the station platform and departed. Time passed, but the train we were waiting for did not come. A true Western blizzard, growing wilder every moment, had set in, and we finally realized that the train was not coming, and that, moreover, it was now impossible to get back to the hotel. The only thing we could do was to spend the night in the railroad station. I was the only woman in the group, and my fellow-passengers were cattlemen who whiled away the hours by smoking, telling stories, and exchanging pocket flasks. The station had a telegraph operator who occupied a tiny box by himself, and he finally invited me to share the privacy of his microscopic quarters. I entered them very gratefully, and he laid a board on the floor, covered it with an overcoat made of buffalo-skins, and cheerfully invited me to go to bed. I went, and slept peacefully until morning. Then we all returned to the hotel, the men going ahead and shoveling a path.

Again, one Sunday, I was snowbound in a train near Faribault, and this time also I was the only woman among a number of cattlemen. They were an odoriferous lot, who smoked diligently and played cards without ceasing, but in deference to my presence they swore only mildly and under their breath. At last they wearied of their game, and one of them rose and came to me.

"I heard you lecture the other night," he said, awkwardly, "and I've bin tellin' the fellers about it. We'd like to have a lecture now."

Their card-playing had seemed to me a sinful thing (I was stricter in my views then than I am to-day), and I was glad to create a diversion. I agreed to give them a lecture, and they went through the train, which consisted of two day coaches, and brought in the remaining passengers. A few of them could sing, and we began with a Moody and Sankey hymn or two and the appealing ditty, "Where is my wandering boy to-night?" in which they all joined with special zest. Then I delivered the lecture, and they listened attentively. When I had finished they seemed to think that some slight return was in order, so they proceeded to make a bed for me. They took the bottoms out of two seats, arranged them crosswise, and one man folded his overcoat into a pillow. Inspired by this, two others immediately donated their fur overcoats for upper and lower coverings. When the bed was ready they waved me toward it with a most hospitable air, and I crept in between the overcoats and slumbered sweetly until I was aroused the next morning by the welcome music of a snow-plow which had been sent from St. Paul to our rescue. To drive fifty or sixty miles in a day to meet a lecture engagement was a frequent experience. I have been driven across the prairies in June when they were like a mammoth flower-bed, and in January when they seemed one huge snow-covered grave—my grave, I thought, at times. Once during a thirty-mile drive, when the thermometer was twenty degrees below zero, I suddenly realized that my face was freezing. I opened my satchel, took out the tissue-paper that protected my best gown, and put the paper over my face as a veil, tucking it inside of my bonnet. When I reached my destination the tissue was a perfect mask, frozen stiff, and I had to be lifted from the sleigh. I was due on the lecture platform in half an hour, so I drank a huge bowl of boiling ginger tea and appeared on time. That night I went to bed expecting an attack of pneumonia as a result of the exposure, but I awoke next morning in superb condition. I possess what is called "an iron constitution," and in those days I needed it.

That same winter, in Kansas, I was chased by wolves, and though I had been more or less intimately associated with wolves in my pioneer life in the Michigan woods, I found the occasion extremely unpleasant. During the long winters of my girlhood wolves had frequently slunk around our log cabin, and at times in the lumber-camps we had even heard them prowling on the roofs. But those were very different creatures from the two huge, starving, tireless animals that hour after hour loped behind the cutter in which I sat with another woman, who, throughout the whole experience, never lost her head nor her control of our frantic horses. They were mad with terror, for, try as they would, they could not outrun the grim things that trailed us, seemingly not trying to gain on us, but keeping always at the same distance, with a patience that was horrible. From time to time I turned to look at them, and the picture they made as they came on and on is one I shall never forget. They were so near that I could see their eyes and slavering jaws, and they were as noiseless as things in a dream. At last, little by little, they began to gain on us, and they were almost within striking distance of the whip, which was our only weapon, when we reached the welcome outskirts of a town and they fell back.

Some of the memories of those days have to do with personal encounters, brief but poignant. Once when I was giving a series of Chautauqua lectures, I spoke at the Chautauqua in Pontiac, Illinois. The State Reformatory for Boys was situated in that town, and, after the lecture the superintendent of the Reformatory invited me to visit it and say a few words to the inmates. I went and spoke for half an hour, carrying away a memory of the place and of the boys which haunted me for months. A year later, while I was waiting for a train in the station at Shelbyville, a lad about sixteen years old passed me and hesitated, looking as if he knew me. I saw that he wanted to speak and dared not, so I nodded to him.

"You think you know me, don't you?" I asked, when he came to my side.

"Yes'm, I do know you," he told me, eagerly. "You are Miss Shaw, and you talked to us boys at Pontiac last year. I'm out on parole now, but I 'ain't forgot. Us boys enjoyed you the best of any show we ever had!"

I was touched by this artless compliment, and anxious to know how I had won it, so I asked, "What did I say that the boys liked?"

The lad hesitated. Then he said, slowly, "Well, you didn't talk as if you thought we were all bad."

"My boy," I told him, "I don't think you are all bad. I know better!"

As if I had touched a spring in him, the lad dropped into the seat by my side; then, leaning toward me, he said, impulsively, but almost in a whisper:

"Say, Miss Shaw, SOME OF US BOYS SAYS OUR PRAYERS!"

Rarely have I had a tribute that moved me more than that shy confidence; and often since then, in hours of discouragement or failure, I have reminded myself that at least there must have been something in me once to make a lad of that age so open up his heart. We had a long and intimate talk, from which grew the abiding interest I feel in boys today.

Naturally I was sometimes inconvenienced by slight misunderstandings between local committees and myself as to the subjects of my lectures, and the most extreme instance of this occurred in a town where I arrived to find myself widely advertised as "Mrs. Anna Shaw, who whistled before Queen Victoria"! Transfixed, I gaped before the billboards, and by reading their additional lettering discovered the gratifying fact that at least I was not expected to whistle now. Instead, it appeared, I was to lecture on "The Missing Link."

As usual, I had arrived in town only an hour or two before the time fixed for my lecture; there was the briefest interval in which to clear up these painful misunderstandings. I repeatedly tried to reach the chairman who was to preside at the entertainment, but failed. At last I went to the hall at the hour appointed, and found the local committee there, graciously waiting to receive me. Without wasting precious minutes in preliminaries, I asked why they had advertised me as the woman who had "whistled before Queen Victoria."

"Why, didn't you whistle before her?" they exclaimed in grieved surprise.

"I certainly did not," I explained. "Moreover, I was never called 'The American Nightingale,' and I have never lectured on 'The Missing Link.' Where DID you get that subject? It was not on the list I sent you."

The members of the committee seemed dazed. They withdrew to a corner and consulted in whispers. Then, with clearing brow, the spokesman returned.

"Why," he said, cheerfully, "it's simple enough! We mixed you up with a Shaw lady that whistles; and we've been discussing the missing link in our debating society, so our citizens want to hear your views."

"But I don't know anything about the missing link," I protested, "and I can't speak on it."

"Now, come," they begged. "Why, you'll have to! We've sold all our tickets for that lecture. The whole town has turned out to hear it."

Then, as I maintained a depressed silence, one of them had a bright idea.

"I'll tell you how to fix it!" he cried. "Speak on any subject you please, but bring in something about the missing link every few minutes. That will satisfy 'em."

"Very well," I agreed, reluctantly. "Open the meeting with a song. Get the audience to sing 'America' or 'The Star-spangled Banner.' That will give me a few minutes to think, and I will see what can be done."

Led by a very nervous chairman, the big audience began to sing, and under the inspiration of the music the solution of our problem flashed into my mind.

"It is easy," I told myself. "Woman is the missing link in our government. I'll give them a suffrage speech along that line."

When the song ended I began my part of the entertainment with a portion of my lecture on "The Fate of Republics," tracing their growth and decay, and pointing out that what our republic needed to give it a stable government was the missing link of woman suffrage. I got along admirably, for every five minutes I mentioned "the missing link," and the audience sat content and apparently interested, while the members of the committee burst into bloom on the platform.

VIII. DRAMA IN THE LECTURE-FIELD

My most dramatic experience occurred in a city in Michigan, where I was making a temperance campaign. It was an important lumber and shipping center, and it harbored much intemperance. The editor of the leading newspaper was with the temperance-workers in our fight there, and he had warned me that the liquor people threatened to "burn the building over my head" if I attempted to lecture. We were used to similar threats, so I proceeded with my preparations and held the meeting in the town skating-rink—a huge, bare, wooden structure.

Lectures were rare in that city, and rumors of some special excitement on this occasion had been circulated; every seat in the rink was filled, and several hundred persons stood in the aisles and at the back of the building. Just opposite the speaker's platform was a small gallery, and above that, in the ceiling, was a trap-door. Before I had been speaking ten minutes I saw a man drop through this trap-door to the balcony and climb from there to the main floor. As he reached the floor he shouted "Fire!" and rushed out into the street. The next instant every person in the rink was up and a panic had started. I was very sure there was no fire, but I knew that many might be killed in the rush which was beginning. So I sprang on a chair and shouted to the people with the full strength of my lungs:

"There is no fire! It's only a trick! Sit down! Sit down!"

The cooler persons in the crowd at once began to help in this calming process.

"Sit down!" they repeated. "It's all right! There's no fire! Sit down!"

It looked as if we had the situation in hand, for the people hesitated, and most of them grew quiet; but just then a few words were hissed up to me that made my heart stop beating. A member of our local committee was standing beside my chair, speaking in a terrified whisper:

"There IS a fire, Miss Shaw," he said. "For God's sake get the people out—QUICKLY!"

The shock was so unexpected that my knees almost gave way. The people were still standing, wavering, looking uncertainly toward us. I raised my voice again, and if it sounded unnatural my hearers probably thought it was because I was speaking so loudly.

"As we are already standing," I cried, "and are all nervous, a little exercise will do us good. So march out, singing. Keep time to the music! Later you can come back and take your seats!"

The man who had whispered the warning jumped into the aisle and struck up "Jesus, Lover of My Soul." Then he led the march down to the door, while the big audience swung into line and followed him, joining in the song. I remained on the chair, beating time and talking to the people as they went; but when the last of them had left the building I almost collapsed; for the flames had begun to eat through the wooden walls and the clang of the fire-engines was heard outside.

As soon as I was sure every one was safe, however, I experienced the most intense anger I had yet known. My indignation against the men who had risked hundreds of lives by setting fire to a crowded building made me "see red"; it was clear that they must be taught a lesson then and there. As soon as I was outside the rink I called a meeting, and the Congregational minister, who was in the crowd, lent us his church and led the way to it. Most of the audience followed us, and we had a wonderful meeting, during which we were able at last to make clear to the people of that town the character of the liquor interests we were fighting. That episode did the temperance cause more good than a hundred ordinary meetings. Men who had been indifferent before became our friends and supporters, and at the following election we carried the town for prohibition by a big majority.

There have been other occasions when our opponents have not fought us fairly. Once, in an Ohio town, a group of politicians, hearing that I was to lecture on temperance in the court-house on a certain night, took possession of the building early in the evening, on the pretense of holding a meeting, and held it against us. When, escorted by a committee of leading women, I reached the building and tried to enter, we found that the men had locked us out. Our audience was gathering and filling the street, and we finally sent a courteous message to the men, assuming that they had forgotten us and reminding them of our position. The messenger reported that the men would leave "about eight," but that the room was "black with smoke and filthy with tobacco-juice." We waited patiently until eight o'clock, holding little outside meetings in groups, as our audience waited with us. At eight we again sent our messenger into the hall, and he brought back word that the men were "not through, didn't know when they would be through, and had told the women not to wait."

Naturally, the waiting townswomen were deeply chagrined by this. So were many men in the outside crowd. We asked if there was no other entrance to the hall except through the locked front doors, and were told that the judge's private room opened into it, and that one of our committee had the key, as she had planned to use this room as a dressing and retiring room for the speakers. After some discussion we decided to storm the hall and take possession. Within five minutes all the women had formed in line and were crowding up the back stairs and into the judge's room. There we unlocked the door, again formed in line, and marched into the hall, singing "Onward, Christian Soldiers!"

There were hundreds of us, and we marched directly to the platform, where the astonished men got up to stare at us. More and more women entered, coming up the back stairs from the street and filling the hall; and when the men realized what it all meant, and recognized their wives, sisters, and women friends in the throng, they sheepishly unlocked the front doors and left us in possession, though we politely urged them to remain. We had a great meeting that night!

Another reminiscence may not be out of place. We were working for a prohibition amendment in the state of Pennsylvania, and the night before election I reached Coatesville. I had just completed six weeks of strenuous campaigning, and that day I had already conducted and spoken at two big outdoor meetings. When I entered the town hall of Coatesville I found it filled with women. Only a few men were there; the rest were celebrating and campaigning in the streets. So I arose and said:

"I would like to ask how many men there are in the audience who intend to vote for the amendment to-morrow?"

Every man in the hall stood up.

"I thought so," I said. "Now I intend to ask your indulgence. As you are all in favor of the amendment, there is no use in my setting its claims before you; and, as I am utterly exhausted, I suggest that we sing the Doxology and go home!"

The audience saw the common sense of my position, so the people laughed and sang the Doxology and departed. As we were leaving the hall one of Coatesville's prominent citizens stopped me.

"I wish you were a man," he said. "The town was to have a big outdoor meeting to-night, and the orator has failed us. There are thousands of men in the streets waiting for the speech, and the saloons are sending them free drinks to get them drunk and carry the town to-morrow."

"Why," I said, "I'll talk to them if you wish."

"Great Scott!" he gasped. "I'd be afraid to let you. Something might happen!"

"If anything happens, it will be in a good cause," I reminded him. "Let us go."

Down-town we found the streets so packed with men that the cars could not get through, and with the greatest difficulty we reached the stand which had been erected for the speaker. It was a gorgeous affair. There were flaring torches all around it, and a "bull's-eye," taken from the head of a locomotive, made an especially brilliant patch of light. The stand had been erected at a point where the city's four principal streets meet, and as far as I could see there were solid masses of citizens extending into these streets. A glee-club was doing its best to help things along, and the music of an organette, an instrument much used at the time in campaign rallies, swelled the joyful tumult. As I mounted the platform the crowd was singing "Vote for Betty and the Baby," and I took that song for my text, speaking of the helplessness of women and children in the face of intemperance, and telling the crowd the only hope of the Coatesville women lay in the vote cast by their men the next day.

Directly in front of me stood a huge and extraordinarily repellent-looking negro. A glance at him almost made one shudder, but before I had finished my first sentence he raised his right arm straight above him and shouted, in a deep and wonderfully rich bass voice, "Hallelujah to the Lamb!" From that point on he punctuated my speech every few moments with good, old-fashioned exclamations of salvation which helped to inspire the crowd. I spoke for almost an hour. Three times in my life, and only three times, I have made speeches that have satisfied me to the degree, that is, of making me feel that at least I was giving the best that was in me. The speech at Coatesville was one of those three. At the end of it the good-natured crowd cheered for ten minutes. The next day Coatesville voted for prohibition, and, rightly or wrongly, I have always believed that I helped to win that victory.

Here, by the way, I may add that of the two other speeches which satisfied me one was made in Chicago, during the World's Fair, in 1893, and the other in Stockholm, Sweden, in 1912. The International Council of Women, it will be remembered, met in Chicago during the Fair, and I was invited to preach the sermon at the Sunday-morning session. The occasion was a very important one, bringing together at least five thousand persons, including representative women from almost every country in Europe, and a large number of women ministers. These made an impressive group, as they all wore their ministerial robes; and for the first time I preached in a ministerial robe, ordered especially for that day. It was made of black crepe de Chine, with great double flowing sleeves, white silk undersleeves, and a wide white silk underfold down the front; and I may mention casually that it looked very much better than I felt, for I was very nervous. My father had come on to Chicago especially to hear my sermon, and had been invited to sit on the platform. Even yet he was not wholly reconciled to my public work, but he was beginning to take a deep interest in it. I greatly desired to please him and to satisfy Miss Anthony, who was extremely anxious that on that day of all days I should do my best.

I gave an unusual amount of time and thought to that sermon, and at last evolved what I modestly believed to be a good one. I never write out a sermon in advance, but I did it this time, laboriously, and then memorized the effort. The night before the sermon was to be delivered Miss Anthony asked me about it, and when I realized how deeply interested she was I delivered it to her then and there as a rehearsal. It was very late, and I knew we would not be interrupted. As she listened her face grew longer and longer and her lips drooped at the corners. Her disappointment was so obvious that I had difficulty in finishing my recitation; but I finally got through it, though rather weakly toward the end, and waited to hear what she would say, hoping against hope that she had liked it better than she seemed to. But Susan B. Anthony was the frankest as well as the kindest of women. Resolutely she shook her head.

"It's no good, Anna," she said; firmly. "You'll have to do better. You've polished and repolished that sermon until there's no life left in it. It's dead. Besides, I don't care for your text."

"Then give me a text," I demanded, gloomily.

"I can't," said Aunt Susan.

I was tired and bitterly disappointed, and both conditions showed in my reply.

"Well," I asked, somberly, "if you can't even supply a text, how do you suppose I'm going to deliver a brand-new sermon at ten o'clock to-morrow morning?"

"Oh," declared Aunt Susan, blithely, "you'll find a text."

I suggested several, but she did not like them. At last I said, "I have it—'Let no man take thy crown.'"

"That's it!" exclaimed Miss Anthony. "Give us a good sermon on that text."

She went to her room to sleep the sleep of the just and the untroubled, but I tossed in my bed the rest of the night, planning the points of the new sermon. After I had delivered it the next morning I went to my father to assist him from the platform. He was trembling, and his eyes were full of tears. He seized my arm and pressed it.

"Now I am ready to die," was all he said.

I was so tired that I felt ready to die, too; but his satisfaction and a glance at Aunt Susan's contented face gave me the tonic I needed. Father died two years later, and as I was campaigning in California I was not with him at the end. It was a comfort to remember, however, that in the twilight of his life he had learned to understand his most difficult daughter, and to give her credit for earnestness of purpose, at least, in following the life that had led her away from him. After his death, and immediately upon my return from California, I visited my mother, and it was well indeed that I did, for within a few months she followed father into the other world for which all of her unselfish life had been a preparation.

Our last days together were perfect. Her attitude was one of serene and cheerful expectancy, and I always think of her as sitting among the primroses and bluebells she loved, which seemed to bloom unceasingly in the windows of her room. I recall, too, with gratitude, a trifle which gave her a pleasure out of all proportion to what I had dreamed it would do. She had expressed a longing for some English heather, "not the hot-house variety, but the kind that blooms on the hills," and I had succeeded in getting a bunch for her by writing to an English friend.

Its possession filled her with joy, and from the time it came until the day her eyes closed in their last sleep it was rarely beyond reach of her hand. At her request, when she was buried we laid the heather on her heart—the heart of a true and loyal woman, who, though her children had not known it, must have longed without ceasing throughout her New World life for the Old World of her youth.

The Scandinavian speech was an even more vital experience than the Chicago one, for in Stockholm I delivered the first sermon ever preached by a woman in the State Church of Sweden, and the event was preceded by an amount of political and journalistic opposition which gave it an international importance. I had also been invited by the Norwegian women to preach in the State Church of Norway, but there we experienced obstacles. By the laws of Norway women are permitted to hold all public offices except those in the army, navy, and church—a rather remarkable militant and spiritual combination. As a woman, therefore, I was denied the use of the church by the Minister of Church Affairs.

The decision created great excitement and much delving into the law. It then appeared that if the use of a State Church is desired for a minister of a foreign country the government can give such permission. It was thought that I might slip in through this loophole, and application was made to the government. The reply came that permission could be received only from the entire Cabinet; and while the Cabinet gentlemen were feverishly discussing the important issue, the Norwegian press became active, pointing out that the Minister of Church Affairs had arrogantly assumed the right of the entire Cabinet in denying the application. The charge was taken up by the party opposed to the government party in Parliament, and the Minister of Church Affairs swiftly turned the whole matter over to his conferees.

The Cabinet held a session, and by a vote of four to three decided NOT to allow a woman to preach in the State Church. I am happy to add that of the three who voted favorably on the question one was the Premier of Norway. Again the newspapers grasped their opportunity—especially the organs of the opposition party. My rooms were filled with reporters, while daily the excitement grew. The question was brought up in Parliament, and I was invited to attend and hear the discussion there. By this time every newspaper in Scandinavia was for or against me; and the result of the whole matter was that, though the State Church of Norway was not opened to me, a most unusual interest had been aroused in my sermon in the State Church of Sweden. When I arrived there to keep my engagement, not only was the wonderful structure packed to its walls, but the waiting crowds in the street were so large that the police had difficulty in opening a way for our party.

I shall never forget my impression of the church itself when I entered it. It will always stand forth in my memory as one of the most beautiful churches I have ever visited. On every side were monuments of dead heroes and statesmen, and the high, vaulted blue dome seemed like the open sky above our heads. Over us lay a light like a soft twilight, and the great congregation filled not only all the pews, but the aisles, the platform, and even the steps of the pulpit. The ushers were young women from the University of Upsala, wearing white university caps with black vizors, and sashes in the university colors. The anthem was composed especially for the occasion by the first woman cathedral organist in Sweden—the organist of the cathedral in Gothenburg—and she had brought with her thirty members of her choir, all of them remarkable singers.

The whole occasion was indescribably impressive, and I realized in every fiber the necessity of being worthy of it. Also, I experienced a sensation such as I had never known before, and which I can only describe as a seeming complete separation of my physical self from my spiritual self. It was as if my body stood aside and watched my soul enter that pulpit. There was no uncertainty, no nervousness, though usually I am very nervous when I begin to speak; and when I had finished I knew that I had done my best.

But all this is a long way from the early days I was discussing, when I was making my first diffident bows to lecture audiences and learning the lessons of the pioneer in the lecture-field. I was soon to learn more, for in 1888 Miss Anthony persuaded me to drop my temperance work and concentrate my energies on the suffrage cause. For a long time I hesitated. I was very happy in my connection with the Woman's Christian Temperance Union, and I knew that Miss Willard was depending on me to continue it. But Miss Anthony's arguments were irrefutable, and she was herself, as always, irresistible.

"You can't win two causes at once," she reminded me. "You're merely scattering your energies. Begin at the beginning. Win suffrage for women, and the rest will follow." As an added argument, she took me with her on her Kansas campaign, and after that no further arguments were needed. From then until her death, eighteen years later, Miss Anthony and I worked shoulder to shoulder.

The most interesting lecture episode of our first Kansas campaign was my debate with Senator John J. Ingalls. Before this, however, on our arrival at Atchison, Mrs. Ingalls gave a luncheon for Miss Anthony, and Rachel Foster Avery and I were also invited. Miss Anthony sat at the right of Senator Ingalls, and I at his left, while Mrs. Ingalls, of course, adorned the opposite end of her table. Mrs. Avery and I had just been entertained for several days at the home of a vegetarian friend who did not know how to cook vegetables, and we were both half starved. When we were invited to the Ingalls home we had uttered in unison a joyous cry, "Now we shall have something to eat!" At the luncheon, however, Senator Ingalls kept Miss Anthony and me talking steadily. He was not in favor of suffrage for women, but he wished to know all sorts of things about the Cause, and we were anxious to have him know them. The result was that I had time for only an occasional mouthful, while down at the end of the table Mrs. Avery ate and ate, pausing only to send me glances of heartfelt sympathy. Also, whenever she had an especially toothsome morsel on the end of her fork she wickedly succeeded in catching my eye and thus adding the last sybaritic touch to her enjoyment.

Notwithstanding the wealth of knowledge we had bestowed upon him, or perhaps because of it, the following night Senator Ingalls made his famous speech against suffrage, and it fell to my lot to answer him. In the course of his remarks he asked this question: "Would you like to add three million illiterate voters to the large body of illiterate voters we have in America to-day?" The audience applauded light-heartedly, but I was disturbed by the sophistry of the question. One of Senator Ingalls's most discussed personal peculiarities was the parting of his hair in the middle. Cartoonists and newspaper writers always made much of this, so when I rose to reply I felt justified in mentioning it.

"Senator Ingalls," I began, "parts his hair in the middle, as we all know, but he makes up for it by parting his figures on one side. Last night he gave you the short side of his figures. At the present time there are in the United States about eighteen million women of voting age. When the Senator asked whether you wanted three million additional illiterate women voters, he forgot to ask also if you didn't want fifteen million additional intelligent women voters! We will grant that it will take the votes of three million intelligent women to wipe out the votes of three million illiterate women. But don't forget that that would still leave us twelve million intelligent votes to the good!"

The audience applauded as gaily as it had applauded Senator Ingalls when he spoke on the other side, and I continued:

"Now women have always been generous to men. So of our twelve million intelligent voters we will offer four million to offset the votes of the four million illiterate men in this country—and then we will still have eight million intelligent votes to add to the other intelligent votes which are cast." The audience seemed to enjoy this.

"The anti-suffragists are fairly safe," I ended, "as long as they remain on the plane of prophecy. But as soon as they tackle mathematics they get into trouble!"

Miss Anthony was much pleased by the wide publicity given to this debate, but Senator Ingalls failed to share her enthusiasm.

It was shortly after this encounter that I had two traveling experiences which nearly cost me my life. One of them occurred in Ohio at the time of a spring freshet. I know of no state that can cover itself with water as completely as Ohio can, and for no apparent reason. On this occasion it was breaking its own record. We had driven twenty miles across country in a buggy which was barely out of the water, and behind horses that at times were almost forced to swim, and when we got near the town where I was to lecture, though still on the opposite side of the river from it, we discovered that the bridge was gone. We had a good view of the town, situated high and dry on a steep bank; but the river which rolled between us and that town was a roaring, boiling stream, and the only possible way to cross it, I found, was to walk over a railroad trestle, already trembling under the force of the water.

There were hundreds of men on the river-bank watching the flood, and when they saw me start out on the empty trestle they set up a cheer that nearly threw me off. The river was wide and the ties far apart, and the roar of the stream below was far from reassuring; but in some way I reached the other side, and was there helped off the trestle by what the newspapers called "strong and willing hands."

Another time, in a desperate resolve to meet a lecture engagement, I walked across the railroad trestle at Elmira, New York, and when I was halfway over I heard shouts of warning to turn back, as a train was coming. The trestle was very high at that point, and I realized that if I turned and faced an oncoming train I would undoubtedly lose my nerve and fall. So I kept on, as rapidly as I could, accompanied by the shrieks of those who objected to witnessing a violent death, and I reached the end of the trestle just as an express-train thundered on the beginning of it. The next instant a policeman had me by the shoulders and was shaking me as if I had been a bad child.

"If you ever do such a thing again," he thundered, "I'll lock you up!"

As soon as I could speak I assured him fervently that I never would; one such experience was all I desired.

Occasionally a flash of humor, conscious or unconscious, lit up the gloom of a trying situation. Thus, in Parkersburg, West Virginia, the train I was on ran into a coal-car. I was sitting in a sleeper, leaning back comfortably with my feet on the seat in front of me, and the force of the collision lifted me up, turned me completely over, and deposited me, head first, two seats beyond. On every side I heard cries and the crash of human bodies against unyielding substances as my fellow-passengers flew through the air, while high and clear above the tumult rang the voice of the conductor:

"Keep your seats!" he yelled. "KEEP YOUR SEATS!"

Nobody in our car was seriously hurt; but, so great is the power of vested authority, no one smiled over that order but me.

Many times my medical experience was useful. Once I was on a train which ran into a buggy and killed the woman in it. Her little daughter, who was with her, was badly hurt, and when the train had stopped the crew lifted the dead woman and the injured child on board, to take them to the next station. As I was the only doctor among the passengers, the child was turned over to me. I made up a bed on the seats and put the little patient there, but no woman in the car was able to assist me. The tragedy had made them hysterical, and on every side they were weeping and nerveless. The men were willing but inefficient, with the exception of one uncouth woodsman whose trousers were tucked into his boots and whose hands were phenomenally big and awkward. But they were also very gentle, as I realized when he began to help me. I knew at once that he was the man I needed, notwithstanding his unkempt hair, his general ungainliness, the hat he wore on the back of his head, and the pink carnation in his buttonhole, which, by its very incongruity, added the final accent to his unprepossessing appearance. Together we worked over the child, making it as comfortable as we could. It was hardly necessary to tell my aide what I wanted done; he seemed to know and even to anticipate my efforts.

When we reached the next station the dead woman was taken out and laid on the platform, and a nurse and doctor who had been telegraphed for were waiting to care for the little girl. She was conscious by this time, and with the most exquisite gentleness my rustic Bayard lifted her in his arms to carry her off the train. Quite unnecessarily I motioned to him not to let her see her dead mother. He was not the sort who needed that warning; he had already turned her face to his shoulder, and, with head bent low above her, was safely skirting the spot where the long, covered figure lay.

Evidently the station was his destination, too, for he remained there; but just as the train pulled out he came hurrying to my window, took the carnation from his buttonhole, and without a word handed it to me. And after the tragic hour in which I had learned to know him the crushed flower, from that man, seemed the best fee I had ever received.

IX. "AUNT SUSAN"

In The Life of Susan B. Anthony it is mentioned that 1888 was a year of special recognition of our great leader's work, but that it was also the year in which many of her closest friends and strongest supporters were taken from her by death. A. Bronson Alcott was among these, and Louisa M. Alcott, as well as Dr. Lozier; and special stress is laid on Miss Anthony's sense of loss in the diminishing circle of her friends—a loss which new friends and workers came forward, eager to supply.

"Chief among these," adds the record, "was Anna Shaw, who, from the time of the International Council in '88, gave her truest allegiance to Miss Anthony."

It is true that from that year until Miss Anthony's death in 1906 we two were rarely separated; and I never read the paragraph I have just quoted without seeing, as in a vision, the figure of "Aunt Susan" as she slipped into my hotel room in Chicago late one night after an evening meeting of the International Council. I had gone to bed—indeed, I was almost asleep when she came, for the day had been as exhausting as it was interesting. But notwithstanding the lateness of the hour, "Aunt Susan," then nearing seventy, was still as fresh and as full of enthusiasm as a young girl. She had a great deal to say, she declared, and she proceeded to say it—sitting in a big easy-chair near the bed, with a rug around her knees, while I propped myself up with pillows and listened.

Hours passed and the dawn peered wanly through the windows, but still Miss Anthony talked of the Cause always of the Cause—and of what we two must do for it. The previous evening she had been too busy to eat any dinner, and I greatly doubt whether she had eaten any luncheon at noon. She had been on her feet for hours at a time, and she had held numerous discussions with other women she wished to inspire to special effort. Yet, after it all, here she was laying out our campaigns for years ahead, foreseeing everything, forgetting nothing, and sweeping me with her in her flight toward our common goal, until I, who am not easily carried off my feet, experienced an almost dizzy sense of exhilaration.

Suddenly she stopped, looked at the gas-jets paling in the morning light that filled the room, and for a fleeting instant seemed surprised. In the next she had dismissed from her mind the realization that we had talked all night. Why should we not talk all night? It was part of our work. She threw off the enveloping rug and rose.

"I must dress now," she said, briskly. "I've called a committee meeting before the morning session."

On her way to the door nature smote her with a rare reminder, but even then she did not realize that it was personal. "Perhaps," she remarked, tentatively, "you ought to have a cup of coffee."

That was "Aunt Susan." And in the eighteen years which followed I had daily illustrations of her superiority to purely human weaknesses. To her the hardships we underwent later, in our Western campaigns for woman suffrage, were as the airiest trifles. Like a true soldier, she could snatch a moment of sleep or a mouthful of food where she found it, and if either was not forthcoming she did not miss it. To me she was an unceasing inspiration—the torch that illumined my life. We went through some difficult years together—years when we fought hard for each inch of headway we gained—but I found full compensation for every effort in the glory of working with her for the Cause that was first in both our hearts, and in the happiness of being her friend. Later I shall describe in more detail the suffrage campaigns and the National and International councils in which we took part; now it is of her I wish to write—of her bigness, her many-sidedness, her humor, her courage, her quickness, her sympathy, her understanding, her force, her supreme common-sense, her selflessness; in short, of the rare beauty of her nature as I learned to know it.

Like most great leaders, she took one's best work for granted, and was chary with her praise; and even when praise was given it usually came by indirect routes. I recall with amusement that the highest compliment she ever paid me in public involved her in a tangle from which, later, only her quick wit extricated her. We were lecturing in an especially pious town which I shall call B——, and just before I went on the platform Miss Anthony remarked, peacefully:

"These people have always claimed that I am irreligious. They will not accept the fact that I am a Quaker—or, rather, they seem to think a Quaker is an infidel. I am glad you are a Methodist, for now they cannot claim that we are not orthodox."

She was still enveloped in the comfort of this reflection when she introduced me to our audience, and to impress my qualifications upon my hearers she made her introduction in these words:

"It is a pleasure to introduce Miss Shaw, who is a Methodist minister. And she is not only orthodox of the orthodox, but she is also my right bower!"

There was a gasp from the pious audience, and then a roar of laughter from irreverent men, in which, I must confess, I light-heartedly joined. For once in her life Miss Anthony lost her presence of mind; she did not know how to meet the situation, for she had no idea what had caused the laughter. It bubbled forth again and again during the evening, and each time Miss Anthony received the demonstration with the same air of puzzled surprise. When we had returned to our hotel rooms I explained the matter to her. I do not remember now where I had acquired my own sinful knowledge, but that night I faced "Aunt Susan" from the pedestal of a sophisticated worldling.

"Don't you know what a right bower is?" I demanded, sternly.

"Of course I do," insisted "Aunt Susan." "It's a right-hand man—the kind one can't do without."

"It is a card," I told her, firmly—"a leading card in a game called euchre."

"Aunt Susan" was dazed. "I didn't know it had anything to do with cards," she mused, mournfully. "What must they think of me?"

What they thought became quite evident. The newspapers made countless jokes at our expense, and there were significant smiles on the faces in the audience that awaited us the next night. When Miss Anthony walked upon the platform she at once proceeded to clear herself of the tacit charge against her.

"When I came to your town," she began, cheerfully, "I had been warned that you were a very religious lot of people. I wanted to impress upon you the fact that Miss Shaw and I are religious, too. But I admit that when I told you she was my right bower I did not know what a right bower was. I have learned that, since last night."

She waited until the happy chortles of her hearers had subsided, and then went on.

"It interests me very much, however," she concluded, "to realize that every one of you seemed to know all about a right bower, and that I had to come to your good, orthodox town to get the information."

That time the joke was on the audience. Miss Anthony's home was in Rochester, New York, and it was said by our friends that on the rare occasions when we were not together, and I was lecturing independently, "all return roads led through Rochester." I invariably found some excuse to go there and report to her. Together we must have worn out many Rochester pavements, for "Aunt Susan's" pet recreation was walking, and she used to walk me round and round the city squares, far into the night, and at a pace that made policemen gape at us as we flew by. Some disrespectful youth once remarked that on these occasions we suggested a race between a ruler and a rubber ball—for she was very tall and thin, while I am short and plump. To keep up with her I literally bounded at her side.

A certain amount of independent lecturing was necessary for me, for I had to earn my living. The National American Woman Suffrage Association has never paid salaries to its officers, so, when I became vice-president and eventually, in 1904, president of the association, I continued to work gratuitously for the Cause in these positions. Even Miss Anthony received not one penny of salary for all her years of unceasing labor, and she was so poor that she did not have a home of her own until she was seventy-five. Then it was a very simple one, and she lived with the utmost economy. I decided that I could earn my bare expenses by making one brief lecture tour each year, and I made an arrangement with the Redpath Bureau which left me fully two-thirds of my time for the suffrage work I loved.

This was one result of my all-night talk with Miss Anthony in Chicago, and it enabled me to carry out her plan that I should accompany her in most of the campaigns in which she sought to arouse the West to the need of suffrage for women. From that time on we traveled and lectured together so constantly that each of us developed an almost uncanny knowledge of the other's mental processes. At any point of either's lecture the other could pick it up and carry it on—a fortunate condition, as it sometimes became necessary to do this. Miss Anthony was subject to contractions of the throat, which for the moment caused a slight strangulation. On such occasions—of which there were several—she would turn to me and indicate her helplessness. Then I would repeat her last sentence, complete her speech, and afterward make my own.

The first time this happened we were in Washington, and "Aunt Susan" stopped in the middle of a word. She could not speak; she merely motioned to me to continue for her, and left the stage. At the end of the evening a prominent Washington man who had been in our audience remarked to me, confidentially:

"That was a nice little play you and Miss Anthony made to-night—very effective indeed."

For an instant I did not catch his meaning, nor the implication in his knowing smile.

"Very clever, that strangling bit, and your going on with the speech," he repeated. "It hit the audience hard."

"Surely," I protested, "you don't think it was a deliberate thing—that we planned or rehearsed it."

He stared at me incredulously. "Are you going to pretend," he demanded, "that it wasn't a put-up job?"

I told him he had paid us a high compliment, and that we must really have done very well if we had conveyed that impression; and I finally convinced him that we not only had not rehearsed the episode, but that neither of us had known what the other meant to say. We never wrote out our speeches, but our subject was always suffrage or some ramification of suffrage, and, naturally, we had thoroughly digested each other's views.

It is said by my friends that I write my speeches on the tips of my fingers— for I always make my points on my fingers and have my fingers named for points. When I plan a speech I decide how many points I wish to make and what those points shall be. My mental preparation follows. Miss Anthony's method was much the same; but very frequently both of us threw over all our plans at the last moment and spoke extemporaneously on some theme suggested by the atmosphere of the gathering or by the words of another speaker.

From Miss Anthony, more than from any one else, I learned to keep cool in the face of interruptions and of the small annoyances and disasters inevitable in campaigning. Often we were able to help each other out of embarrassing situations, and one incident of this kind occurred during our campaign in South Dakota. We were holding a meeting on the hottest Sunday of the hottest month in the year—August—and hundreds of the natives had driven twenty, thirty, and even forty miles across the country to hear us. We were to speak in a sod church, but it was discovered that the structure would not hold half the people who were trying to enter it, so we decided that Miss Anthony should speak from the door, in order that those both inside and outside might hear her. To elevate her above her audience, she was given an empty dry-goods box to stand on.

This makeshift platform was not large, and men, women, and children were seated on the ground around it, pressing up against it, as close to the speaker as they could get. Directly in front of Miss Anthony sat a woman with a child about two years old—a little boy; and this infant, like every one else in the packed throng, was dripping with perspiration and suffering acutely under the blazing sun. Every woman present seemed to have brought children with her, doubtless because she could not leave them alone at home; and babies were crying and fretting on all sides. The infant nearest Miss Anthony fretted most strenuously; he was a sturdy little fellow with a fine pair of lungs, and he made it very difficult for her to lift her voice above his dismal clamor. Suddenly, however, he discovered her feet on the drygoods box, about on a level with his head. They were clad in black stockings and low shoes; they moved about oddly; they fascinated him. With a yelp of interest he grabbed for them and began pinching them to see what they were. His howls ceased; he was happy.

Miss Anthony was not. But it was a great relief to have the child quiet, so she bore the infliction of the pinching as long as she could. When endurance had found its limit she slipped back out of reach, and as his new plaything receded the boy uttered shrieks of disapproval. There was only one way to stop his noise; Miss Anthony brought her feet forward again, and he resumed the pinching of her ankles, while his yelps subsided to contented murmurs. The performance was repeated half a dozen times. Each time the ankles retreated the baby yelled. Finally, for once at the end of her patience, "Aunt Susan" leaned forward and addressed the mother, whose facial expression throughout had shown a complete mental detachment from the situation.

"I think your little boy is hot and thirsty," she said, gently. "If you would take him out of the crowd and give him a drink of water and unfasten his clothes, I am sure he would be more comfortable." Before she had finished speaking the woman had sprung to her feet and was facing her with fierce indignation.

"This is the first time I have ever been insulted as a mother," she cried; "and by an old maid at that!" Then she grasped the infant and left the scene, amid great confusion. The majority of those in the audience seemed to sympathize with her. They had not seen the episode of the feet, and they thought Miss Anthony was complaining of the child's crying. Their children were crying, too, and they felt that they had all been criticized. Other women rose and followed the irate mother, and many men gallantly followed them. It seemed clear that motherhood had been outraged.

Miss Anthony was greatly depressed by the episode, and she was not comforted by a prediction one man made after the meeting.

"You've lost at least twenty votes by that little affair," he told her.

"Aunt Susan" sighed. "Well," she said, "if those men knew how my ankles felt I would have won twenty votes by enduring the torture as long as I did."

The next day we had a second meeting. Miss Anthony made her speech early in the evening, and by the time it was my turn to begin all the children in the audience—and there were many—were both tired and sleepy. At least half a dozen of them were crying, and I had to shout to make my voice heard above their uproar. Miss Anthony remarked afterward that there seemed to be a contest between me and the infants to see which of us could make more noise. The audience was plainly getting restless under the combined effect, and finally a man in the rear rose and added his voice to the tumult.

"Say, Miss Shaw," he yelled, "don't you want these children put out?"

It was our chance to remove the sad impression of yesterday, and I grasped it.

"No, indeed," I yelled back. "Nothing inspires me like the voice of a child!"

A handsome round of applause from mothers and fathers greeted this noble declaration, after which the blessed babies and I resumed our joint vocal efforts. When the speech was finished and we were alone together, Miss Anthony put her arm around my shoulder and drew me to her side.

"Well, Anna," she said, gratefully, "you've certainly evened us up on motherhood this time."

That South Dakota campaign was one of the most difficult we ever made. It extended over nine months; and it is impossible to describe the poverty which prevailed throughout the whole rural community of the State. There had been three consecutive years of drought. The sand was like powder, so deep that the wheels of the wagons in which we rode "across country" sank half-way to the hubs; and in the midst of this dry powder lay withered tangles that had once been grass. Every one had the forsaken, desperate look worn by the pioneer who has reached the limit of his endurance, and the great stretches of prairie roads showed innumerable canvas-covered wagons, drawn by starved horses, and followed by starved cows, on their way "Back East." Our talks with the despairing drivers of these wagons are among my most tragic memories. They had lost everything except what they had with them, and they were going East to leave "the woman" with her father and try to find work. Usually, with a look of disgust at his wife, the man would say: "I wanted to leave two years ago, but the woman kept saying, 'Hold on a little longer.'"

Both Miss Anthony and I gloried in the spirit of these pioneer women, and lost no opportunity to tell them so; for we realized what our nation owes to the patience and courage of such as they were. We often asked them what was the hardest thing to bear in their pioneer life, and we usually received the same reply:

"To sit in our little adobe or sod houses at night and listen to the wolves howl over the graves of our babies. For the howl of the wolf is like the cry of a child from the grave."

Many days, and in all kinds of weather, we rode forty and fifty miles in uncovered wagons. Many nights we shared a one-room cabin with all the members of the family. But the greatest hardship we suffered was the lack of water. There was very little good water in the state, and the purest water was so brackish that we could hardly drink it. The more we drank the thirstier we became, and when the water was made into tea it tasted worse than when it was clear. A bath was the rarest of luxuries. The only available fuel was buffalo manure, of which the odor permeated all our food. But despite these handicaps we were happy in our work, for we had some great meetings and many wonderful experiences.

When we reached the Black Hills we had more of this genuine campaigning. We traveled over the mountains in wagons, behind teams of horses, visiting the mining-camps; and often the gullies were so deep that when our horses got into them it was almost impossible to get them out. I recall with special clearness one ride from Hill City to Custer City. It was only a matter of thirty miles, but it was thoroughly exhausting; and after our meeting that same night we had to drive forty miles farther over the mountains to get the early morning train from Buffalo Gap. The trail from Custer City to Buffalo Gap was the one the animals had originally made in their journeys over the pass, and the drive in that wild region, throughout a cold, piercing October night, was an unforgetable experience. Our host at Custer City lent Miss Anthony his big buffalo overcoat, and his wife lent hers to me. They also heated blocks of wood for our feet, and with these protections we started. A full moon hung in the sky. The trees were covered with hoar-frost, and the cold, still air seemed to sparkle in the brilliant light. Again Miss Anthony talked to me throughout the night—of the work, always of the work, and of what it would mean to the women who followed us; and again she fired my soul with the flame that burned so steadily in her own.

It was daylight when we reached the little station at Buffalo Gap where we were to take the train. This was not due, however, for half an hour, and even then it did not come. The station was only large enough to hold the stove, the ticket-office, and the inevitable cuspidor. There was barely room in which to walk between these and the wall. Miss Anthony sat down on the floor. I had a few raisins in my bag, and we divided them for breakfast. An hour passed, and another, and still the train did not come. Miss Anthony, her back braced against the wall, buried her face in her hands and dropped into a peaceful abyss of slumber, while I walked restlessly up and down the platform. The train arrived four hours late, and when eventually we had reached our destination we learned that the ministers of the town had persuaded the women to give up the suffrage meeting scheduled for that night, as it was Sunday.

This disappointment, following our all-day and all-night drive to keep our appointment, aroused Miss Anthony's fighting spirit. She sent me out to rent the theater for the evening, and to have some hand-bills printed and distributed, announcing that we would speak. At three o'clock she made the concession to her seventy years of lying down for an hour's rest. I was young and vigorous, so I trotted around town to get somebody to preside, somebody to introduce us, somebody to take up the collection, and somebody who would provide music—in short, to make all our preparations for the night meeting.

When evening came the crowd which had assembled was so great that men and women sat in the windows and on the stage, and stood in the flies. Night attractions were rare in that Dakota town, and here was something new. Nobody went to church, so the churches were forced to close. We had a glorious meeting. Both Miss Anthony and I were in excellent fighting trim, and Miss Anthony remarked that the only thing lacking to make me do my best was a sick headache. The collection we took up paid all our expenses, the church singers sang for us, the great audience was interested, and the whole occasion was an inspiring success.

The meeting ended about half after ten o'clock, and I remember taking Miss Anthony to our hotel and escorting her to her room. I also remember that she followed me to the door and made some laughing remark as I left for my own room; but I recall nothing more until the next morning when she stood beside me telling me it was time for breakfast. She had found me lying on the cover of my bed, fully clothed even to my bonnet and shoes. I had fallen there, utterly exhausted, when I entered my room the night before, and I do not think I had even moved from that time until the moment—nine hours later—when I heard her voice and felt her hand on my shoulder.

After all our work, we did not win Dakota that year, but Miss Anthony bore the disappointment with the serenity she always showed. To her a failure was merely another opportunity, and I mention our experience here only to show of what she was capable in her gallant seventies. But I should misrepresent her if I did not show her human and sentimental side as well. With all her detachment from human needs she had emotional moments, and of these the most satisfying came when she was listening to music. She knew nothing whatever about music, but was deeply moved by it; and I remember vividly one occasion when Nordica sang for her, at an afternoon reception given by a Chicago friend in "Aunt Susan's" honor. As it happened, she had never heard Nordica sing until that day; and before the music began the great artiste and the great leader met, and in the moment of meeting became friends. When Nordica sang, half an hour later, she sang directly to Miss Anthony, looking into her eyes; and "Aunt Susan" listened with her own eyes full of tears. When the last notes had been sung she went to the singer and put both arms around her. The music had carried her back to her girlhood and to the sentiment of sixteen.

"Oh, Nordica," she sighed, "I could die listening to such singing!"

Another example of her unquenchable youth has also a Chicago setting. During the World's Fair a certain clergyman made an especially violent stand in favor of closing the Fair grounds on Sunday. Miss Anthony took issue with him.

"If I had charge of a young man in Chicago at this time," she told the clergyman, "I would much rather have him locked inside the Fair grounds on Sunday or any other day than have him going about on the outside."

The clergyman was horrified. "Would you like to have a son of yours go to Buffalo Bill's Wild West Show on Sunday?" he demanded.

"Of course I would," admitted Miss Anthony. "In fact, I think he would learn more there than from the sermons preached in some churches."

Later this remark was repeated to Colonel Cody ("Buffalo Bill"), who, of course, was delighted with it. He at once wrote to Miss Anthony, thanking her for the breadth of her views, and offering her a box for his "Show." She had no strong desire to see the performance, but some of us urged her to accept the invitation and to take us with her. She was always ready to do anything that would give us pleasure, so she promised that we should go the next afternoon. Others heard of the jaunt and begged to go also, and Miss Anthony blithely took every applicant under her wing, with the result that when we arrived at the box-office the next day there were twelve of us in the group. When she presented her note and asked for a box, the local manager looked doubtfully at the delegation.

"A box only holds six," he objected, logically. Miss Anthony, who had given no thought to that slight detail, looked us over and smiled her seraphic smile.

"Why, in that case," she said, cheerfully, "you'll have to give us two boxes, won't you?"

The amused manager decided that he would, and handed her the tickets; and she led her band to their places in triumph. When the performance began Colonel Cody, as was his custom, entered the arena from the far end of the building, riding his wonderful horse and bathed, of course, in the effulgence of his faithful spot-light. He rode directly to our boxes, reined his horse in front of Miss Anthony, rose in his stirrups, and with his characteristic gesture swept his slouch-hat to his saddle-bow in salutation. "Aunt Susan" immediately rose, bowed in her turn and, for the moment as enthusiastic as a girl, waved her handkerchief at him, while the big audience, catching the spirit of the scene, wildly applauded. It was a striking picture this meeting of the pioneer man and woman; and, poor as I am, I would give a hundred dollars for a snapshot of it.

On many occasions I saw instances of Miss Anthony's prescience—and one of these was connected with the death of Frances E. Willard. "Aunt Susan" had called on Miss Willard, and, coming to me from the sick-room, had walked the floor, beating her hands together as she talked of the visit.

"Frances Willard is dying," she exclaimed, passionately. "She is dying, and she doesn't know it, and no one around her realizes it. She is lying there, seeing into two worlds, and making more plans than a thousand women could carry out in ten years. Her brain is wonderful. She has the most extraordinary clearness of vision. There should be a stenographer in that room, and every word she utters should be taken down, for every word is golden. But they don't understand. They can't realize that she is going. I told Anna Gordon the truth, but she won't believe it."

Miss Willard died a few days later, with a suddenness which seemed to be a terrible shock to those around her.

Of "Aunt Susan's" really remarkable lack of selfconsciousness we who worked close to her had a thousand extraordinary examples. Once, I remember, at the New Orleans Convention, she reached the hall a little late, and as she entered the great audience already assembled gave her a tremendous reception. The exercises of the day had not yet begun, and Miss Anthony stopped short and looked around for an explanation of the outburst. It never for a moment occurred to her that the tribute was to her.

"What has happened, Anna?" she asked at last.

"You happened, Aunt Susan," I had to explain.

Again, on the great "College Night" of the Baltimore Convention, when President M. Carey Thomas of Bryn Mawr College had finished her wonderful tribute to Miss Anthony, the audience, carried away by the speech and also by the presence of the venerable leader on the platform, broke into a whirlwind of applause. In this "Aunt Susan" artlessly joined, clapping her hands as hard as she could. "This is all for you, Aunt Susan," I whispered, "so it isn't your time to applaud."

"Aunt Susan" continued to clap. "Nonsense," she said, briskly. "It's not for me. It's for the Cause—the Cause!"

Miss Anthony told me in 1904 that she regarded her reception in Berlin, during the meeting of the International Council of Women that year, as the climax of her career. She said it after the unexpected and wonderful ovation she had received from the German people, and certainly throughout her inspiring life nothing had happened that moved her more deeply.

For some time Mrs. Carrie Chapman Catt, of whose splendid work for the Cause I shall later have more to say, had cherished the plan of forming an International Suffrage Alliance. She believed the time had come when the suffragists of the entire world could meet to their common benefit; and

Miss Anthony, always Mrs. Catt's devoted friend and admirer, agreed with her. A committee was appointed to meet in Berlin in 1904, just before the meeting of the International Council of Women, and Miss Anthony was appointed chairman of the committee. At first the plan of the committee was not welcomed by the International Council; there was even a suspicion that its purpose was to start a rival organization. But it met, a constitution was framed, and officers were elected, Mrs. Catt—the ideal choice for the place—being made president. As a climax to the organization, a great public mass-meeting had been arranged by the German suffragists, but at the special plea of the president of the International Council Miss Anthony remained away from this meeting. It was represented to her that the interests of the Council might suffer if she and other of its leading speakers were also leaders in the suffrage movement. In the interest of harmony, there fore, she followed the wishes of the Council's president—to my great unhappiness and to that of other suffragists.

When the meeting was opened the first words of the presiding officer were, "Where is Susan B. Anthony?" and the demonstration that followed the question was the most unexpected and overwhelming incident of the gathering. The entire audience rose, men jumped on their chairs, and the cheering continued without a break for ten minutes. Every second of that time I seemed to see Miss Anthony, alone in her hotel room, longing with all her big heart to be with us, as we longed to have her. I prayed that the loss of a tribute which would have meant so much might be made up to her, and it was. Afterward, when we burst in upon her and told her of the great demonstration the mere mention of her name had caused, her lips quivered and her brave old eyes filled with tears. As we looked at her I think we all realized anew that what the world called stoicism in Susan B. Anthony throughout the years of her long struggle had been, instead, the splendid courage of an indomitable soul—while all the time the woman's heart had longed for affection and recognition. The next morning the leading Berlin newspaper, in reporting the debate and describing the spontaneous tribute to Miss Anthony, closed with these sentences: "The Americans call her 'Aunt Susan.' She is our 'Aunt Susan,' too!"

Throughout the remainder of Miss Anthony's visit she was the most honored figure at the International Council. Every time she entered the great convention-hall the entire audience rose and remained standing until she was seated; each mention of her name was punctuated by cheers; and the enthusiasm when she appeared on the platform to say a few words was beyond bounds. When the Empress of Germany gave her reception to the officers of the Council, she crowned the hospitality of her people in a characteristically gracious way. As soon as Miss Anthony was presented to her the Empress invited her to be seated, and to remain seated, although every one else, including the august lady herself, was standing. A little later, seeing the intrepid warrior of eighty-four on her feet with the other delegates, the Empress sent one of her aides across the room with this message: "Please tell my friend Miss Anthony that I especially wish her to be seated. We must not let her grow weary."

In her turn, Miss Anthony was fascinated by the Empress. She could not keep her eyes off that charming royal lady. Probably the thing that most impressed her was the ability of her Majesty as a linguist. Receiving women from every civilized country on the globe, the Empress seemed to address each in her own tongue-slipping from one language into the next as easily as from one topic to another.

"And here I am," mourned "Aunt Susan," "speaking only one language, and that not very well."

At this Berlin quinquennial, by the way, I preached the Council sermon, and the occasion gained a certain interest from the fact that I was the first ordained woman to preach in a church in Germany. It then took on a tinge of humor from the additional fact that, according to the German law, as suddenly revealed to us by the police, no clergyman was permitted to preach unless clothed in clerical robes in the pulpit. It happened that I had not taken my clerical robes with me—I am constantly forgetting those clerical robes!—so the pastor of the church kindly offered me his robes.

Now the pastor was six feet tall and broad in proportion, and I, as I have already confessed, am very short. His robes transformed me into such an absurd caricature of a preacher that it was quite impossible for me to wear them. What, then, were we to do? Lacking clerical robes, the police would not allow me to utter six words. It was finally decided that the clergyman should meet the letter of the law by entering the pulpit in his robes and standing by my side while I delivered my sermon. The law soberly accepted this solution of the problem, and we offered the congregation the extraordinary tableau of a pulpit combining a large and impressive pastor standing silently beside a small and inwardly convulsed woman who had all she could do to deliver her sermon with the solemnity the occasion required.

At this same conference I made one of the few friendships I enjoy with a member of a European royal family, for I met the Princess Blank of Italy, who overwhelmed me with attention during my visit, and from whom I still receive charming letters. She invited me to visit her in her castle in Italy, and to accompany her to her mother's castle in Austria, and she finally insisted on knowing exactly why I persistently refused both invitations.

"Because, my dear Princess," I explained, "I am a working-woman."

"Nobody need KNOW that," murmured the Princess, calmly.

"On the contrary," I assured her, "it is the first thing I should explain."

"But why?" the Princess wanted to know.

I studied her in silence for a moment. She was a new and interesting type to me, and I was glad to exchange viewpoints with her.

"You are proud of your family, are you not?" I asked. "You are proud of your great line?"

The Princess drew herself up. "Assuredly," she said.

"Very well," I continued. "I am proud, too. What I have done I have done unaided, and, to be frank with you, I rather approve of it. My work is my patent of nobility, and I am not willing to associate with those from whom it would have to be concealed or with those who would look down upon it."

The Princess sighed. I was a new type to her, too, as new as she was to me; but I had the advantage of her, for I could understand her point of view, whereas she apparently could not follow mine. She was very gracious to me, however, showing me kindness and friendship in a dozen ways, giving me an immense amount of her time and taking rather more of my time than I could spare, but never forgetting for a moment that her blood was among the oldest in Europe, and that all her traditions were in keeping with its honorable age.

After the Berlin meeting Miss Anthony and I were invited to spend a week-end at the home of Mrs. Jacob Bright, that "Aunt Susan" might renew her acquaintance with Annie Besant. This visit is among my most vivid memories. Originally "Aunt Susan" had greatly admired Mrs. Besant, and had openly lamented the latter's concentration on theosophical interests— when, as Miss Anthony put it, "there are so many live problems here in this world." Now she could not conceal her disapproval of the "other-worldliness" of Mrs. Besant, Mrs. Bright, and her daughter. Some remarkable and, to me, most amusing discussions took place among the three; but often, during Mrs. Besant's most sustained oratorical flights, Miss Anthony's interest would wander, and she would drop a remark that showed she had not heard a word. She had a great admiration for Mrs. Besant's intellect; but she disapproved of her flowing and picturesque white robes, of her bare feet, of her incessant cigarette-smoking; above all, of her views. At last, one day.{sic} the climax of the discussions came.

"Annie," demanded "Aunt Susan," "why don't you make that aura of yours do its gallivanting in this world, looking up the needs of the oppressed, and investigating the causes of present wrongs? Then you could reveal to us workers just what we should do to put things right, and we could be about it."

Mrs. Besant sighed and said that life was short and aeons were long, and that while every one would be perfected some time, it was useless to deal with individuals here.

"But, Annie!" exclaimed Miss Anthony, pathetically. "We ARE here! Our business is here! It's our duty to do what we can here."

Mrs. Besant seemed not to hear her. She was in a trance, gazing into the aeons.

"I'd rather have one year of your ability, backed up with common sense, for the work of making this world better," cried the exasperated "Aunt Susan," "than a million aeons in the hereafter!"

Mrs. Besant sighed again. It was plain that she could not bring herself back from the other world, so Miss Anthony, perforce, accompanied her to it.

"When your aura goes visiting in the other world," she asked, curiously, "does it ever meet your old friend Charles Bradlaugh?"

"Oh yes," declared Mrs. Besant. "Frequently."

"Wasn't he very much surprised," demanded Miss Anthony, with growing interest, "to discover that he was not dead?"

Mrs. Besant did not seem to know what emotion Mr. Bradlaugh had experienced when that revelation came.

"Well," mused "Aunt Susan," "I should think he would have been surprised. He was so certain he was going to be dead that it must have been astounding to discover he wasn't. What was he doing in the other world?"

Mrs. Besant heaved a deeper sigh. "I am very much discouraged over Mr. Bradlaugh," she admitted, wanly. "He is hovering too near this world. He cannot seem to get away from his mundane interests. He is as much concerned with parliamentary affairs now as when he was on this plane."

"Humph!" said Miss Anthony; "that's the most sensible thing I've heard yet about the other world. It encourages me. I've always felt sure that if I entered the other life before women were enfranchised nothing in the glories of heaven would interest me so much as the work for women's freedom on earth. Now," she ended, "I shall be like Mr. Bradlaugh. I shall hover round and continue my work here."

When Mrs. Besant had left the room Mrs. Bright felt that it was her duty to admonish "Aunt Susan" to be more careful in what she said.

"You are making too light of her creed," she expostulated. "You do not realize the important position Mrs. Besant holds. Why, in India, when she walks from her home to her school all those she meets prostrate themselves. Even the learned men prostrate themselves and put their faces on the ground as she goes by."

"Aunt Susan's" voice, when she replied, took on the tones of one who is sorely tried. "But why in Heaven's name does any sensible Englishwoman want a lot of heathen to prostrate themselves as she goes up the street?" she demanded, wearily. "It's the most foolish thing I ever heard."

The effort to win Miss Anthony over to the theosophical doctrine was abandoned. That night, after we had gone to our rooms, "Aunt Susan" summed up her conclusions on the interview:

"It's a good thing for the world," she declared, "that some of us don't know so much. And it's a better thing for this world that some of us think a little earthly common sense is more valuable than too much heavenly knowledge."

X. THE PASSING OF "AUNT SUSAN"

On one occasion Miss Anthony had the doubtful pleasure of reading her own obituary notices, and her interest in them was characteristically naive. She had made a speech at Lakeside, Ohio, during which, for the first time in her long experience, she fainted on the platform. I was not with her at the time, and in the excitement following her collapse it was rumored that she had died. Immediately the news was telegraphed to the Associated Press of New York, and from there flashed over the country. At Miss Anthony's home in Rochester a reporter rang the bell and abruptly informed her sister, Miss Mary Anthony, who came to the door, that "Aunt Susan" was dead. Fortunately Miss Mary had a cool head.

"I think," she said, "that if my sister had died I would have heard about it. Please have your editors telegraph to Lakeside."

The reporter departed, but came back an hour later to say that his newspaper had sent the telegram and the reply was that Susan B. Anthony was dead.

"I have just received a better telegram than that," remarked Mary Anthony. "Mine is from my sister; she tells me that she fainted to-night, but soon recovered and will be home to-morrow."

Nevertheless, the next morning the American newspapers gave much space to Miss Anthony's obituary notices, and "Aunt Susan" spent some interesting hours reading them. One that pleased her vastly was printed in the Wichita Eagle, whose editor, Mr. Murdock, had been almost her bitterest opponent. He had often exhausted his brilliant vocabulary in editorial denunciations of suffrage and suffragists, and Miss Anthony had been the special target of his scorn. But the news of her death seemed to be a bitter blow to him; and of all the tributes the American press gave to Susan B. Anthony dead, few equaled in beauty and appreciation the one penned by Mr. Murdock and published in the Eagle. He must have been amused when, a few days later, he received a letter from "Aunt Susan" herself, thanking him warmly for his changed opinion of her and hoping that it meant the conversion of his soul to our Cause. It did not, and Mr. Murdock, though never again quite as bitter as he had been, soon resumed the free editorial expression of his antisuffrage sentiments. Times have changed, however, and to-day his son, now a member of Congress, is one of our strongest supporters in that body.

In 1905 it became plain that Miss Anthony's health was failing. Her visits to Germany and England the previous year, triumphant though they had been, had also proved a drain on her vitality; and soon after her return to America she entered upon a task which helped to exhaust her remaining strength. She had been deeply interested in securing a fund of $50,000 to enable women to enter Rochester University, and, one morning, just after we had held a session of our executive committee in her Rochester home, she read a newspaper announcement to the effect that at four o'clock that afternoon the opportunity to admit women to the university would expire, as the full fifty thousand dollars had not been raised. The sum of eight thousand dollars was still lacking.

With characteristic energy, Miss Anthony undertook to save the situation by raising this amount within the time limit. Rushing to the telephone, she called a cab and prepared to go forth on her difficult quest; but first, while she was putting on her hat and coat, she insisted that her sister, Mary Anthony, should start the fund by contributing one thousand dollars from her meager savings, and this Miss Mary did. "Aunt Susan" made every second count that day, and by half after three o'clock she had secured the necessary pledges. Several of the trustees of the university, however, had not seemed especially anxious to have the fund raised, and at the last moment they objected to one pledge for a thousand dollars, on the ground that the man who had given it was very old and might die before the time set to pay it; then his family, they feared, might repudiate the obligation. Without a word Miss Anthony seized the pledge and wrote her name across it as an indorsement. "I am good for it," she then said, quietly, "if the gentleman who signed it is not."

That afternoon she returned home greatly fatigued. A few hours later the girl students who had been waiting admission to the university came to serenade her in recognition of her successful work for them, but she was too ill to see them. She was passing through the first stage of what proved to be her final breakdown.

In 1906, when the date of the annual convention of the National American Woman Suffrage Association in Baltimore was drawing near, she became convinced that it would be her last convention. She was right. She showed a passionate eagerness to make it one of the greatest conventions ever held in the history of the movement; and we, who loved her and saw that the flame of her life was burning low, also bent all our energies to the task of realizing her hopes. In November preceding the convention she visited me and her niece, Miss Lucy Anthony, in our home in Mount Airy, Philadelphia, and it was clear that her anxiety over the convention was weighing heavily upon her. She visibly lost strength from day to day. One morning she said abruptly, "Anna, let's go and call on President M. Carey Thomas, of Bryn Mawr."

I wrote a note to Miss Thomas, telling her of Miss Anthony's desire to see her, and received an immediate reply inviting us to luncheon the following day. We found Miss Thomas deep in the work connected with her new college buildings, over which she showed us with much pride. Miss Anthony, of course, gloried in the splendid results Miss Thomas had achieved, but she was, for her, strangely silent and preoccupied. At luncheon she said:

"Miss Thomas, your buildings are beautiful; your new library is a marvel; but they are not the cause of our presence here."

"No," Miss Thomas said; "I know you have something on your mind. I am waiting for you to tell me what it is."

"We want your co-operation, and that of Miss Garrett," began Miss Anthony, promptly, "to make our Baltimore Convention a success. We want you to persuade the Arundel Club of Baltimore, the most fashionable club in the city, to give a reception to the delegates; and we want you to arrange a college night on the programme—a great college night, with the best college speakers ever brought together."

These were large commissions for two extremely busy women, but both Miss Thomas and Miss Garrett—realizing Miss Anthony's intense earnestness—promised to think over the suggestions and see what they could do. The next morning we received a telegram from them stating that Miss Thomas would arrange the college evening, and that Miss Garrett would reopen her Baltimore home, which she had closed, during the convention. She also invited Miss Anthony and me to be her guests there, and added that she would try to arrange the reception by the Arundel Club.

"Aunt Susan" was overjoyed. I have never seen her happier than she was over the receipt of that telegram. She knew that whatever Miss Thomas and Miss Garrett undertook would be accomplished, and she rightly regarded the success of the convention as already assured. Her expectations were more than realized. The college evening was undoubtedly the most brilliant occasion of its kind ever arranged for a convention. President Ira Remsen of Johns Hopkins University presided, and addresses were made by President Mary E. Woolley of Mount Holyoke, Professor Lucy Salmon of Vassar, Professor Mary Jordan of Smith, President Thomas herself, and many others.

From beginning to end the convention was probably the most notable yet held in our history. Julia Ward Howe and her daughter, Florence Howe Hall, were also guests of Miss Garrett, who, moreover, entertained all the speakers of "College Night." Miss Anthony, now eighty-six, arrived in Baltimore quite ill, and Mrs. Howe, who was ninety, was taken ill soon after she reached there. The two great women made a dramatic exchange on the programme, for on the first night, when Miss Anthony was unable to speak, Mrs. Howe took her place, and on the second night, when Mrs. Howe had succumbed, Miss Anthony had recovered sufficiently to appear for her. Clara Barton was also an honored figure at the convention, and Miss Anthony's joy in the presence of all these old and dear friends was overflowing. With them, too, were the younger women, ready to take up and carry on the work the old leaders were laying down; and "Aunt Susan," as she surveyed them all, felt like a general whose superb army is passing in review before him. At the close of the college programme, when the final address had been made by Miss Thomas, Miss Anthony rose and in a few words expressed her feeling that her life-work was done, and her consciousness of the near approach of the end. After that night she was unable to appear, and was indeed so ill that she was confined to her bed in Miss Garrett's most hospitable home. Nothing could have been more thoughtful or more beautiful than the care Miss Garrett and Miss Thomas bestowed on her. They engaged for her one of the best physicians in Baltimore, who, in turn, consulted with the leading specialists of Johns Hopkins, and they also secured a trained nurse. This final attention required special tact, for Miss Anthony's fear of "giving trouble" was so great that she was not willing to have a nurse. The nurse, therefore, wore a housemaid's uniform, and "Aunt Susan" remained wholly unconscious that she was being cared for by one of the best nurses in the famous hospital.

Between sessions of the convention I used to sit by "Aunt Susan's" bed and tell her what was going on. She was triumphant over the immense success of the convention, but it was clear that she was still worrying over the details of future work. One day at luncheon Miss Thomas asked me, casually:

"By the way, how do you raise the money to carry on your work?"

When I told her the work was wholly dependent on voluntary contributions and on the services of those who were willing to give themselves gratuitously to it, Miss Thomas was greatly surprised. She and Miss Garrett asked a number of practical questions, and at the end of our talk they looked at each other.

"I don't think," said Miss Thomas, "that we have quite done our duty in this matter."

The next day they invited a number of us to dinner, to again discuss the situation; and they admitted that they had sat up throughout the previous night, talking the matter over and trying to find some way to help us. They had also discussed the situation with Miss Anthony, to her vast content, and had finally decided that they would try to raise a fund of $60,000, to be paid in yearly instalments of $12,000 for five years—part of these annual instalments to be used as salaries for the active officers. The mere mention of so large a fund startled us all. We feared that it could not possibly be raised. But Miss Anthony plainly believed that now the last great wish of her life had been granted. She was convinced that Miss Thomas and Miss Garrett could accomplish anything—even the miracle of raising $60,000 for the suffrage cause—and they did, though "Aunt Susan" was not here to glory over the result when they had achieved it.

On the 15th of February we left Baltimore for Washington, where Miss Anthony was to celebrate her eighty-sixth birthday. For many years the National American Woman Suffrage Association had celebrated our birthdays together, as hers came on the 15th of the month and mine on the 14th. There had been an especially festive banquet when she was seventy-four and I was forty-seven, and our friends had decorated the table with floral "4's" and "7's"—the centerpiece representing "74" during the first half of the banquet, and "47" the latter half. This time "Aunt Susan" should not have attempted the Washington celebration, for she was still ill and exhausted by the strain of the convention. But notwithstanding her sufferings and the warnings of her physicians, she insisted on being present; so Miss Garrett sent the trained nurse to Washington with her, and we all tried to make the journey the least possible strain on the patient's vitality.

On our arrival in Washington we went to the Shoreham, where, as always, the proprietor took pains to give Miss Anthony a room with a view of the Washington monument, which she greatly admired. When I entered her room a little later I found her standing at a window, holding herself up with hands braced against the casement on either side, and so absorbed in the view that she did not hear my approach. When I spoke to her she answered without turning her head.

"That," she said, softly, "is the most beautiful monument in the world."

I stood by her side, and together we looked at it in silence I realizing with a sick heart that "Aunt Susan" knew she was seeing it for the last time.

The birthday celebration that followed our executive meeting was an impressive one. It was held in the Church of Our Father, whose pastor, the Rev. John Van Schaick, had always been exceedingly kind to Miss Anthony. Many prominent men spoke. President Roosevelt and other statesmen sent most friendly letters, and William H. Taft had promised to be present. He did not come, nor did he, then or later, send any excuse for not coming—an omission that greatly disappointed Miss Anthony, who had always admired him. I presided at the meeting, and though we all did our best to make it gay, a strange hush hung over the assemblage a solemn stillness, such as one feels in the presence of death. We became more and more conscious that Miss Anthony was suffering, and we hastened the exercises all we could. When I read President Roosevelt's long tribute to her, Miss Anthony rose to comment on it.

"One word from President Roosevelt in his message to Congress," she said, a little wearily, "would be worth a thousand eulogies of Susan B. Anthony. When will men learn that what we ask is not praise, but justice?"

At the close of the meeting, realizing how weak she was, I begged her to let me speak for her. But she again rose, rested her hand on my shoulder, and, standing by my side, uttered the last words she ever spoke in public, pleading with women to consecrate themselves to the Cause, assuring them that no power could prevent its ultimate success, but reminding them also that the time of its coming would depend wholly on their work and their loyalty. She ended with three words—very fitting words from her lips, expressing as they did the spirit of her life-work—"FAILURE IS IMPOSSIBLE."

The next morning she was taken to her home in Rochester, and one month from that day we conducted her funeral services. The nurse who had accompanied her from Baltimore remained with her until two others had been secured to take her place, and every care that love or medical science could suggest was lavished on the patient. But from the first it was plain that, as she herself had foretold, "Aunt Susan's" soul was merely waiting for the hour of its passing.

One of her characteristic traits was a dislike to being seen, even by those nearest to her, when she was not well. During the first three weeks of her last illness, therefore, I did what she wished me to do—I continued our work, trying to do hers as well as my own. But all the time my heart was in her sick-room, and at last the day came when I could no longer remain away from her. I had awakened in the morning with a strong conviction that she needed me, and at the breakfast-table I announced to her niece, Miss Lucy Anthony, the friend who for years has shared my home, that I was going at once to "Aunt Susan."

"I shall not even wait to telegraph," I declared. "I am sure she has sent for me; I shall take the first train."

The journey brought me very close to death. As we were approaching Wilkes-Barre our train ran into a wagon loaded with powder and dynamite, which had been left on the track. The horses attached to it had been unhitched by their driver, who had spent his time in this effort, when he saw the train coming, instead of in signaling to the engineer. I was on my way to the dining-car when the collision occurred, and, with every one else who happened to be standing, I was hurled to the floor by the impact; flash after flash of blinding light outside, accompanied by a terrific roar, added to the panic of the passengers. When the train stopped we learned how narrow had been our escape from an especially unpleasant form of death. The dynamite in the wagon was frozen, and therefore had not exploded; it was the explosion of the powder that had caused the flashes and the din. The dark-green cars were burned almost white, and as we stood staring at them, a silent, stunned group, our conductor said, quietly, "You will never be as near death again, and escape, as you have been to-day."

The accident caused a long delay, and it was ten o'clock at night when I reached Rochester and Miss Anthony's home. As I entered the house Miss Mary Anthony rose in surprise to greet me.

"How did you get here so soon?" she cried. And then: "We sent for you this afternoon. Susan has been asking for you all day."

When I reached my friend's bedside one glance at her face showed me the end was near; and from that time until it came, almost a week later, I remained with her; while again, as always, she talked of the Cause, and of the life-work she must now lay down. The first thing she spoke of was her will, which she had made several years before, and in which she had left the small property she possessed to her sister Mary, her niece Lucy, and myself, with instructions as to the use we three were to make of it. Now she told me we were to pay no attention to these instructions, but to give every dollar of her money to the $60,000 fund Miss Thomas and Miss Garrett were trying to raise. She was vitally interested in this fund, as its success meant that for five years the active officers of the National American Woman Suffrage Association, including myself as president, would for the first time receive salaries for our work. When she had given her instructions on this point she still seemed depressed.

"I wish I could live on," she said, wistfully. "But I cannot. My spirit is eager and my heart is as young as it ever was, but my poor old body is worn out. Before I go I want you to give me a promise: Promise me that you will keep the presidency of the association as long as you are well enough to do the work."

"But how can I promise that?" I asked. "I can keep it only as long as others wish me to keep it."

"Promise to make them wish you to keep it," she urged. "Just as I wish you to keep it."

I would have promised her anything then. So, though I knew that to hold the presidency would tie me to a position that brought in no living income, and though for several years past I had already drawn alarmingly upon my small financial reserve, I promised her that I would hold the office as long as the majority of the women in the association wished me to do so. "But," I added, "if the time comes when I believe that some one else can do better work in the presidency than I, then let me feel at liberty to resign it."

This did not satisfy her.

"No, no," she objected. "You cannot be the judge of that. Promise me you will remain until the friends you most trust tell you it is time to withdraw, or make you understand that it is time. Promise me that."

I made the promise. She seemed content, and again began to talk of the future.

"You will not have an easy path," she warned me. "In some ways it will be harder for you than it has ever been for me. I was so much older than the rest of you, and I had been president so long, that you girls have all been willing to listen to me. It will be different with you. Other women of your own age have been in the work almost as long as you have been; you do not stand out from them by age or length of service, as I did. There will be inevitable jealousies and misunderstandings; there will be all sorts of criticism and misrepresentation. My last word to you is this: No matter what is done or is not done, how you are criticized or misunderstood, or what efforts are made to block your path, remember that the only fear you need have is the fear of not standing by the thing you believe to be right. Take your stand and hold it; then let come what will, and receive blows like a good soldier."

I was too much overcome to answer her; and after a moment of silence she, in her turn, made me a promise.

"I do not know anything about what comes to us after this life ends," she said. "But if there is a continuance of life beyond it, and if I have any conscious knowledge of this world and of what you are doing, I shall not be far away from you; and in times of need I will help you all I can. Who knows? Perhaps I may be able to do more for the Cause after I am gone than while I am here."

Nine years have passed since then, and in each day of them all it seems to me, in looking back, I have had some occasion to recall her words. When they were uttered I did not fully comprehend all they meant, or the clearness of the vision that had suggested them. It seemed to me that no position I could hold would be of sufficient importance to attract jealousy or personal attacks. The years have brought more wisdom; I have learned that any one who assumes leadership, or who, like myself, has had leadership forced upon her, must expect to bear many things of which the world knows nothing. But with this knowledge, too, has come the memory of "Aunt Susan's" last promise, and again and yet again in hours of discouragement and despair I have been helped by the blessed conviction that she was keeping it.

During the last forty-eight hours of her life she was unwilling that I should leave her side. So day and night I knelt by her bed, holding her hand and watching the flame of her wonderful spirit grow dim. At times, even then, it blazed up with startling suddenness. On the last afternoon of her life, when she had lain quiet for hours, she suddenly began to utter the names of the women who had worked with her, as if in a final roll-call. Many of them had preceded her into the next world; others were still splendidly active in the work she was laying down. But young or old, living or dead, they all seemed to file past her dying eyes that day in an endless, shadowy review, and as they went by she spoke to each of them.

Not all the names she mentioned were known in suffrage ranks; some of these women lived only in the heart of Susan B. Anthony, and now, for the last time, she was thanking them for what they had done. Here was one who, at a moment of special need, had given her small savings; here was another who had won valuable recruits to the Cause; this one had written a strong editorial; that one had made a stirring speech. In these final hours it seemed that not a single sacrifice or service, however small, had been forgotten by the dying leader. Last of all, she spoke to the women who had been on her board and had stood by her loyally so long—Rachel Foster Avery, Alice Stone Blackwell, Carrie Chapman Catt, Mrs. Upton, Laura Clay, and others. Then, after lying in silence for a long time with her cheek on my hand, she murmured: "They are still passing before me—face after face, hundreds and hundreds of them, representing all the efforts of fifty years. I know how hard they have worked I know the sacrifices they have made. But it has all been worth while!"

Just before she lapsed into unconsciousness she seemed restless and anxious to say something, searching my face with her dimming eyes.

"Do you want me to repeat my promise?" I asked, for she had already made me do so several times. She made a sign of assent, and I gave her the assurance she desired. As I did so she raised my hand to her lips and kissed it—her last conscious action. For more than thirty hours after that I knelt by her side, but though she clung to my hand until her own hand grew cold, she did not speak again.

She had told me over and over how much our long friendship and association had meant to her, and the comfort I had given her. But whatever I may have been to her, it was as nothing compared with what she was to me. Kneeling close to her as she passed away, I knew that I would have given her a dozen lives had I had them, and endured a thousand times more hardship than we had borne together, for the inspiration of her companionship and the joy of her affection. They were the greatest blessings I have had in all my life, and I cherish as my dearest treasure the volume of her History of Woman Suffrage on the fly-leaf of which she had written this inscription:

REVEREND ANNA HOWARD SHAW:

This huge volume IV I present to you with the love that a mother beareth, and I hope you will find in it the facts about women, for you will find them nowhere else. Your part will be to see that the four volumes are duly placed in the libraries of the country, where every student of history may have access to them.

With unbounded love and faith,

SUSAN B. ANTHONY.

That final line is still my greatest comfort. When I am misrepresented or misunderstood, when I am accused of personal ambition or of working for personal ends, I turn to it and to similar lines penned by the same hand, and tell myself that I should not allow anything to interfere with the serenity of my spirit or to disturb me in my work. At the end of eighteen years of the most intimate companionship, the leader of our Cause, the greatest woman I have ever known, still felt for me "unbounded love and faith." Having had that, I have had enough.

For two days after "Aunt Susan's" death she lay in her own home, as if in restful slumber, her face wearing its most exquisite look of peaceful serenity; and here her special friends, the poor and the unfortunate of the city, came by hundreds to pay their last respects. On the third day there was a public funeral, held in the Congregational church, and, though a wild blizzard was raging, every one in Rochester seemed included in the great throng of mourners who came to her bier in reverence and left it in tears. The church services were conducted by the pastor, the Rev. C. C. Albertson, a lifelong friend of Miss Anthony's, assisted by the Rev. William C. Gannett. James G. Potter, the Mayor of the city, and Dr. Rush Rhees, president of Rochester University, occupied prominent places among the distinguished mourners, and Mrs. Jerome Jeffries, the head of a colored school, spoke in behalf of the negro race and its recognition of Miss Anthony's services. College clubs, medical societies, and reform groups were represented by delegates sent from different states, and Miss Anna Gordon had come on from Illinois to represent the Woman's National Christian Temperance Union. Mrs. Catt delivered a eulogy in which she expressed the love and recognition of the organized suffrage women of the world for Miss Anthony, as the one to whom they had all looked as their leader. William Lloyd Garrison spoke of Miss Anthony's work with his father and other antislavery leaders, and Mrs. Jean Brooks Greenleaf spoke in behalf of the New York State Suffrage Association. Then, as "Aunt Susan" had requested, I made the closing address. She had asked me to do this and to pronounce the benediction, as well as to say the final words at her grave.

It was estimated that more than ten thousand persons were assembled in and around the church, and after the benediction those who had been patiently waiting out in the storm were permitted to pass inside in single file for a last look at their friend. They found the coffin covered by a large American flag, on which lay a wreath of laurel and palms; around it stood a guard of honor composed of girl students of Rochester University in their college caps and gowns. All day students had mounted guard, relieving one another at intervals. On every side there were flowers and floral emblems sent by various organizations, and just over "Aunt Susan's" head floated the silk flag given to her by the women of Colorado. It contained four gold stars, representing the four enfranchised states, while the other stars were in silver. On her breast was pinned the jeweled flag given to her on her eightieth birthday by the women of Wyoming—the first place in the world where in the constitution of the state women were given equal political rights with men. Here the four stars representing the enfranchised states were made of diamonds, the others of silver enamel. Just before the lid was fastened on the coffin this flag was removed and handed to Mary Anthony, who presented it to me. From that day I have worn it on every occasion of importance to our Cause, and each time a state is won for woman suffrage I have added a new diamond star. At the time I write this—in 1914—there are twelve.

As the funeral procession went through the streets of Rochester it was seen that all the city flags were at half-mast, by order of the City Council. Many houses were draped in black, and the grief of the citizens manifested itself on every side. All the way to Mount Hope Cemetery the snow whirled blindingly around us, while the masses that had fallen covered the earth as far as we could see a fitting winding-sheet for the one who had gone. Under the fir-trees around her open grave I obeyed "Aunt Susan's" wish that I should utter the last words spoken over her body as she was laid to rest:

"Dear friend," I said, "thou hast tarried with us long. Now thou hast gone to thy well-earned rest. We beseech the Infinite Spirit Who has upheld thee to make us worthy to follow in thy steps and to carry on thy work. Hail and farewell."

XI. THE WIDENING SUFFRAGE STREAM

In my chapters on Miss Anthony I bridged the twenty years between 1886 and 1906, omitting many of the stirring suffrage events of that long period, in my desire to concentrate on those which most vitally concerned her. I must now retrace my steps along the widening suffrage stream and describe, consecutively at least, and as fully as these incomplete reminiscences will permit, other incidents that occurred on its banks.

Of these the most important was the union in 1889 of the two great suffrage societies—the American Association, of which Lucy Stone was the president, and the National Association, headed by Susan B. Anthony and Elizabeth Cady Stanton. At a convention held in Washington these societies were merged as The National American Woman Suffrage Association—the name our association still bears—and Mrs. Stanton was elected president. She was then nearly eighty and past active work, but she made a wonderful presiding officer at our subsequent meetings, and she was as picturesque as she was efficient.

Miss Anthony, who had an immense admiration for her and a great personal pride in her, always escorted her to the capital, and, having worked her utmost to make the meeting a success, invariably gave Mrs. Stanton credit for all that was accomplished. She often said that Mrs. Stanton was the brains of the new association, while she herself was merely its hands and feet; but in truth the two women worked marvelously together, for Mrs. Stanton was a master of words and could write and speak to perfection of the things Susan B. Anthony saw and felt but could not herself express. Usually Miss Anthony went to Mrs. Stanton's house and took charge of it while she stimulated the venerable president to the writing of her annual address. Then, at the subsequent convention, she would listen to the report with as much delight and pleasure as if each word of it had been new to her. Even after Mrs. Stanton's resignation from the presidency—at the end, I think, of three years—and Miss Anthony's election as her successor, "Aunt Susan" still went to her old friend whenever an important resolution was to be written, and Mrs. Stanton loyally drafted it for her.

Mrs. Stanton was the most brilliant conversationalist I have ever known; and the best talk I have heard anywhere was that to which I used to listen in the home of Mrs. Eliza Wright Osborne, in Auburn, New York, when Mrs. Stanton, Susan B. Anthony, Emily Howland, Elizabeth Smith Miller, Ida Husted Harper, Miss Mills, and I were gathered there for our occasional week-end visits. Mrs. Osborne inherited her suffrage sympathies, for she was the daughter of Martha Wright, who, with Mrs. Stanton and Lucretia Mott, called the first suffrage convention in Seneca Falls, New York. I must add in passing that her son, Thomas Mott Osborne, who is doing such admirable work in prison reform at Sing Sing, has shown himself worthy of the gifted and high-minded mother who gave him to the world.

Most of the conversation in Mrs. Osborne's home was contributed by Mrs. Stanton and Miss Anthony, while the rest of us sat, as it were, at their feet. Many human and feminine touches brightened the lofty discussions that were constantly going on, and the varied characteristics of our leaders cropped up in amusing fashion. Mrs. Stanton, for example, was rarely accurate in giving figures or dates, while Miss Anthony was always very exact in such matters. She frequently corrected Mrs. Stanton's statements, and Mrs. Stanton usually took the interruption in the best possible spirit, promptly admitting that "Aunt Susan" knew best. On one occasion I recall, however, she held fast to her opinion that she was right as to the month in which a certain incident had occurred.

"No, Susan," she insisted, "you're wrong for once. I remember perfectly when that happened, for it was at the time I was beginning to wean Harriet."

Aunt Susan, though somewhat staggered by the force of this testimony, still maintained that Mrs. Stanton must be mistaken, whereupon the latter repeated, in exasperation, "I tell you it happened when I was weaning Harriet." And she added, scornfully, "What event have you got to reckon from?"

Miss Anthony meekly subsided.

Mrs. Stanton had wonderful blue eyes, which held to the end of her life an expression of eternal youth. During our conventions she usually took a little nap in the afternoon, and when she awoke her blue eyes always had an expression of pleased and innocent surprise, as if she were gazing on the world for the first time—the round, unwinking, interested look a baby's eyes have when something attractive is held up before them.

Let me give in a paragraph, before I swing off into the bypaths that always allure me, the consecutive suffrage events of the past quarter of a century. Having done this, I can dwell on each as casually as I choose, for it is possible to describe only a few incidents here and there; and I shall not be departing from the story of my life, for my life had become merged in the suffrage cause.

Of the preliminary suffrage campaigns in Kansas, made in company with "Aunt Susan," I have already written, and it remains only to say that during the second Kansas campaign yellow was adopted as the suffrage color. In

1890, '92, and '93 we again worked in Kansas and in South Dakota, with such indefatigable and brilliant speakers as Mrs. Catt (to whose efforts also were largely due the winning of Colorado in '93), Mrs. Laura Johns of Kansas, Mrs. Julia Nelson, Henry B. Blackwell, Dr. Helen V. Putnam of Dakota, Mrs. Emma Smith DeVoe, Rev. Olympia Browne of Wisconsin, and Dr. Mary Seymour Howell of New York. In '94, '95, and '96 special efforts were devoted to Idaho, Utah, California, and Washington, and from then on our campaigns were waged steadily in the Western states.

The Colorado victory gave us two full suffrage states, for in 1869 the Territory of Wyoming had enfranchised women under very interesting conditions, not now generally remembered. The achievement was due to the influence of one woman, Esther Morris, a pioneer who was as good a neighbor as she was a suffragist. In those early days, in homes far from physicians and surgeons, the women cared for one another in sickness, and Esther Morris, as it happened, once took full and skilful charge of a neighbor during the difficult birth of the latter's child. She had done the same thing for many other women, but this woman's husband was especially grateful. He was also a member of the Legislature, and he told Mrs. Morris that if there was any measure she wished put through for the women of the territory he would be glad to introduce it. She immediately took him at his word by asking him to introduce a bill enfranchising women, and he promptly did so.

The Legislature was Democratic, and it pounced upon the measure as a huge joke. With the amiable purpose of embarrassing the Governor of the territory, who was a Republican and had been appointed by the President, the members passed the bill and put it up to him to veto. To their combined horror and amazement, the young Governor did nothing of the kind. He had come, as it happened, from Salem, Ohio, one of the first towns in the United States in which a suffrage convention was held. There, as a boy, he had heard Susan B. Anthony make a speech, and he had carried into the years the impression it made upon him. He signed that bill; and, as the Legislature could not get a two-thirds vote to kill it, the disgusted members had to make the best of the matter. The following year a Democrat introduced a bill to repeal the measure, but already public sentiment had changed and he was laughed down. After that no further effort was ever made to take the ballot away from the women of Wyoming.

When the territory applied for statehood, it was feared that the woman-suffrage clause in the constitution might injure its chance of admission, and the women sent this telegram to Joseph M. Carey:

"Drop us if you must. We can trust the men of Wyoming to enfranchise us after our territory becomes a state."

Mr. Carey discussed this telegram with the other men who were urging upon Congress the admission of their territory, and the following reply went back:

"We may stay out of the Union a hundred years, but we will come in with our women."

There is great inspiration in those two messages—and a great lesson, as well.

In 1894 we conducted a campaign in New York, when an effort was made to secure a clause to enfranchise women in the new state constitution; and for the first time in the history of the woman-suffrage movement many of the influential women in the state and city of New York took an active part in the work. Miss Anthony was, as always, our leader and greatest inspiration. Mrs. John Brooks Greenleaf was state president, and Miss Mary Anthony was the most active worker in the Rochester headquarters. Mrs. Lily Devereaux Blake had charge of the campaign in New York City, and Mrs. Marianna Chapman looked after the Brooklyn section, while a most stimulating sign of the times was the organization of a committee of New York women of wealth and social influence, who established their headquarters at Sherry's. Among these were Mrs. Josephine Shaw Lowell, Mrs. Joseph H. Choate, Dr. Mary Putnam Jacobi, Mrs. J. Warren Goddard, and Mrs. Robert Abbe. Miss Anthony, then in her seventy-fifth year, spoke in every county of the state sixty in all. I spoke in forty, and Mrs. Catt, as always, made a superb record. Miss Harriet May Mills, a graduate of Cornell, and Miss Mary G. Hay, did admirable organization work in the different counties. Our disappointment over the result was greatly soothed by the fact that only two years later both Idaho and Utah swung into line as full suffrage states, though California, in which we had labored with equal zeal, waited fifteen years longer.

Among these campaigns, and overlapping them, were our annual conventions—each of which I attended from 1888 on—and the national and international councils, to a number of which, also, I have given preliminary mention. When Susan B. Anthony died in 1906, four American states had granted suffrage to woman. At the time I write—1914—the result of the American women's work for suffrage may be briefly tabulated thus:

SUFFRAGE STATUS

FULL SUFFRAGE FOR WOMEN

State	Year Won	Number of Electoral Votes

Wyoming	1869	3
Colorado	1893	6
Idaho	1896	4
Utah	1896	4
Washington	1910	7
California	1911	13
Arizona	1912	3
Kansas	1912	10
Oregon	1912	5
Alaska	1913	—
Nevada	1914	3
Montana	1914	4

PRESIDENTIAL AND MUNICIPAL SUFFRAGE FOR WOMEN

State	Year Won	Number of Electoral Votes
Illinois	1913	29

STATES WHERE AMENDMENT HAS PASSED ONE LEGISLATURE AND

MUST PASS ANOTHER

State	House	Senate	Number Goes to Voters	Electoral Votes
Iowa	81-26	31-15	1916	13
Massachusetts	169-39	34-2	1915	18
New Jersey	49-4	15-3	1915	14
New York	125-5	40-2	1915	45
North Dakota	77-29	31-19	1916	5
Pennsylvania	131-70	26-22	1915	38

To tabulate the wonderful work done by the conventions and councils is not possible, but a consecutive list of the meetings would run like this:

First National Convention, Washington, D.C., 1887.

First International Council of Women, Washington, D.C., 1888.

National Suffrage Convention, Washington, D.C., 1889.

National Suffrage Convention, Washington, D.C., 1890.

National Suffrage Convention, Washington, D.C., 1891.

National Suffrage Convention, Washington, D.C., 1892.

National Suffrage Convention, Washington, D.C., 1893.

International Council, Chicago, 1893.

National Suffrage Convention, Washington, D.C., 1894.

National Suffrage Convention, Atlanta, Ga., 1895.

National Suffrage Convention, Washington, D.C., 1896.

National Suffrage Convention, Des Moines, Iowa, 1897.

National Suffrage Convention, Washington, D.C., 1898.

National Suffrage Convention, Grand Rapids, Mich., 1899.

International Council, London, England, 1899.

National Suffrage Convention, Washington, D.C., 1900.

National Suffrage Convention, Minneapolis, Minn., 1901.

National Suffrage Convention, Washington, D.C., 1902.

National Suffrage Convention, New Orleans, La., 1903.

National Suffrage Convention, Washington, D.C., 1904.

International Council of Women, Berlin, Germany, 1904.

Formation of Intern'l Suffrage Alliance, Berlin, Germany, 1904.

National Suffrage Convention, Portland, Oregon, 1905.

National Suffrage Convention, Baltimore, Md., 1906.

International Suffrage Alliance, Copenhagen, Denmark, 1906.

National Suffrage Convention, Chicago, III., 1907.

International Suffrage Alliance, Amsterdam, Holland, 1908.

National Suffrage Convention, Buffalo, N. Y., 1908.

New York Headquarters established, 1909.

National Suffrage Convention, Seattle, Wash., 1909.

International Suffrage Alliance, London, England, 1909.

National Suffrage Convention, Washington, D.C., 1910.

International Council, Genoa, Italy, 1911.

National Suffrage Convention, Louisville, Ky., 1911.

International Suffrage Alliance, Stockholm, Sweden, 1911.

National Suffrage Convention, Philadelphia, Pa., 1912.

International Council, The Hague, Holland, 1913

National Suffrage Convention, Washington, D.C.; 1913.

International Suffrage Alliance, Budapest, Hungary, 1913.

National Suffrage Convention, Nashville, Tenn., 1914.

International Council, Rome, Italy, 1914.

The winning of the suffrage states, the work in the states not yet won, the conventions, gatherings, and international councils in which women of every nation have come together, have all combined to make this quarter of a century the most brilliant period for women in the history of the world. I have set forth the record baldly and without comment, because the bare facts are far more eloquent than words. It must not be forgotten, too, that these great achievements of the progressive women of to-day have been accomplished against the opposition of a large number of their own sex—who, while they are out in the world's arena fighting against progress for their sisters, still shatter the ear-drum with their incongruous war-cry, "Woman's place is in the home!" here: We were attending the Republican state nominating convention at Mitchell—Miss Anthony, Mrs. Catt, other leaders, and myself—having been told that it would be at once the largest and the most interesting gathering ever held in the state as it proved to be. All the leading politicians of the state were there, and in the wake of the white men had come tribes of Indians with their camp outfits, their wives and their children—the groups forming a picturesque circle of tents and tepees around the town. It was a great occasion for them, an Indian powwow, for by the law all Indians who had lands in severalty were to be permitted to vote the following year. They were present, therefore, to study the ways of the white man, and an edifying exhibition of these was promptly offered them.

The crowd was so great that it was only through the courtesy of Major Pickler, a member of Congress and a devoted believer in suffrage, that Miss Anthony, Mrs. Catt, and the rest of us were able to secure passes to the convention, and when we reached the hall we were escorted to the last row of seats on the crowded platform. As the space between us and the speakers was filled by rows upon rows of men, as well as by the band and their instruments, we could see very little that took place. Some of our friends pointed out this condition to the local committee and asked that we be given seats on the floor, but received the reply that there was "absolutely no room on the floor except for delegates and distinguished visitors." Our persistent friends then suggested that at least a front seat should be given to Miss Anthony, who certainly came under the head of a "distinguished visitor"; but this was not done—probably because a large number of the best seats were filled by Russian laborers wearing badges inscribed "Against Woman Suffrage and Susan B. Anthony." We remained, perforce, in our rear seats, finding such interest as we could in the back view of hundreds of heads.

Just before the convention was called to order it was announced that a delegation of influential Indians was waiting outside, and a motion to invite the red men into the hall was made and carried with great enthusiasm. A committee of leading citizens was appointed to act as escort, and these gentlemen filed out, returning a few moments later with a party of Indian warriors in full war regalia, even to their gay blankets, their feathered head-dresses, and their paint. When they appeared the band struck up a stirring march of welcome, and the entire audience cheered while the Indians, flanked by the admiring committee, stalked solemnly down the aisle and were given seats of honor directly in front of the platform.

All we could see of them were the brilliant feathers of their war-bonnets, but we got the full effect of their reception in the music and the cheers. I dared not look at Miss Anthony during this remarkable scene, and she, craning her venerable neck to get a glimpse of the incident from her obscure corner, made no comment to me; but I knew what she was thinking. The following year these Indians would have votes. Courtesy, therefore, must be shown them. But the women did not matter, the politicians reasoned, for even if they were enfranchised they would never support the element represented at that convention. It was not surprising that, notwithstanding our hard work, we did not win the state, though all the conditions had seemed most favorable; for the state was new, the men and women were working side by side in the fields, and there was discontent in the ranks of the political parties.

After the election, when we analyzed the vote county by county, we discovered that in every county whose residents were principally Americans the amendment was carried, whereas in all counties populated largely by foreigners it was lost. In certain counties—those inhabited by Russian Jews—the vote was almost solidly against us, and this notwithstanding the fact that the wives of these Russian voters were doing a man's work on their farms in addition to the usual women's work in their homes. The fact that our Cause could be defeated by ignorant laborers newly come to our country was a humiliating one to accept; and we realized more forcibly than ever before the difficulty of the task we had assumed—a task far beyond any ever undertaken by a body of men in the history of democratic government throughout the world. We not only had to bring American men back to a belief in the fundamental principles of republican government, but we had also to educate ignorant immigrants, as well as our own Indians, whose degree of civilization was indicated by their war-paint and the flaunting feathers of their head-dresses.

The Kansas campaign, which Miss Anthony, Mrs. Catt, Mrs. Johns, and I conducted in 1894, held a special interest, due to the Populist movement. There were so many problems before the people—prohibition, free silver, and the Populist propaganda—that we found ourselves involved in the bitterest campaign ever fought out in the state. Our desire, of course, was to get the indorsement of the different political parties and religious bodies, We succeeded in obtaining that of three out of four of the Methodist Episcopal conferences—the Congregational, the Epworth League, and the Christian Endeavor League—as well as that of the State Teachers' Association, the Woman's Christian Temperance Union, and various other religious and philanthropic societies. To obtain the indorsement of the political parties was much more difficult, and we were facing conditions in which partial success was worse than complete failure. It had long been an unwritten law before it became a written law in our National Association that we must not take partisan action or line up with any one political party. It was highly important, therefore, that either all parties should support us or that none should.

The Populist convention was held in Topeka before either the Democratic or Republican convention, and after two days of vigorous fighting, led by Mrs. Anna Diggs and other prominent Populist women, a suffrage plank was added to the platform. The Populist party invited me, as a minister, to open the convention with prayer. This was an innovation, and served as a wedge for the admission of women representatives of the Suffrage Association to address the convention. We all did so, Miss Anthony speaking first, Mrs. Catt second, and I last; after which, for the first time in history, the Doxology was sung at a political convention.

At the Democratic convention we made the same appeal, and were refused. Instead of indorsing us, the Democrats put an anti-suffrage plank in their platform—but this, as the party had little standing in Kansas, probably did us more good than harm. Trouble came thick and fast, however, when the Republicans, the dominant party in the state, held their convention; and a mighty struggle began over the admission of a suffrage plank. There was a Woman's Republican Club in Kansas, which held its convention in Topeka at the same time the Republicans were holding theirs. There was also a Mrs. Judith Ellen Foster, who, by stirring up opposition in this Republican Club against the insertion of a suffrage plank, caused a serious split in the convention. Miss Anthony, Mrs. Catt, and I, of course, urged the Republican women to stand by their sex, and to give their support to the Republicans only on condition that the latter added suffrage to their platform. At no time, and in no field of work, have I ever seen a more bitter conflict in progress than that which raged for two days during this Republican women's convention. Liquor-dealers, joint-keepers, "boot-leggers," and all the lawless element of Kansas swung into line at a special convention held under the auspices of the Liquor League of Kansas City, and cast their united weight against suffrage by threatening to deny their votes to any candidate or political party favoring our Cause. The Republican women's convention finally adjourned with nothing accomplished except the passing of a resolution mildly requesting the Republican party to indorse woman suffrage. The result was, of course, that it was not indorsed by the Republican convention, and that it was defeated at the following election.

It was at the time of these campaigns that I was elected Vice-President of the National Association and Lecturer at Large, and the latter office brought in its train a glittering variety of experiences. On one occasion an episode occurred which "Aunt Susan" never afterward wearied of describing. There was a wreck somewhere on the road on which I was to travel to meet a lecture engagement, and the trains going my way were not running. Looking up the track, however, I saw a train coming from the opposite direction. I at once grasped my hand-luggage and started for it.

"Wait! Wait!" cried Miss Anthony. "That train's going the wrong way!"

"At least it's going SOMEWHERE!" I replied, tersely, as the train stopped, and I climbed the steps.

Looking back when the train had started again, I saw "Aunt Susan" standing in the same spot on the platform and staring after it with incredulous eyes; but I was right, for I discovered that by going up into another state I could get a train which would take me to my destination in time for the lecture that night. It was a fine illustration of my pet theory that if one intends to get somewhere it is better to start, even in the wrong direction, than to stand still.

Again and again in our work we had occasion to marvel over men's lack of understanding of the views of women, even of those nearest and dearest to them; and we had an especially striking illustration of this at one of our hearings in Washington. A certain distinguished gentleman (we will call him Mr. H——) was chairman of the Judiciary, and after we had said what we wished to say, he remarked:

"Your arguments are logical. Your cause is just. The trouble is that women don't want suffrage. My wife doesn't want it. I don't know a single woman who does want it."

As it happened for this unfortunate gentleman, his wife was present at the hearing and sitting beside Miss Anthony. She listened to his words with surprise, and then whispered to "Aunt Susan":

"How CAN he say that? I want suffrage, and I've told him so a hundred times in the last twenty years."

"Tell him again NOW," urged Miss Anthony. "Here's your chance to impress it on his memory."

"Here!" gasped the wife. "Oh, I wouldn't dare."

"Then may I tell him?"

"Why—yes! He can think what he pleases, but he has no right to publicly misrepresent me."

The assent, hesitatingly begun, finished on a sudden note of firmness. Miss Anthony stood up.

"It may interest Mr. H——," she said, "to know that his wife DOES wish to vote, and that for twenty years she has wished to vote, and has often told him so, though he has evidently forgotten it. She is here beside me, and has just made this explanation."

Mr. H—— stammered and hesitated, and finally decided to laugh. But there was no mirth in the sound he made, and I am afraid his wife had a bad quarter of an hour when they met a little later in the privacy of their home.

Among other duties that fell to my lot at this period were numerous suffrage debates with prominent opponents of the Cause. I have already referred to the debate in Kansas with Senator Ingalls. Equaling this in importance was a bout with Dr. Buckley, the distinguished Methodist debater, which had been arranged for us at Chautauqua by Bishop Vincent of the Methodist Church. The bishop was not a believer in suffrage, nor was he one of my admirers. I had once aroused his ire by replying to a sermon he had delivered on "God's Women," and by proving, to my own satisfaction at least, that the women he thought were God's women had done very little, whereas the work of the world had been done by those he believed were not "God's Women." There was considerable interest, therefore, in the Buckley-Shaw debate he had arranged; we all knew he expected Dr. Buckley to wipe out that old score, and I was determined to make it as difficult as possible for the distinguished gentleman to do so. We held the debate on two succeeding days, I speaking one afternoon and Dr. Buckley replying the following day. On the evening before I spoke, however, Dr. Buckley made an indiscreet remark, which, blown about Chautauqua on the light breeze of gossip, was generally regarded as both unchivalrous and unfair.

As the hall in which we were to speak was enormous, he declared that one of two things would certainly happen. Either I would scream in order to be heard by my great audience, or I would be unable to make myself heard at all. If I screamed it would be a powerful argument against women as public speakers; if I could not be heard, it would be an even better argument. In either case, he summed up, I was doomed to failure. Following out this theory, he posted men in the extreme rear of the great hall on the day of my lecture, to report to him whether my words reached them, while he himself graciously occupied a front seat. Bishop Vincent's antagonistic feeling was so strong, however, that though, as the presiding officer of the occasion, he introduced me to the audience, he did not wait to hear my speech, but immediately left the hall—and this little slight added to the public's interest in the debate. It was felt that the two gentlemen were not quite "playing fair," and the champions of the Cause were especially enthusiastic in their efforts to make up for these failures in courtesy. My friends turned out in force to hear the lecture, and on the breast of every one of them flamed the yellow bow that stood for suffrage, giving to the vast hall something of the effect of a field of yellow tulips in full bloom.

When Dr. Buckley rose to reply the next day these friends were again awaiting him with an equally jocund display of the suffrage color, and this did not add to his serenity. During his remarks he made the serious mistake of losing his temper; and, unfortunately for him, he directed his wrath toward a very old man who had thoughtlessly applauded by pounding on the floor with his cane when Dr. Buckley quoted a point I had made. The doctor leaned forward and shook his fist at him.

"Think she's right, do you?" he asked.

"Yes," admitted the venerable citizen, briskly, though a little startled by the manner of the question.

"Old man," shouted Dr. Buckley, "I'll make you take that back if you've got a grain of sense in your head!"

The insult cost him his audience. When he realized this he lost all his self-possession, and, as the Buffalo Courier put it the next day, "went up and down the platform raving like a Billingsgate fishwife." He lost the debate, and the supply of yellow ribbon left in the surrounding counties was purchased that night to be used in the suffrage celebration that followed. My friends still refer to the occasion as "the day we wiped up the earth with Dr. Buckley"; but I do not deserve the implied tribute, for Dr. Buckley would have lost his case without a word from me. What really gave me some satisfaction, however, was the respective degree of freshness with which he and I emerged from our combat. After my speech Miss Anthony and I were given a reception, and stood for hours shaking hands with hundreds of men and women. Later in the evening we had a dinner and another reception, which, lasting, as they did, until midnight, kept us from our repose. Dr. Buckley, poor gentleman, had to be taken to his hotel immediately after his speech, given a hot bath, rubbed down, and put tenderly to bed; and not even the sympathetic heart of Susan B. Anthony yearned over him when she heard of his exhaustion.

It was also at Chautauqua, by the way, though a number of years earlier, that I had my much misquoted encounter with the minister who deplored the fashion I followed in those days of wearing my hair short. This young man, who was rather a pompous person, saw fit to take me to task at a table where a number of us were dining together.

"Miss Shaw," he said, abruptly, "I have been asked very often why you wear your hair short, and I have not been able to explain. Of course"—this kindly—"I know there is some good reason. I ventured to advance the theory that you have been ill and that your hair has fallen out. Is that it?"

"No," I told him. "There is a reason, as you suggest. But it is not that one."

"Then why—" he insisted.

"I am rather sensitive about it," I explained. "I don't know that I care to discuss the subject."

The young minister looked pained. "But among friends—" he protested.

"True," I conceded. "Well, then, among friends, I will admit frankly that it is a birthmark. I was born with short hair."

That was the last time my short hair was criticized in my presence, but the young minister was right in his disapproval and I was wrong, as I subsequently realized. A few years later I let my hair grow long, for I had learned that no woman in public life can afford to make herself conspicuous by any eccentricity of dress or appearance. If she does so she suffers for it herself, which may not disturb her, and to a greater or less degree she injures the cause she represents, which should disturb her very much.

XII. BUILDING A HOME

It is not generally known that the meeting of the International Council of Women held in Chicago during the World's Fair was suggested by Miss Anthony, as was also the appointment of the Exposition's "Board of Lady Managers." "Aunt Susan" kept her name in the background, that she might not array against these projects the opposition of those prejudiced against woman suffrage. We both spoke at the meetings, however, as I have already explained, and one of our most chastening experiences occurred on "Actress Night." There was a great demand for tickets for this occasion, as every one seemed anxious to know what kind of speeches our leading women of the stage would make; and the programme offered such magic names as Helena Modjeska, Julia Marlowe, Georgia Cayvan, Clara Morris, and others of equal appeal. The hall was soon filled, and to keep out the increasing throng the doors were locked and the waiting crowd was directed to a second hall for an overflow meeting.

As it happened, Miss Anthony and I were among the earliest arrivals at the main hall. It was the first evening we had been free to do exactly as we pleased, and we were both in high spirits, looking forward to the speeches, congratulating each other on the good seats we had been given on the platform, and rallying the speakers on their stage fright; for, much to our amusement, we had found them all in mortal terror of their audience. Georgia Cayvan, for example, was so nervous that she had to be strengthened with hot milk before she could speak, and Julia Marlowe admitted freely that her knees were giving way beneath her. They really had something of an ordeal before them, for it was decided that each actress must speak twice going immediately from the hall to the overflow meeting and repeating there the speech she had just made. But in the mean time some one had to hold the impatient audience in the second hall, and as it was a duty every one else promptly repudiated, a row of suddenly imploring faces turned toward Miss Anthony and me. I admit that we responded to the appeal with great reluctance. We were SO comfortable where we were—and we were also deeply interested in the first intimate glimpse we were having of these stars in the dramatic sky. We saw our duty, however, and with deep sighs we rose and departed for the second hall, where a glance at the waiting throng did not add to our pleasure in the prospect before us.

When I walked upon the stage I found myself facing an actually hostile audience. They had come to look at and listen to the actresses who had been promised them, and they thought they were being deprived of that privilege by an interloper. Never before had I gazed out on a mass of such unresponsive faces or looked into so many angry eyes. They were exchanging views on their wrongs, and the general buzz of conversation continued when I appeared. For some moments I stood looking at them, my hands behind my back. If I had tried to speak they would undoubtedly have gone on talking; my silence attracted their attention and they began to wonder what I intended to do. When they had stopped whispering and moving about, I spoke to them with the frankness of an overburdened heart.

"I think," I said, slowly and distinctly, "that you are the most disagreeable audience I ever faced in my life."

They gasped and stared, almost open-mouthed in their surprise.

"Never," I went on, "have I seen a gathering of people turn such ugly looks upon a speaker who has sacrificed her own enjoyment to come and talk to them. Do you think I want to talk to you?" I demanded, warming to my subject. "I certainly do not. Neither does Miss Anthony want to talk to you, and the lady who spoke to you a few moments ago, and whom you treated so rudely, did not wish to be here. We would all much prefer to be in the other hall, listening to the speakers from our comfortable seats on the stage. To entertain you we gave up our places and came here simply because the committee begged us to do so. I have only one thing more to say. If you care to listen to me courteously I am willing to waste time on you; but don't imagine that I will stand here and wait while you criticize the management."

By this time I felt as if I had a child across my knee to whom I was administering maternal chastisement, and the uneasiness of my audience underlined the impression. They listened rather sulkily at first; then a few of the best-natured among them laughed, and the laugh grew and developed into applause. The experience had done them good, and they were a chastened band when Clara Morris appeared, and I gladly yielded the floor to her.

All the actresses who spoke that night delivered admirable addresses, but no one equaled Madame Modjeska, who delivered exquisitely a speech written, not by herself, but by a friend and countrywoman, on the condition of Polish women under the regime of Russia. We were all charmed as we listened, but none of us dreamed what that address would mean to Modjeska. It resulted in her banishment from Poland, her native land, which she was never again permitted to enter. But though she paid so heavy a price for the revelation, I do not think she ever really regretted having given to America the facts in that speech.

During this same period I embarked upon a high adventure. I had always longed for a home, and my heart had always been loyal to Cape Cod. Now I decided to have a home at Wianno, across the Cape from my old parish at East Dennis. Deep-seated as my home-making aspiration had been, it was realized largely as the result of chance. A special hobby of mine has always been auction sales. I dearly love to drop into auction-rooms while sales are in progress, and bid up to the danger-point, taking care to stop just in time to let some one else get the offered article. But of course I sometimes failed to stop at the psychological moment, and the result was a sudden realization that, in the course of the years, I had accumulated an extraordinary number of articles for which I had no shelter and no possible use.

The crown jewel of the collection was a bedroom set I had picked up in Philadelphia. Usually, cautious friends accompanied me on my auction-room expeditions and restrained my ardor; but this time I got away alone and found myself bidding at the sale of a solid bog-wood bedroom set which had been exhibited as a show-piece at the World's Fair, and was now, in the words of the auctioneer, "going for a song." I sang the song. I offered twenty dollars, thirty dollars, forty dollars, and other excited voices drowned mine with higher bids. It was very thrilling. I offered fifty dollars, and there was a horrible silence, broken at last by the auctioneer's final, "Going, going, GONE!" I was mistress of the bog-wood bedroom set—a set wholly out of harmony with everything else I possessed, and so huge and massive that two men were required to lift the head-board alone. Like many of the previous treasures I had acquired, this was a white elephant; but, unlike some of them, it was worth more than I had paid for it. I was offered sixty dollars for one piece alone, but I coldly refused to sell it, though the tribute to my judgment warmed my heart. I had not the faintest idea what to do with the set, however, and at last I confided my dilemma to my friend, Mrs. Ellen Dietrick, who sagely advised me to build a house for it. The idea intrigued me. The bog-wood furniture needed a home, and so did I.

The result of our talk was that Mrs. Dietrick promised to select a lot for me at Wianno, where she herself lived, and even promised to supervise the building of my cottage, and to attend to all the other details connected with it. Thus put, the temptation was irresistible. Besides Mrs. Dietrick, many other delightful friends lived at Wianno—the Garrisons, the Chases of Rhode Island, the Wymans, the Wellingtons—a most charming community. I gave Mrs. Dietrick full authority to use her judgment in every detail connected with the undertaking, and the cottage was built. Having put her hand to this plow of friendship, Mrs. Dietrick did the work with characteristic thoroughness. I did not even visit Wianno to look at my land.

She selected it, bought it, engaged a woman architect—Lois Howe of Boston—and followed the latter's work from beginning to end. The only stipulation I made was that the cottage must be far up on the beach, out of sight of everybody—really in the woods; and this was easily met, for along that coast the trees came almost to the water's edge.

The cottage was a great success, and for many years I spent my vacations there, filling the place with young people. From the time of my sister Mary's death I had had the general oversight of her two daughters, Lola and Grace, as well as of Nicolas and Eleanor, the two motherless daughters of my brother John. They were all with me every summer in the new home, together with Lucy Anthony, her sister and brother, Mrs. Rachel Foster Avery, and other friends. We had special fishing costumes made, and wore them much of the time. My nieces wore knickerbockers, and I found vast contentment in short, heavy skirts over bloomers. We lived out of doors, boating, fishing, and clamming all day long, and, as in my early pioneer days in Michigan, my part of the work was in the open. I chopped all the wood, kept the fires going, and looked after the grounds.

Rumors of our care-free and unconventional life began to circulate, and presently our Eden was invaded by the only serpent I have ever found in the newspaper world—a girl reporter from Boston. She telegraphed that she was coming to see us; and though, when she came, we had been warned of her propensities and received her in conventional attire, formally entertaining her with tea on the veranda, she went away and gave free play to a hectic fancy. She wrote a sensational full-page article for a Sunday newspaper, illustrated with pictures showing us all in knickerbockers. In this striking work of art I carried a fish net and pole and wore a handkerchief tied over my head. The article, which was headed THE ADAMLESS EDEN, was almost libelous, and I admit that for a long time it dimmed our enjoyment of our beloved retreat. Then, gradually, my old friends died, Mrs. Dietrick among the first; others moved away; and the character of the entire region changed. It became fashionable, privacy was no longer to be found there, and we ceased to visit it. For five years I have not even seen the cottage.

In 1908 I built the house I now occupy (in Moylan, Pennsylvania), which is the realization of a desire I have always had—to build on a tract which had a stream, a grove of trees, great boulders and rocks, and a hill site for the house with a broad outlook, and a railroad station conveniently near. The friend who finally found the place for me had begun his quest with the pessimistic remark that I would better wait for it until I got to Paradise; but two years later he telegraphed me that he had discovered it on this planet, and he was right. I have only eight acres of land, but no one could ask a more ideal site for a cottage; and on the place is my beloved forest, including a grove of three hundred firs. From every country I have visited I have brought back a tiny tree for this little forest, and now it is as full of memories as of beauty.

To the surprise of my neighbors, I built my house with its back toward the public road, facing the valley and the stream. "But you will never see anybody go by," they protested. I answered that the one person in the house who was necessarily interested in passers-by was my maid, and she could see them perfectly from the kitchen, which faced the road. I enjoy my views from the broad veranda that overlooks the valley, the stream, and the country for miles around.

Every suffragist I have ever met has been a lover of home; and only the conviction that she is fighting for her home, her children, for other women, or for all of these, has sustained her in her public work. Looking back on many campaign experiences, I am forced to admit that it is not always the privations we endure which make us think most tenderly of home. Often we are more overcome by the attentions of well-meaning friends. As an example of this I recall an incident of one Oregon campaign. I was to speak in a small city in the southern part of the state, and on reaching the station, hot, tired, and covered with the grime of a midsummer journey, I found awaiting me a delegation of citizens, a brass-band, and a white carriage drawn by a pair of beautiful white horses. In this carriage, and devotedly escorted by the citizens and the band, the latter playing its hardest, I was driven to the City Hall and there met by the mayor, who delivered an address, after which I was crowned with a laurel wreath. Subsequently, with this wreath still resting upon my perspiring brow, I was again driven through the streets of the city; and if ever a woman felt that her place was in the home and longed to be in her place, I felt it that day.

An almost equally trying occasion had San Francisco for its setting. The city had arranged a Fourth of July celebration, at which Miss Anthony and I were to speak. Here we rode in a carriage decorated with flowers—yellow roses—while just in front of us was the mayor in a carriage gorgeously festooned with purple blossoms. Behind us, for more than a mile, stretched a procession of uniformed policemen, soldiers, and citizens, while the sidewalks were lined with men and women whose enthusiastic greetings came to Miss Anthony from every side. She was enchanted over the whole experience, for to her it meant, as always, not a personal tribute, but a triumph of the Cause. But I sat by her side acutely miserable; for across my shoulders and breast had been draped a huge sash with the word "Orator" emblazoned on it, and this was further embellished by a striking rosette with streamers which hung nearly to the bottom of my gown. It is almost unnecessary to add that this remarkable decoration was furnished by a committee of men, and was also worn by all the men speakers of the day.

Possibly I was overheated by the sash, or by the emotions the sash aroused in me, for I was stricken with pneumonia the following day and experienced my first serious illness, from which, however, I soon recovered.

On our way to California in 1895 Miss Anthony and I spent a day at Cheyenne, Wyoming, as the guests of Senator and Mrs. Carey, who gave a dinner for us. At the table I asked Senator Carey what he considered the best result of the enfranchisement of Wyoming women, and even after the lapse of twenty years I am able to give his reply almost word for word, for it impressed me deeply at the time and I have since quoted it again and again.

"There have been many good results," he said, "but the one I consider above all the others is the great change for the better in the character of our candidates for office. Consider this for a moment: Since our women have voted there has never been an embezzlement of public funds, or a scandalous misuse of public funds, or a disgraceful condition of graft. I attribute the better character of our public officials almost entirely to the votes of the women."

"Those are inspiring facts," I conceded, "but let us be just. There are three men in Wyoming to every woman, and no candidate for office could be elected unless the men voted for him, too. Why, then, don't they deserve as much credit for his election as the women?"

"Because," explained Senator Carey, promptly, "women are politically an uncertain factor. We can go among men and learn beforehand how they are going to vote, but we can't do that with women; they keep us guessing. In the old days, when we went into the caucus we knew what resolutions put into our platforms would win the votes of the ranchmen, what would win the miners, what would win the men of different nationalities; but we did not know how to win the votes of the women until we began to nominate our candidates. Then we immediately discovered that if the Democrats nominated a man of immoral character for office, the women voted for his Republican opponent, and we learned our first big lesson—that whatever a candidate's other qualifications for office may be, he must first of all have a clean record. In the old days, when we nominated a candidate we asked, 'Can he hold the saloon vote?' Now we ask, 'Can he hold the women's vote?' Instead of bidding down to the saloon, we bid up to the home."

Following the dinner there was a large public meeting, at which Miss Anthony and I were to speak. Mrs. Jenkins, who was president of the Suffrage Association of the state, presided and introduced us to the assemblage. Then she added: "I have introduced you ladies to your audience. Now I would like to introduce your audience to you." She began with the two Senators and the member of Congress, then introduced the Governor, the Lieutenant-Governor, the state Superintendent of Education, and numerous city and state officials. As she went on Miss Anthony grew more and more excited, and when the introductions were over, she said: "This is the first time I have ever seen an audience assembled for woman suffrage made up of the public officials of a state. No one can ever persuade me now that men respect women without political power as much as they respect women who have it; for certainly in no other state in the Union would it be possible to gather so many public officials under one roof to listen to the addresses of women."

The following spring we again went West, with Mrs. Catt, Lucy Anthony, Miss Hay and Miss Sweet, her secretary, to carry on the Pacific coast campaign of '96, arranged by Mrs. Cooper and her daughter Harriet, of Oakland—both women of remarkable executive ability. Headquarters were secured in San Francisco, and Miss Hay was put in charge, associated with a large group of California women. It was the second time in the history of campaigns—the first being in New York—that all the money to carry on the work was raised by the people of the state.

The last days of the campaign were extremely interesting, and one of their important events was that the Hon. Thomas Reed, then Speaker of the House of Representatives, for the first time came out publicly for suffrage. Mr. Reed had often expressed himself privately as in favor of the Cause— but he had never made a public statement for us. At Oakland, one day, the indefatigable and irresistible "Aunt Susan" caught him off his guard by persuading his daughter, Kitty Reed, who was his idol, to ask him to say just one word in favor of our amendment. When he arose we did not know whether he had promised what she asked, and as his speech progressed our hearts sank lower and lower, for all he said was remote from our Cause. But he ended with these words:

"There is an amendment of the constitution pending, granting suffrage to women. The women of California ought to have suffrage. The men of California ought to give it to them—and the next speaker, Dr. Shaw, will tell you why."

The word was spoken. And though it was not a very strong word, it came from a strong man, and therefore helped us.

Election day, as usual, brought its surprises and revelations. Mrs. Cooper asked her Chinese cook how the Chinese were voting—i. e., the native-born Chinamen who were entitled to vote—and he replied, blithely, "All Chinamen vote for Billy McKee and 'NO' to women!" It is an interesting fact that every Chinese vote was cast against us.

All day we went from one to another of the polling-places, and I shall always remember the picture of Miss Anthony and the wife of Senator Sargent wandering around the polls arm in arm at eleven o'clock at night, their tired faces taking on lines of deeper depression with every minute; for the count was against us. However, we made a fairly good showing. When the final counts came in we found that we had won the state from the north down to Oakland, and from the south up to San Francisco; but there was not a sufficient majority to overcome the adverse votes of San Francisco and Oakland. With more than 230,000 votes cast, we were defeated by only 10,000 majority. In San Francisco the saloon element and the most aristocratic section of the city made an equal showing against us, while the section occupied by the middle working-class was largely in favor of our amendment. I dwell especially on this campaign, partly because such splendid work was done by the women of California, and also because, during the same election, Utah and Idaho granted full suffrage to women. This gave us four suffrage states—Wyoming, Colorado, Utah, and Idaho— and we prepared for future struggles with very hopeful hearts.

It was during this California campaign, by the way, that I unwittingly caused much embarrassment to a worthy young man. At a mass-meeting held in San Francisco, Rabbi Vorsanger, who was not in favor of suffrage for women, advanced the heartening theory that in a thousand years more they might possibly be ready for it. After a thousand years of education for women, of physically developed women, of uncorseted women, he said, we might have the ideal woman, and could then begin to talk about freedom for her.

When the rabbi sat down there was a shout from the audience for me to answer him, but all I said was that the ideal woman would be rather lonely, as it would certainly take another thousand years to develop an ideal man capable of being a mate for her. On the following night Prof. Howard Griggs, of Stanford University, made a speech on the modern woman—a speech so admirably thought out and delivered that we were all delighted with it. When he had finished the audience again called on me, and I rose and proceeded to make what my friends frankly called "the worst break" of my experience. Rabbi Vorsanger's ideal woman was still in my mind, and I had been rather hard on the men in my reply to the rabbi the night before; so now I hastened to give this clever young man his full due. I said that though the rabbi thought it would take a thousand years to make an ideal woman, I believed that, after all, it might not take as long to make the ideal man. We had something very near it in a speaker who could reveal such ability, such chivalry, and such breadth of view as Professor Griggs had just shown that he possessed.

That night I slept the sleep of the just and the well-meaning, and it was fortunate I did, for the morning newspapers had a surprise for me that called for steady nerves and a sense of humor. Across the front page of every one of them ran startling head-lines to this effect:

DR. SHAW HAS FOUND HER IDEAL MAN

The Prospects Are That She Will

Remain in California

Professor Griggs was young enough to be my son, and he was already married and the father of two beautiful children; but these facts were not permitted to interfere with the free play of fancy in journalistic minds. For a week the newspapers were filled with all sorts of articles, caricatures, and editorials on my ideal man, which caused me much annoyance and some amusement, while they plunged Professor Griggs into an abysmal gloom. In the end, however, the experience proved an excellent one for him, for the publicity attending his speech made him decide to take up lecturing as a profession, which he eventually did with great success. But neither of us has yet heard the last of the Ideal Man episode. Only a few years ago, on his return to California after a long absence, one of the leading Sunday newspapers of the state heralded Professor Griggs's arrival by publishing a full-page article bearing his photograph and mine and this flamboyant heading:

SHE MADE HIM

And Dr. Shaw's Ideal Man Became the

Idol of American Women and

Earns $30,000 a Year

We had other unusual experiences in California, and the display of affluence on every side was not the least impressive of them. In one town, after a heavy rain, I remember seeing a number of little boys scraping the dirt from the gutters, washing it, and finding tiny nuggets of gold. We learned that these boys sometimes made two or three dollars a day in this way, and that the streets of the town—I think it was Marysville—contained so much gold that a syndicate offered to level the whole town and repave the streets in return for the right to wash out the gold. This sounds like the kind of thing Americans tell to trustful visitors from foreign lands, but it is quite true. Nuggets, indeed, were so numerous that at one of our meetings, when we were taking up a collection, I cheerfully suggested that our audience drop a few into the box, as we had not had a nugget since we reached the state. There were no nuggets in the subsequent collection, but there was a note which read: "If Dr. Shaw will accept a gold nugget, I will see that she does not leave town without one." I read this aloud, and added, "I have never refused a gold nugget in my life."

The following day brought me a pin made of a very beautiful gold nugget, and a few days later another Californian produced a cluster of smaller nuggets which he had washed out of a panful of earth and insisted on my accepting half of them. I was not accustomed to this sort of generosity, but it was characteristic of the spirit of the state. Nowhere else, during our campaign experiences, were we so royally treated in every way. As a single example among many, I may mention that Mrs. Leland Stanford once happened to be on a train with us and to meet Miss Anthony. As a result of this chance encounter she gave our whole party passes on all the lines of the Southern Pacific Railroad, for use during the entire campaign. Similar generosity was shown us on every side, and the question of finance did not burden us from the beginning to the end of the California work.

In our Utah and Idaho campaigns we had also our full share of new experiences, and of these perhaps the most memorable to me was the sermon I preached in the Mormon Tabernacle at Salt Lake City. Before I left New York the Mormon women had sent me the invitation to preach this sermon, and when I reached Salt Lake City and the so-called "Gentile" women heard of the plan, they at once invited me to preach to the "Gentiles" on the evening of the same Sunday, in the Salt Lake City Opera House.

On the morning of the sermon I approached the Mormon Tabernacle with much more trepidation than I usually experienced before entering a pulpit. I was not sure what particular kind of trouble I would get into, but I had an abysmal suspicion that trouble of some sort lay in wait for me, and I shivered in the anticipation of it. Fortunately, my anxiety was not long drawn out. I arrived only a few moments before the hour fixed for the sermon, and found the congregation already assembled and the Tabernacle filled with the beautiful music of the great organ. On the platform, to which I was escorted by several leading dignitaries of the church, was the characteristic Mormon arrangement of seats. The first row was occupied by the deacons, and in the center of these was the pulpit from which the deacons preach. Above these seats was a second row, occupied by ordained elders, and there they too had their own pulpit. The third row was occupied by, the bishops and the highest dignitaries of the church, with the pulpit from which the bishops preach; and behind them all, an effective human frieze, was the really wonderful Mormon choir.

As I am an ordained elder in my church, I occupied the pulpit in the middle row of seats, with the deacons below me and the bishops just behind. Scattered among the congregation were hundreds of "Gentiles" ready to leap mentally upon any concession I might make to the Mormon faith; while the Mormons were equally on the alert for any implied criticism of them and their church. The problem of preaching a sermon which should offer some appeal to both classes, without offending either, was a perplexing one, and I solved it to the best of my ability by delivering a sermon I had once given in my own church to my own people. When I had finished I was wholly uncertain of its effect, but at the end of the services one of the bishops leaned toward me from his place in the rear, and, to my mingled horror and amusement, offered me this tribute, "That is one of the best Mormon sermons ever preached in this Tabernacle."

I thanked him, but inwardly I was aghast. What had I said to give him such an impression? I racked my brain, but could recall nothing that justified it. I passed the day in a state of nervous apprehension, fully expecting some frank criticism from the "Gentiles" on the score of having delivered a Mormon sermon to ingratiate myself into the favor of the Mormons and secure their votes for the constitutional amendment. But nothing of the kind was said. That evening, after the sermon to the "Gentiles," a reception was given to our party, and I drew my first deep breath when the wife of a well-known clergyman came to me and introduced herself in these words:

"My husband could not come here to-night, but he heard your sermon this morning. He asked me to tell you how glad he was that under such unusual conditions you held so firmly to the teachings of Christ."

The next day I was still more reassured. A reception was given us at the home of one of Brigham Young's daughters, and the receiving-line was graced by the presiding elder of the Methodist Episcopal Church. He was a bluff and jovial gentleman, and when he took my hand he said, warmly, "Well, Sister Shaw, you certainly gave our Mormon friends the biggest dose of Methodism yesterday that they ever got in their lives."

After this experience I reminded myself again that what Frances Willard so frequently said is true; All truth is our truth when it has reached our hearts; we merely rechristen it according to our individual creeds.

During the visit I had an interesting conversation with a number of the younger Mormon women. I was to leave the city on a midnight train, and about twenty of them, including four daughters of Brigham Young, came to my hotel to remain with me until it was time to go to the station. They filled the room, sitting around in school-girl fashion on the floor and even on the bed. It was an unusual opportunity to learn some things I wished to know, and I could not resist it.

"There are some questions I would like to ask you," I began, "and one or two of them may seem impertinent. But they won't be asked in that spirit— and please don't answer any that embarrass you."

They exchanged glances, and then told me to ask as many questions as I wished.

"First of all," I said, "I would like to know the real attitude toward polygamy of the present generation of Mormon women. Do you all believe in it?"

They assured me that they did.

"How many of you," I then asked, "are polygamous wives?"

There was not one in the group. "But," I insisted, "if you really believe in polygamy, why is it that some of your husbands have not taken more than one wife?"

There was a moment of silence, while each woman looked around as if waiting for another to answer. At last one of them said, slowly:

"In my case, I alone was to blame. For years I could not force myself to consent to my husband's taking another wife, though I tried hard. By the time I had overcome my objection the law was passed prohibiting polygamy."

A second member of the group hastened to tell her story. She had had a similar spiritual struggle, and just as she reached the point where she was willing to have her husband take another wife, he died. And now the room was filled with eager voices. Four or five women were telling at once that they, too, had been reluctant in the beginning, and that when they had reached the point of consent this, that, or another cause had kept the husbands from marrying again. They were all so passionately in earnest that they stared at me in puzzled wonder when I broke into the sudden laughter I could not restrain.

"What fortunate women you all were!" I exclaimed, teasingly. "Not one of you arrived at the point of consenting to the presence of a second wife in your home until it was impossible for your husband to take her."

They flushed a little at that, and then laughed with me; but they did not defend themselves against the tacit charge, and I turned the conversation into less personal channels. I learned that many of the Mormon young men were marrying girls outside of the Church, and that two sons of a leading Mormon elder had married and were living very happily with Catholic girls.

At this time the Mormon candidate for Congress (a man named Roberts) was a bitter opponent of woman suffrage. The Mormon women begged me to challenge him to a debate on the subject, which I did, but Mr. Roberts declined the challenge. The ground of his refusal, which he made public through the newspapers, was chastening to my spirit. He explained that he would not debate with me because he was not willing to lower himself to the intellectual plane of a woman.

XIII. PRESIDENT OF "THE NATIONAL"

In 1900 Miss Anthony, then over eighty, decided that she must resign the presidency of our National Association, and the question of the successor she would choose became an important one. It was conceded that there were only two candidates in her mind—Mrs. Carrie Chapman Catt and myself—and for several months we gave the suffrage world the unusual spectacle of rivals vigorously pushing each other's claims. Miss Anthony was devoted to us both, and I think the choice was a hard one for her to make. On the one hand, I had been vice-president at large and her almost constant companion for twelve years, and she had grown accustomed to think of me as her successor. On the other hand, Mrs. Catt had been chairman of the organization committee, and through her splendid executive ability had built up our organization in many states. From Miss Anthony down, we all recognized her steadily growing powers; she had, moreover, abundant means, which I had not.

In my mind there was no question of her superior qualification for the presidency. She seemed to me the logical and indeed the only possible successor to Miss Anthony; and I told "Aunt Susan" so with all the eloquence I could command, while simultaneously Mrs. Catt was pouring into Miss Anthony's other ear a series of impassioned tributes to me. It was an unusual situation and a very pleasant one, and it had two excellent results: it simplified "Aunt Susan's" problem by eliminating the element of personal ambition, and it led to her eventual choice of Mrs. Catt as her successor.

I will admit here for the first time that in urging Mrs. Catt's fitness for the office I made the greatest sacrifice of my life. My highest ambition had been to succeed Miss Anthony, for no one who knew her as I did could underestimate the honor of being chosen by her to carry on her work.

At the convention in Washington that year she formally refused the nomination for re-election, as we had all expected, and then, on being urged to choose her own successor, she stepped forward to do so. It was a difficult hour, for her fiery soul resented the limitations imposed by her worn-out body, and to such a worker the most poignant experience in life is to be forced to lay down one's work at the command of old age. On this she touched briefly, but in a trembling voice; and then, in furtherance of the understanding between the three of us, she presented the name of Mrs. Catt to the convention with all the pride and hope a mother could feel in the presentation of a daughter.

Her faith was fully justified. Mrs. Catt made an admirable president, and during every moment of the four years she held the office she had Miss Anthony's whole-hearted and enthusiastic support, while I, too, in my continued office of vice-president, did my utmost to help her in every way. In 1904, however, Mrs. Catt was elected president of the International Suffrage Alliance, as I have mentioned before, and that same year she resigned the presidency of our National Association, as her health was not equal to the strain of carrying the two offices.

Miss Anthony immediately urged me to accept the presidency of the National Association, which I was now most unwilling to do; I had lost my ambition to be president, and there were other reasons, into which I need not go again, why I felt that I could not accept the post. At last, however, Miss Anthony actually commanded me to take the place, and there was nothing to do but obey her. She was then eighty-four, and, as it proved, within two years of her death. It was no time for me to rebel against her wishes; but I yielded with the heaviest heart I have ever carried, and after my election to the presidency at the national convention in Washington I left the stage, went into a dark corner of the wings, and for the first time since my girlhood "cried myself sick."

In the work I now took up I found myself much alone. Mrs. Catt was really ill, and the strength of "Aunt Susan" must be saved in every way. Neither could give me much help, though each did all she should have done, and more. Mrs. Catt, whose husband had recently died, was in a deeply despondent frame of mind, and seemed to feel that the future was hopelessly dark. My own panacea for grief is work, and it seemed to me that both physically and mentally she would be helped by a wise combination of travel and effort. During my lifetime I have cherished two ambitions, and only two: the first, as I have already confessed, had been to succeed Miss Anthony as president of our association; the second was to go around the world, carrying the woman-suffrage ideal to every country, and starting in each a suffrage society. Long before the inception of the International Suffrage Alliance I had dreamed this dream; and, though it had receded as I followed it through life, I had never wholly lost sight of it. Now I realized that for me it could never be more than a dream. I could never hope to have enough money at my disposal to carry it out, and it occurred to me that if Mrs. Catt undertook it as president of the International Suffrage Alliance the results would be of the greatest benefit to the Cause and to her.

In my first visit to her after her husband's death I suggested this plan, but she replied that it was impossible for her to consider it. I did not lose thought of it, however, and at the next International Conference, held in Copenhagen in 1907, I suggested to some of the delegates that we introduce the matter as a resolution, asking Mrs. Catt to go around the world in behalf of woman suffrage. They approved the suggestion so heartily that I followed it up with a speech setting forth the whole plan and Mrs. Catt's peculiar fitness for the work. Several months later Mrs. Catt and Dr. Aletta Jacobs, president of the Holland Suffrage Association, started on their world tour; and not until after they had gone did I fully realize that the two great personal ambitions of my life had been realized, not by me, but by another, and in each case with my enthusiastic co-operation.

In 1904, following my election to the presidency, a strong appeal came from the Board of Managers of the exposition to be held in Portland, Oregon, urging us to hold our next annual convention there during the exposition. It was the first time an important body of men had recognized us in this manner, and we gladly responded. So strong a political factor did the men of Oregon recognize us to be that every political party in the state asked to be represented on our platform; and one entire evening of the convention was given over to the representatives chosen by the various parties to indorse the suffrage movement. Thus we began in Oregon the good work we continued in 1906, and of which we reaped the harvest in 1912.

Next to "Suffrage Night," the most interesting feature of the exposition to us was the unveiling of the statue of Saccawagea, the young Indian girl who led the Lewis and Clark expedition through the dangerous passes of the mountain ranges of the Northwest until they reached the Pacific coast. This statue, presented to the exposition by the women of Oregon, is the belated tribute of the state to its most dauntless pioneer; and no one can look upon the noble face of the young squaw, whose outstretched hand points to the ocean, without marveling over the ingratitude of the nation that ignored her supreme service. To Saccawagea is due the opening up of the entire western country. There was no one to guide Lewis and Clark except this Indian, who alone knew the way; and she led the whole party, carrying her papoose on her back. She was only sixteen, but she brought every man safely through an experience of almost unparalleled hardship and danger, nursing them in sickness and setting them an example of unfaltering courage and endurance, until she stood at last on the Pacific coast, where her statue stands now, pointing to the wide sweep of the Columbia River as it flows into the sea.

This recognition by women is the only recognition she ever received. Both Lewis and Clark were sincerely grateful to her and warmly recommended her to the government for reward; but the government allowed her absolutely nothing, though each man in the party she had led was given a large tract of land. Tradition says that she was bitterly disappointed, as well she might have been, and her Indian brain must have been sadly puzzled.

But she was treated little worse than thousands of the white pioneer women who have followed her; and standing: there to-day on the bank of her river, she still seems sorrowfully reflective over the strange ways of the nation she so nobly served.

The Oregon campaign of 1906 was the carrying out of one of Miss Anthony's dearest wishes, and we who loved her set about this work soon after her death. In the autumn preceding her passing, headquarters had been established in Oregon, and Miss Laura Gregg had been placed in charge, with Miss Gale Laughlin as her associate. As the money for this effort was raised by the National Association, it was decided, after some discussion, to let the National Association develop the work in Oregon, which was admittedly a hard state to carry and full of possible difficulties which soon became actual ones.

As a beginning, the Legislature had failed to submit an amendment; but as the initiative and referendum was the law in Oregon, the amendment was submitted through initiative patent. The task of securing the necessary signatures was not an easy one, but at last a sufficient number of signatures were secured and verified, and the authorities issued the necessary proclamation for the vote, which was to take place at a special election held on the 5th of June. Our campaign work had been carried on as extensively as possible, but the distances were great and the workers few, and as a result of the strain upon her Miss Gregg's health soon failed alarmingly.

All this was happening during Miss Anthony's last illness, and it added greatly to our anxieties.

She instructed me to go to Oregon immediately after her death and to take her sister Mary and her niece Lucy with me, and we followed these orders within a week of her funeral, arriving in Portland on the third day of April. I had attempted too much, however, and I proved it by fainting as I got off the train, to the horror of the friendly delegation waiting to receive us. The Portland women took very tender care of me, and in a few days I was ready for work, but we found conditions even worse than we had expected. Miss Gregg had collapsed utterly and was unable to give us any information as to what had been done or planned, and we had to make a new foundation. Miss Laura Clay, who had been in the Portland work for a few weeks, proved a tower of strength, and we were soon aided further by Ida Porter Boyer, who came on to take charge of the publicity department. During the final six weeks of the campaign Alice Stone Blackwell, of Boston, was also with us, while Kate Gordon took under her special charge the organization of the city of Portland and the parlor-meeting work. Miss Clay went into the state, where Emma Smith DeVoe and other speakers were also working, and I spent my time between the office headquarters and "the road," often working at my desk until it was time to rush off and take a train for some town where I was to hold a night meeting. Miss Mary and Miss Lucy Anthony confined themselves to office-work in the Portland headquarters, where they gave us very valuable assistance. I have always believed that we would have carried Oregon that year if the disaster of the California earthquake had not occurred to divert the minds of Western men from interest in anything save that great catastrophe.

On election day it seemed as if the heavens had opened to pour floods upon us. Never before or since have I seen such incessant, relentless rain. Nevertheless, the women of Portland turned out in force, led by Mrs. Sarah Evans, president of the Oregon State Federation of Women's Clubs, while all day long Dr. Pohl took me in her automobile from one polling-place to another. At each we found representative women patiently enduring the drenching rain while they tried to persuade men to vote for us. We distributed sandwiches, courage, and inspiration among them, and tried to cheer in the same way the women watchers, whose appointment we had secured that year for the first time. Two women had been admitted to every polling-place—but the way in which we had been able to secure their presence throws a high-light on the difficulties we were meeting. We had to persuade men candidates to select these women as watchers; and the only men who allowed themselves to be persuaded were those running on minority tickets and hopeless of election—the prohibitionists, the socialists, and the candidates of the labor party.

The result of the election taught us several things. We had been told that all the prohibitionists and socialists would vote for us. Instead, we discovered that the percentage of votes for woman suffrage was about the same in every party, and that whenever the voter had cast a straight vote, without independence enough to "scratch" his ticket, that vote was usually against us. On the other hand, when the ticket was "scratched" the vote was usually in our favor, whatever political party the man belonged to.

Another interesting discovery was that the early morning vote was favorable to our Cause the vote cast by working-men on their way to their employment. During the middle of the forenoon and afternoon, when the idle class was at the polls, the vote ran against us. The late vote, cast as men were returning from their work, was again largely in our favor—and we drew some conclusions from this.

Also, for the first time in the history of any campaign, the anti-suffragists had organized against us. Portland held a small body of women with antisuffrage sentiments, and there were others in the state who formed themselves into an anti-suffrage society and carried on a more or less active warfare. In this campaign, for the first time, obscene cards directed against the suffragists were circulated at the polls; and while I certainly do not accuse the Oregon anti-suffragists of circulating them, it is a fact that the cards were distributed as coming from the anti-suffragists—undoubtedly by some vicious element among the men which had its own good reason for opposing us. The "antis" also suffered in this campaign from the "pernicious activity" of their spokesman—a lawyer with an unenviable reputation. After the campaign was over this man declared that it had cost the opponents of our measure $300,000.

In 1907 Mrs. O. H. P. Belmont began to show an interest in suffrage work, and through the influence of several leaders in the movement, notably that of Mrs. Ida Husted Harper, she decided to assist in the establishment of national headquarters in the State of New York. For a long time the association's headquarters had been in Warren, Ohio, the home of Mrs. Harriet Taylor Upton, then national treasurer, and it was felt that their removal to a larger city would have a great influence in developing the work. In 1909 Mrs. Belmont attended as a delegate the meeting of the International Suffrage Alliance in London, and her interest in the Cause deepened. She became convinced that the headquarters of the association should be in New York City, and at our Seattle convention that same year I presented to the delegates her generous offer to pay the rent and maintain a press department for two years, on condition that our national headquarters were established in New York.

This proposition was most gratefully accepted, and we promptly secured headquarters in one of the most desirable buildings on Fifth Avenue. The wisdom of the change was demonstrated at once by the extraordinary growth of the work. During our last year in Warren, for example, the proceeds from the sale of our literature were between $1,200 and $1,300. During the first year in New York our returns from such sales were between $13,000 and $14,000, and an equal growth was evident in our other departments.

At the end of two years Mrs. Belmont ceased to support the press department or to pay the rent, but her timely aid had put us on our feet, and we were able to continue our splendid progress and to meet our expenses.

The special event of 1908 was the successful completion of the fund President M. Carey Thomas of Bryn Mawr and Miss Mary Garrett had promised in 1906 to raise for the Cause. For some time after Miss Anthony's death nothing more was said of this, but I knew those two indefatigable friends were not idle, and "Aunt Susan" had died in the blessed conviction that their success was certain. In 1907 I received a letter from Miss Thomas telling me that the project was progressing; and later she sent an outline of her plan, which was to ask a certain number of wealthy persons to give five hundred dollars a year each for a term of years. In all, a fund of $60,000 was to be raised, of which we were to have $12,000 a year for five years; $4,500 of the $12,000 was to be paid in salaries to three active officers, and the remaining $7,500 was to go toward the work of the association. The entire fund was to be raised by May 1, 1908, she added, or the plan would be dropped.

I was on a lecture tour in Ohio in April, 1908, when one night, as I was starting for the hall where the lecture was to be given, my telephone bell rang. "Long distance wants you," the operator said, and the next minute a voice I recognized as that of Miss Thomas was offering congratulations. "The last dollar of the $60,000," she added, "was pledged at four o'clock this afternoon."

I was so overcome by the news that I dropped the receiver and shook in a violent nervous attack, and this trembling continued throughout my lecture. It had not seemed possible that such a burden could be lifted from my shoulders; $7,500 a year would greatly aid our work, and $4,500 a year, even though divided among three officers, would be a most welcome help to each. As subsequently arranged, the salaries did not come to us through the National Association treasury; they were paid directly by Miss Thomas and Miss Garrett as custodians of the fund. So it is quite correct to say that no salaries have ever been paid by the National Association to its officers.

Three years later, in 1911, another glorious surprise came to me in a very innocent-looking letter. It was one of many in a heavy mail, and I opened it absent-mindedly, for the day had been problem-filled.

The writer stated very simply that she wished to put a large amount into my hands to invest, to draw on, and to use for the Cause as I saw fit. The matter was to be a secret between us, and she wished no subsequent accounting, as she had entire faith in my ability to put the money to the best possible use.

The proposition rather dazed me, but I rallied my forces and replied that I was infinitely grateful, but that the amount she mentioned was a large one and I would much prefer to share the responsibility of disbursing it. Could she not select one more person, at least, to share the secret and act with me? She replied, telling me to make the selection, if I insisted on having a confidante, and I sent her the names of Miss Thomas and Miss Garrett, suggesting that as Miss Thomas had done so much of the work in connection with the $60,000 fund, Miss Garrett might be willing to accept the detail work of this fund. My friend replied that either of these ladies would be perfectly satisfactory to her. She knew them both, she said, and I was to arrange the matter as I chose, as it rested wholly in my hands.

I used this money in subsequent state campaigns, and I am very sure that to it was largely due the winning of Arizona, Kansas, and Oregon in 1912, and of Montana and Nevada in 1914. It enabled us for the first time to establish headquarters, secure an office force, and engage campaign speakers. I also spent some of it in the states we lost then but will win later—Ohio, Wisconsin, and Michigan—using in all more than fifteen thousand dollars. In September, 1913, I received another check from the same friend, showing that she at least was satisfied with the results we had achieved.

"It goes to you with my love," she wrote, "and my earnest hopes for further success—not the least of this a crowning of your faithful, earnest, splendid work for our beloved Cause. How blessed it is that you are our president and leader!"

I had talked to this woman only twice in my life, and I had not seen her for years when her first check came; so her confidence in me was an even greater gift than her royal donation toward our Cause.

XIV. RECENT CAMPAIGNS

The interval between the winning of Idaho and Utah in 1896 and that of Washington in 1910 seemed very long to lovers of the Cause. We were working as hard as ever—harder, indeed, for the opposition against us was growing stronger as our opponents realized what triumphant woman suffrage would mean to the underworld, the grafters, and the whited sepulchers in public office. But in 1910 we were cheered by our Washington victory, followed the next year by the winning of California. Then, with our splendid banner year of 1912 came the winning of three states—Arizona, Kansas, and Oregon—preceded by a campaign so full of vim and interest that it must have its brief chronicle here.

To begin, we conducted in 1912 the largest number of campaigns we had ever undertaken, working in six states in which constitutional amendments were pending—Ohio, Michigan, Wisconsin, Oregon, Arizona, and Kansas. Personally, I began my work in Ohio in August, with the modest aspiration of speaking in each of the principal towns in every one of these states. In Michigan I had the invaluable assistance of Mrs. Lawrence Lewis, of Philadelphia, and I visited at this time the region of my old home, greatly changed since the days of my girlhood, and talked to the old friends and neighbors who had turned out in force to welcome me. They showed their further interest in the most satisfactory way, by carrying the amendment in their part of the state.

At least four and five speeches a day were expected, and as usual we traveled in every sort of conveyance, from freight-cars to eighty horse-power French automobiles. In Eau Clair, Wisconsin, I spoke at the races immediately after the passing of a procession of cattle. At the end of the procession rode a woman in an ox-cart, to represent pioneer days. She wore a calico gown and a sunbonnet, and drove her ox-team with genuine skill; and the last touch to the picture she made was furnished by the presence of a beautiful biplane which whirred lightly in the air above her. The obvious comparison was too good to ignore, so I told my hearers that their women to-day were still riding in ox-teams while the men soared in the air, and that women's work in the world's service could be properly done only when they too were allowed to fly.

In Oregon we were joined by Miss Lucy Anthony. There, at Pendleton, I spoke during the great "round up," holding the meeting at night on the street, in which thousands of horsemen—cowboys, Indians, and ranchmen—were riding up and down, blowing horns, shouting, and singing. It seemed impossible to interest an audience under such conditions, but evidently the men liked variety, for when we began to speak they quieted down and closed around us until we had an audience that filled the streets in every direction and as far as our voices could reach. Never have we had more courteous or enthusiastic listeners than those wild and happy horsemen. Best of all, they not only cheered our sentiments, but they followed up their cheers with their votes. I spoke from an automobile, and when I had finished one of the cowboys rode close to me and asked for my New York address. "You will hear from me later," he said, when he had made a note of it. In time I received a great linen banner, on which he had made a superb pen-and-ink sketch of himself and his horse, and in every corner sketches of scenes in the different states where women voted, together with drawings of all the details of cowboy equipment. Over these were drawn the words:

WOMAN SUFFRAGE—WE ARE ALL FOR IT.

The banner hangs to-day in the National Headquarters.

In California Mr. Edwards presented me with the money to purchase the diamond in Miss Anthony's flag pin representing the victory of his state the preceding year; and in Arizona one of the highlights of the campaign was the splendid effort of Mrs. Frances Munds, the state president, and Mrs. Alice Park, of Palo Alto, California, who were carrying on the work in their headquarters with tremendous courage, and, as it seemed to me, almost unaided. Mrs. Park's specialty was the distribution of suffrage literature, which she circulated with remarkable judgment. The Governor of Arizona was in favor of our Cause, but there were so few active workers available that to me, at least, the winning of the state was a happy surprise.

In Kansas we stole some of the prestige of Champ Clark, who was making political speeches in the same region. At one station a brass-band and a great gathering were waiting for Mr. Clark's train just as our train drew in; so the local suffragists persuaded the band to play for us, too, and I made a speech to the inspiring accompaniment of "Hail to the Chief." The passengers on our train were greatly impressed, thinking it was all for us; the crowd at the station were glad to be amused until the great man came, and I was glad of the opportunity to talk to so many representative men— so we were all happy.

In the Soldiers' Home at Leavenworth I told the old men of the days when my father and brothers left us in the wilderness, and my mother and I cared for the home while they fought at the front—and I have always believed that much of the large vote we received at Leavenworth was cast by those old soldiers.

No one who knows the conditions doubts that we really won Michigan that year as well as the three other states, but strange things were done in the count. For example, in one precinct in Detroit forty more votes were counted against our amendment than there were voters in the district. In other districts there were seven or eight more votes than voters. Under these conditions it is not surprising that, after the vigorous recounting following the first wide-spread reports of our success, Michigan was declared lost to us.

The campaign of 1914, in which we won Montana and Nevada, deserves special mention here. I must express also my regret that as this book will be on the presses before the campaign of 1915 is ended, I cannot include in these reminiscences the results of our work in New York and other states.

As a beginning of the 1914 campaign I spent a day in Chicago, on the way to South Dakota, to take my part in a moving-picture suffrage play. It was my first experience as an actress, and I found it a taxing one. As a modest beginning I was ordered to make a speech in thirty-three seconds—something of a task, as my usual time allowance for a speech is one hour. The manager assured me, however, that a speech of thirty-three seconds made twenty-seven feet of film—enough, he thought, to convert even a lieutenant-governor!

The Dakota campaigns, as usual, resolved themselves largely into feats of physical endurance, in which I was inspired by the fine example of the state presidents—Mrs. John Pyle of South Dakota and Mrs. Clara V. Darrow of North Dakota. Every day we made speeches from the rear platform of the trains on which we were traveling—sometimes only two or three, sometimes half a dozen. One day I rode one hundred miles in an automobile and spoke in five different towns. Another day I had to make a journey in a freight-car. It was, with a few exceptions, the roughest traveling I had yet known, and it took me six hours to reach my destination. While I was gathering up hair-pins and pulling myself together to leave the car at the end of the ride I asked the conductor how far we had traveled.

"Forty miles," said he, tersely.

"That means forty miles AHEAD," I murmured. "How far up and down?"

"Oh, a hundred miles up and down," grinned the conductor, and the exchange of persiflage cheered us both.

Though we did not win, I have very pleasant memories of North Dakota, for Mrs. Darrow accompanied me during the entire campaign, and took every burden from my shoulders so efficiently that I had nothing to do but make speeches.

In Montana our most interesting day was that of the State Fair, which ended with a suffrage parade that I was invited to lead. On this occasion the suffragists wished me to wear my cap and gown and my doctor's hood, but as I had not brought those garments with me, we borrowed and I proudly wore the cap and gown of the Unitarian minister. It was a small but really beautiful parade, and all the costumes for it were designed by the state president, Miss Jeannette Rankin, to whose fine work, by the way, combined with the work of her friends, the winning of Montana was largely due.

In Butte the big strike was on, and the town was under martial law. A large banquet was given us there, and when we drove up to the club-house where this festivity was to be held we were stopped by two armed guards who confronted us with stern faces and fixed bayonets. The situation seemed so absurd that I burst into happy laughter, and thus deeply offended the earnest young guards who were grasping the fixed bayonets. This sad memory was wiped out, however, by the interest of the banquet—a very delightful affair, attended by the mayor of Butte and other local dignitaries.

In Nevada the most interesting feature of the campaign was the splendid work of the women. In each of the little towns there was the same spirit of ceaseless activity and determination. The president of the State Association, Miss Anne Martin, who was at the head of the campaign work, accompanied me one Sunday when we drove seventy miles in a motor and spoke four times, and she was also my companion in a wonderful journey over the mountains. Miss Martin was a tireless and worthy leader of the fine workers in her state.

In Missouri, under the direction of Mrs. Walter McNabb Miller, and in Nebraska, where Mrs. E. Draper Smith was managing the campaign, we had some inspiring meetings. At Lincoln Mrs. William Jennings Bryan introduced me to the biggest audience of the year, and the programme took on a special interest from the fact that it included Mrs. Bryan's debut as a speaker for suffrage. She is a tall and attractive woman with an extremely pleasant voice, and she made an admirable speech—clear, terse, and much to the point, putting herself on record as a strong supporter of the woman-suffrage movement. There was also an amusing aftermath of this occasion, which Secretary Bryan himself confided to me several months later when I met him in Atlantic City. He assured me, with the deep sincerity he assumes so well, that for five nights after my speech in Lincoln his wife had kept him awake listening to her report of it—and he added, solemnly, that he now knew it "by heart."

A less pleasing memory of Nebraska is that I lost my voice there and my activities were sadly interrupted. But I was taken to the home of Mr. and

Mrs. Francis A. Brogan, of Omaha, and supplied with a trained nurse, a throat specialist, and such care and comfort that I really enjoyed the enforced rest—knowing, too, that the campaign committee was carrying on our work with great enthusiasm.

In Missouri one of our most significant meetings was in Bowling Green, the home of Champ Clark, Speaker of the House. Mrs. Clark gave a reception, made a speech, and introduced me at the meeting, as Mrs. Bryan had done in Lincoln. She is one of the brightest memories of my Missouri experience, for, with few exceptions, she is the most entertaining woman I have ever met. Subsequently we had an all-day motor journey together, during which Mrs. Clark rarely stopped talking and I even more rarely stopped laughing.

XV. CONVENTION INCIDENTS

From 1887 to 1914 we had a suffrage convention every year, and I attended each of them. In preceding chapters I have mentioned various convention episodes of more or less importance. Now, looking back over them all as I near the end of these reminiscences, I recall a few additional incidents which had a bearing on later events. There was, for example, the much-discussed attack on suffrage during the Atlanta convention of 1895, by a prominent clergyman of that city whose name I mercifully withhold. On the Sunday preceding our arrival this gentleman preached a sermon warning every one to keep away from our meetings, as our effort was not to secure the franchise for women, but to encourage the intermarriage of the black and white races. Incidentally he declared that the suffragists were trying to break up the homes of America and degrade the morals of women, and that we were all infidels and blasphemers. He ended with a personal attack on me, saying that on the previous Sunday I had preached in the Epworth Memorial Methodist Church of Cleveland, Ohio, a sermon which was of so blasphemous a nature that nothing could purify the church after it except to burn it down.

As usual at our conventions, I had been announced to preach the sermon at our Sunday conference, and I need hardly point out that the reverend gentleman's charge created a deep public interest in this effort. I had already selected a text, but I immediately changed my plans and announced that I would repeat the sermon I had delivered in Cleveland and which the Atlanta minister considered so blasphemous. The announcement brought out an audience which filled the Opera House and called for a squad of police officers to keep in order the street crowd that could not secure entrance. The assemblage had naturally expected that I would make some reply to the clergyman's attack, but I made no reference whatever to him. I merely repeated, with emphasis, the sermon I had delivered in Cleveland.

At the conclusion of the service one of the trustees of my reverend critic's church came and apologized for his pastor. He had a high regard for him, the trustee said, but in this instance there could be no doubt in the mind of any one who had heard both sermons that of the two mine was the tolerant, the reverent, and the Christian one. The attack made many friends for us, first because of its injustice, and next because of the good-humored tolerance with which the suffragists accepted it.

The Atlanta convention, by the way, was arranged and largely financed by the Misses Howard—three sisters living in Columbus, Georgia, and each an officer of the Georgia Woman Suffrage Association. It is a remarkable fact that in many of our Southern states the suffrage movement has been led by three sisters. In Kentucky the three Clay sisters were for many years leaders in the work. In Texas the three Finnegan sisters did splendid work; in Louisiana the Gordon sisters were our stanchest allies, while in Virginia we had the invaluable aid of Mary Johnston, the novelist, and her two sisters. We used to say, laughingly, if there was a failure to organize any state in the South, that it must be due to the fact that no family there had three sisters to start the movement.

From the Atlanta convention we went directly to Washington to attend the convention of the National Council of Women, and on the first day of this council Frederick Douglass came to the meeting. Mr. Douglass had a special place in the hearts of suffragists, for the reason that at the first convention ever held for woman suffrage in the United States (at Seneca Falls, New York) he was the only person present who stood by Elizabeth Cady Stanton when she presented her resolution in favor of votes for women. Even Lucretia Mott was startled by this radical step, and privately breathed into the ear of her friend, "Elizabeth, thee is making us ridiculous!" Frederick Douglass, however, took the floor in defense of Mrs. Stanton's motion, a service we suffragists never forgot.

Therefore, when the presiding officer of the council, Mrs. May Wright Sewall, saw Mr. Douglass enter the convention hall in Washington on this particular morning, she appointed Susan B. Anthony and me a committee to escort him to a seat on the platform, which we gladly did. Mr. Douglass made a short speech and then left the building, going directly to his home. There, on entering his hall, he had an attack of heart failure and dropped dead as he was removing his overcoat. His death cast a gloom over the convention, and his funeral, which took place three days later, was attended by many prominent men and women who were among the delegates. Miss Anthony and I were invited to take part in the funeral services, and she made a short address, while I offered a prayer.

The event had an aftermath in Atlanta, for it led our clerical enemy to repeat his charges against us, and to offer the funeral of Frederick Douglass as proof that we were hand in glove with the negro race.

Under the gracious direction of Miss Kate Gordon and the Louisiana Woman Suffrage Association, we held an especially inspiring convention in New Orleans in 1903. In no previous convention were arrangements more perfect, and certainly nowhere else did the men of a community co-operate more generously with the women in entertaining us. A club of men paid the rent of our hall, chartered a steamboat and gave us a ride on the Mississippi, and in many other ways helped to make the occasion a success. Miss Gordon, who was chairman of the programme committee, introduced the innovation of putting me before the audience for twenty minutes every evening, at the close of the regular session, as a target for questions. Those present were privileged to ask any questions they pleased, and I answered them—if I could.

We were all conscious of the dangers attending a discussion of the negro question, and it was understood among the Northern women that we must take every precaution to avoid being led into such discussion. It had not been easy to persuade Miss Anthony of the wisdom of this course; her way was to face issues squarely and out in the open. But she agreed that we must respect the convictions of the Southern men and women who were entertaining us so hospitably.

On the opening night, as I took my place to answer questions, almost the first slip passed up bore these words:

What is your purpose in bringing your convention to the South? Is it the desire of suffragists to force upon us the social equality of black and white women? Political equality lays the foundation for social equality. If you give the ballot to women, won't you make the black and white woman equal politically and therefore lay the foundation for a future claim of social equality?

I laid the paper on one side and did not answer the question. The second night it came to me again, put in the same words, and again I ignored it. The third night it came with this addition:

Evidently you do not dare to answer this question. Therefore our conclusion is that this is your purpose.

When I had read this I went to the front of the platform.

"Here," I said, "is a question which has been asked me on three successive nights. I have not answered it because we Northern women had decided not to enter into any discussion of the race question. But now I am told by the writer of this note that we dare not answer it. I wish to say that we dare to answer it if you dare to have it answered—and I leave it to you to decide whether I shall answer it or not."

I read the question aloud. Then the audience called for the answer, and I gave it in these words, quoted as accurately as I can remember them:

"If political equality is the basis of social equality, and if by granting political equality you lay the foundation for a claim of social equality, I can only answer that you have already laid that claim. You did not wait for woman suffrage, but disfranchised both your black and your white women, thus making them politically equal. But you have done more than that. You have put the ballot into the hands of your black men, thus making them the political superiors of your white women. Never before in the history of the world have men made former slaves the political masters of their former mistresses!"

The point went home and it went deep. I drove it in a little further.

"The women of the South are not alone," I said, "in their humiliation. All the women of America share it with them. There is no other nation in the world in which women hold the position of political degradation our American women hold to-day. German women are governed by German men; French women are governed by French men. But in these United States American women are governed by every race of men under the light of the sun. There is not a color from white to black, from red to yellow, there is not a nation from pole to pole, that does not send its contingent to govern American women. If American men are willing to leave their women in a position as degrading as this they need not be surprised when American women resolve to lift themselves out of it."

For a full moment after I had finished there was absolute silence in the audience. We did not know what would happen. Then, suddenly, as the truth of the statement struck them, the men began to applaud—and the danger of that situation was over.

Another episode had its part in driving the suffrage lesson home to Southern women. The Legislature had passed a bill permitting tax-paying women to vote at any election where special taxes were to be imposed for improvements, and the first election following the passage of this bill was one in New Orleans, in which the question of better drainage for the city was before the public. Miss Gordon and the suffrage association known as the Era Club entered enthusiastically into the fight for good drainage. According to the law women could vote by proxy if they preferred, instead of in person, so Miss Gordon drove to the homes of the old conservative Creole families and other families whose women were unwilling to vote in public, and she collected their proxies while incidentally she showed them what position they held under the law.

With each proxy it was necessary to have the signature of a witness, but according to the Louisiana law no woman could witness a legal document. Miss Gordon was driven from place to place by her colored coachman, and after she had secured the proxy of her temporary hostess it was usually discovered that there was no man around the place to act as a witness. This was Miss Gordon's opportunity. With a smile of great sweetness she would say, "I will have Sam come in and help us out"; and the colored coachman would get down from his box, and by scrawling his signature on the proxy of the aristocratic lady he would give it the legal value it lacked. In this way Miss Gordon secured three hundred proxies, and three hundred very conservative women had an opportunity to compare their legal standing with Sam's. The drainage bill was carried and interest in woman suffrage developed steadily.

The special incident of the Buffalo convention of 1908 was the receipt of a note which was passed up to me as I sat on the platform. When I opened it a check dropped out—a check so large that I was sure it had been sent by mistake. However, after asking one or two friends on the platform if I had read it correctly, I announced to the audience that if a certain amount were subscribed immediately I would reveal a secret—a very interesting secret. Audiences are as curious as individuals. The amount was at once subscribed. Then I held up a check for $10,000, given for our campaign work by Mrs. George Howard Lewis, in memory of Susan B. Anthony, and I read to the audience the charming letter that accompanied it. The money was used during the campaigns of the following year—part of it in Washington, where an amendment was already submitted.

In a previous chapter I have described the establishment of our New York headquarters as a result of the generous offer of Mrs. O. H. P. Belmont at the Seattle convention in 1909. During our first year in these beautiful Fifth Avenue rooms Mrs. Pankhurst made her first visit to America, and we gave her a reception there. This, however, was before the adoption of the destructive methods which have since marked the activities of the band of militant suffragists of which Mrs. Pankhurst is president. There has never been any sympathy among American suffragists for the militant suffrage movement in England, and personally I am wholly opposed to it. I do not believe in war in any form; and if violence on the part of men is undesirable in achieving their ends, it is much more so on the part of women; for women never appear to less advantage than in physical combats with men. As for militancy in America, no generation that attempted it could win. No victory could come to us in any state where militant methods were tried. They are undignified, unworthy—in other words, un-American.

The Washington convention of 1910 was graced by the presence of President Taft, who, at the invitation of Mrs. Rachel Foster Avery, made an address. It was understood, of course, that he was to come out strongly for woman suffrage; but, to our great disappointment, the President, a most charming and likable gentleman, seemed unable to grasp the significance of the occasion. He began his address with fulsome praise of women, which was accepted in respectful silence. Then he got round to woman suffrage, floundered helplessly, became confused, and ended with the most unfortunately chosen words he could have uttered: "I am opposed," he said, "to the extension of suffrage to women not fitted to vote. You would hardly expect to put the ballot into the hands of barbarians or savages in the jungle!"

The dropping of these remarkable words into a suffrage convention was naturally followed by an oppressive silence, which Mr. Taft, now wholly bereft of his self-possession, broke by saying that the best women would not vote and the worst women would.

In his audience were many women from suffrage states—high-minded women, wives and mothers, who had voted for Mr. Taft. The remarks to which they had just listened must have seemed to them a poor return. Some one hissed—some man, some woman—no one knows which except the culprit—and a demonstration started which I immediately silenced. Then the President finished his address. He was very gracious to us when he left, shaking hands with many of us, and being especially cordial to Senator Owens's aged mother, who had come to the convention to hear him make his maiden speech on woman suffrage. I have often wondered what he thought of that speech as he drove back to the White House. Probably he regretted as earnestly as we did that he had made it.

In 1912, at an official board meeting at Bryn Mawr, Mrs. Stanley McCormack was appointed to fill a vacancy on the National Board. Subsequently she contributed $6,000 toward the payment of debts incident to our temporary connection with the Woman's Journal of Boston, and did much efficient work for us, To me, personally, the entrance of Mrs. Stanley McCormack into our work has been a source of the deepest gratification and comfort. I can truly say of her what Susan B. Anthony said of me, "She is my right bower." At Nashville, in 1914, she was elected first vice-president, and to a remarkable degree she has since relieved me of the burden of the technical work of the presidency, including the oversight of the work at headquarters. To this she gives all her time, aided by an executive secretary who takes charge of the routine work of the association. She has thus made it possible for me to give the greater part of my time to the field in which such inspiring opportunities still confront us—campaign work in the various states.

To Mrs. Medill McCormack also we are indebted for most admirable work and enthusiastic support. At the Washington (D.C.) convention in 1913 she was made the chairman of the Congressional Committee, with Mrs. Antoinette Funk, Mrs. Helen Gardner of Washington, and Mrs. Booth of Chicago as her assistants. The results they achieved were so brilliant that they were unanimously re-elected to the same positions this year, with the addition of Miss Jeannette Rankin, whose energy and service had helped to win for us the state of Montana.

It was largely due to the work of this Congressional Committee, supported by the large number of states which had been won for suffrage, that we secured such an excellent vote in the Lower House of Congress on the bill to amend the national Constitution granting suffrage to the women of the United States. This measure, known as the Susan B. Anthony bill, had been introduced into every Congress for forty-three years by the National Woman Suffrage Association. In 1914, for the first time, it was brought out of committee, debated, and voted upon in the Lower House. We received 174 votes in favor of it to 204 against it. The previous spring, in the same Congress, the same bill passed the Senate by 35 votes for it to 33 votes against it.

The most interesting features of the Washington convention of 1913 were the labor mass-meetings led by Jane Addams and the hearing before the Rules Committee of the Lower House of Congress—the latter the first hearing ever held before this Committee for the purpose of securing a Committee on Suffrage in the Lower House to correspond with a similar committee in the Senate. For many years we had had hearings before the Judiciary Committee of the Lower House, which was such a busy committee that it had neither time nor interest to give to our measure. We therefore considered it necessary to have a special committee of our own. The hearing began on the morning of Wednesday, the third of December, and lasted for two hours. Then the anti-suffragists were given time, and their hearing began the following day, continued throughout that day and during the morning of the next day, when our National Association was given an opportunity for rebuttal argument in the afternoon. It was the longest hearing in the history of the suffrage movement, and one of the most important.

During the session of Congress in 1914 another strenuous effort was made to secure the appointment of a special suffrage committee in the Lower House. But when success began to loom large before us the Democrats were called in caucus by the minority leader, Mr. Underwood, of Alabama, and they downed our measure by a vote of 127 against it to 58 for it. This was evidently done by the Democrats because of the fear that the united votes of Republican and Progressive members, with those of certain Democratic members, would carry the measure; whereas if this caucus were called, and an unfavorable vote taken, "the gentlemen's agreement" which controls Democratic party action in Congress would force Democrats in favor of suffrage to vote against the appointment of the committee, which of course would insure its defeat.

The caucus blocked the appointment of the committee, but it gave great encouragement to the suffragists of the country, for they knew it to be a tacit admission that the measure would receive a favorable vote if it came before Congress unhampered.

Another feature of the 1913 convention was the new method of electing officers, by which a primary vote was taken on nominations, and afterward a regular ballot was cast; one officer was added to the members of the official board, making nine instead of eight, the former number. The new officers elected were Mrs. Breckenridge of Kentucky, the great-granddaughter of Henry Clay, and Mrs. Catherine Ruutz-Rees of Greenwich, Connecticut. The old officers were re-elected—Miss Jane Addams as first vice-president, Mrs. Breckenridge and Mrs. Ruutz-Rees as second and third vice-presidents, Mrs. Mary Ware Dennett as corresponding secretary, Mrs. Susan Fitzgerald as recording secretary, Mrs. Stanley McCormack as treasurer, Mrs. Joseph Bowen of Chicago and Mrs. James Lees Laidlaw of New York City as auditors.

It would be difficult to secure a group of women of more marked ability, or better-known workers in various lines of philanthropic and educational work, than the members composing this admirable board. At the convention of 1914, held in Nashville, several of them resigned, and at present (in 1914) the "National's" affairs are in the hands of this inspiring group, again headed by the much-criticized and chastened writer of these reminiscences:

Mrs. Stanley McCormack, first vice-president.

Mrs. Desha Breckenridge, second vice-president.

Dr. Katharine B. Davis, third vice-president.

Mrs. Henry Wade Rogers, treasurer.

Mrs. John Clark, corresponding secretary.

Mrs. Susan Walker Fitzgerald, recording secretary.

Mrs. Medill McCormack,   }

                    } Auditors

Mrs. Walter McNabb Miller, of Missouri }

In a book of this size, and covering the details of my own life as well as the development of the great Cause, it is, of course, impossible to mention by name each woman who has worked for us—though, indeed, I would like to make a roll of honor and give them all their due. In looking back I am surprised to see how little I have said about many women with whom I have worked most closely—Rachel Foster Avery, for example, with whom I lived happily for several years; Ida Husted Harper, the historian of the suffrage movement and the biographer of Miss Anthony, with whom I made many delightful voyages to Europe; Alice Stone Blackwell, Rev. Mary Saffard, Jane Addams, Katharine Waugh McCullough, Ella Stewart, Mrs.

Mary Wood Swift, Mrs. Mary S. Sperry, Mary Cogshall, Florence Kelly, Mrs. Ogden Mills Reid and Mrs. Norman Whitehouse (to mention only two of the younger "live wires" in our New York work), Sophonisba Breckenridge, Mrs. Clara B. Arthur, Rev. Caroline Bartlett Crane, Mrs. James Lees Laidlaw, Mrs. Raymond Brown, the splendidly executive president of our New York State Suffrage Association, and my benefactress, Mrs. George Howard Lewis of Buffalo. To all of them, and to thousands of others, I make my grateful acknowledgment of indebtedness for friendship and for help.

XVI. COUNCIL EPISODES

I have said much of the interest attending the international meetings held in Chicago, London, Berlin, and Stockholm. That I have said less about those in Copenhagen, Geneva, The Hague, Budapest, and other cities does not mean that these were less important, and certainly the wonderful women leaders of Europe who made them so brilliant must not be passed over in silence.

First, however, the difference between the Suffrage Alliance meetings and the International Council meetings should be explained. The Council meetings are made up of societies from the various nations which are auxiliary to the International Council—these societies representing all lines of women's activities, whether educational, industrial, or social, while the membership, including more than eleven million women, represents probably the largest organization of women in the world. The International Suffrage Alliance represents the suffrage interest primarily, whereas the International Council has only a suffrage department. So popular did this International Alliance become after its formation in Berlin by Mrs. Catt, in 1904, that at the Copenhagen meeting, only three years later, more than sixteen different nations were represented by regular delegates.

It was unfortunate, therefore, that I chose this occasion to make a spectacular personal failure in the pulpit. I had been invited to preach the convention sermon, and for the first time in my life I had an interpreter. Few experiences, I believe, can be more unpleasant than to stand up in a pulpit, utter a remark, and then wait patiently while it is repeated in a tongue one does not understand, by a man who is putting its gist in his own words and quite possibly giving it his own interpretative twist. I was very unhappy, and I fear I showed it, for I felt, as I looked at the faces of those friends who understood Danish, that they were not getting what I was giving them. Nor were they, for I afterward learned that the interpreter, a good orthodox brother, had given the sermon an ultra-orthodox bias which those who knew my creed certainly did not recognize. The whole experience greatly disheartened me, but no doubt it was good for my soul.

During the Copenhagen meeting we were given a banquet by the City Council, and in the course of his speech of welcome one of the city fathers airily remarked that he hoped on our next visit to Copenhagen there would be women members in the Council to receive us. At the time this seemed merely a pleasant jest, but two years from that day a bill was enacted by Parliament granting municipal suffrage to the women of Denmark, and seven women were elected to the City Council of Copenhagen. So rapidly does the woman suffrage movement grow in these inspiring days!

Recalling the International Council of 1899 in London, one of my most vivid pictures has Queen Victoria for its central figure. The English court was in mourning at the time and no public audiences were being held; but we were invited to Windsor with the understanding that, although the Queen could not formally receive us, she would pass through our lines, receiving Lady Aberdeen and giving the rest of us an opportunity to courtesy and obtain Her Majesty's recognition of the Cause. The Queen arranged with her chamberlain that we should be given tea and a collation; but before this refreshment was served, indeed immediately after our arrival, she entered her familiar little pony-cart and was driven slowly along lines of bowing women who must have looked like a wheat-field in a high wind.

Among us was a group of Indian women, and these, dressed in their native costumes, contributed a picturesque bit of brilliant color to the scene as they deeply salaamed. They arrested the eye of the Queen, who stopped and spoke a few cordial words to them. This gave the rest of us an excellent opportunity to observe her closely, and I admit that my English blood stirred in me suddenly and loyally as I studied the plump little figure. She was dressed entirely and very simply in black, with a quaint flat black hat and a black cape. The only bit of color about her was a black-and-white parasol with a gold handle. It was, however, her face which held me, for it gave me a wholly different impression of the Queen from those I had received from her photographs. Her pictured eyes were always rather cold, and her pictured face rather haughty; but there was a very sweet and winning softness in the eyes she turned upon the Indian women, and her whole expression was unexpectedly gentle and benignant. Behind her, as a personal attendant, strode an enormous East-Indian in full native costume, and closely surrounding her were gentlemen of her household, each in uniform.

By this time my thoughts were on my courtesy, which I desired to make conventional if not graceful; but nature has not made it easy for me to double to the earth as Lady Aberdeen and the Indian women were doing, and I fear I accomplished little save an exhibition of good intentions. The Queen, however, was getting into the spirit of the occasion. She stopped to speak to a Canadian representative, and she would, I think, have ended by talking to many others; but, just at the psychological moment, a woman rushed out of the line, seized Her Majesty's hand and kissed it—and Victoria, startled and possibly fearing a general onslaught, hurriedly passed on.

Another picture I recall was made by the Duchess of Sutherland, the Countess of Aberdeen, and the Countess of Warwick standing together to receive us at the foot of the marble stairway in Sutherland House. All of them literally blazed with jewels, and the Countess of Aberdeen wore the famous Aberdeen emerald. At Lady Battersea's reception I had my first memorial meeting with Mary Anderson Navarro, and was able to thank her for the pleasure she had given me in Boston so long ago. Then I reproached her mildly for taking herself away from us, pointing out that a great gift had been given her which she should have continued to share with the world.

"Come and see my baby," laughed Madame Navarro. "That's the best argument I can offer to refute yours."

At the same reception I had an interesting talk with James Bryce. He had recently written his American Commonwealth, and I had just read it. It was, therefore, the first subject I introduced in our conversation. Mr. Bryce's comment amused me. He told me he had quite changed his opinion toward the suffrage aspirations of women, because so many women had read his book that he really believed they were intelligent, and he had come to feel much more kindly toward them. These were not his exact words, but his meaning was unmistakable and his mental attitude artlessly sincere. And, on reflection, I agree with him that the American Commonwealth is something of an intellectual hurdle for the average human mind.

In 1908 the International Council was held in Geneva, and here, for the first time, we were shown, as entertainment, the dances of a country—the scene being an especially brilliant one, as all the dancers wore their native costumes. Also, for the first time in the history of Geneva, the buildings of Parliament were opened to women and a woman's organization was given the key to the city. At that time the Swiss women were making their fight for a vote in church matters, and we helped their cause as much as we could. To-day many Swiss women are permitted to exercise this right—the first political privilege free Switzerland has given them.

The International Alliance meeting in Amsterdam in 1909 was the largest held up to that time, and much of its success was due to Dr. Aletta Jacobs, the president of the National Suffrage Association of Holland. Dr. Jacobs had some wonderful helpers among the women of her country, and she herself was an ideal leader—patient, enthusiastic, and tireless. That year the governments of Australia, Norway, and Finland paid the expenses of the delegates from those countries—a heartening innovation. One of the interesting features of the meeting was a cantata composed for the occasion and given by the Queen's Royal Band, under the direction of a woman— Catharine van Rennes, one of the most distinguished composers and teachers in Holland. She wrote both words and music of her cantata and directed it admirably; and the musicians of the Queen's Band entered fully into its spirit and played like men inspired. That night we had more music, as well as a never-to-be-forgotten exhibition of folk-dancing.

The same year, in June, we held the meeting of the International Council in Toronto, and, as Canada has never been eagerly interested in suffrage, an unsuccessful effort was made to exclude this subject from the programme. I was asked to preside at the suffrage meetings on the artless and obvious theory that I would thus be kept too busy to say much. I had hoped that the Countess of Aberdeen, who was the president of the International Council, would take the chair; but she declined to do this, or even to speak, as the Earl of Aberdeen had recently been appointed Viceroy of Ireland, and she desired to spare him any embarrassment which might be caused by her public activities. We recognized the wisdom of her decision, but, of course, regretted it; and I was therefore especially pleased when, on suffrage night, the countess, accompanied by her aides in their brilliant uniforms, entered the hall. We had not been sure that she would be with us, but she entered in her usual charming and gracious manner, took a seat beside me on the platform, and showed a deep interest in the programme and the great gathering before us.

As the meeting went on I saw that she was growing more and more enthusiastic, and toward the end of the evening I quietly asked her if she did not wish to say a few words. She said she would say a very few. I had put myself at the end of the programme, intending to talk about twenty minutes; but before beginning my speech I introduced the countess, and by this time she was so enthusiastic that, to my great delight, she used up my twenty minutes in a capital speech in which she came out vigorously for woman suffrage. It gave us the best and timeliest help we could have had, and was a great impetus to the movement.

In London, at the Alliance Council of 1911, we were entertained for the first time by a suffrage organization of men, and by the organized actresses of the nation, as well as by the authors.

In Stockholm, the following year, we listened to several of the most interesting women speakers in the world—Selma Lagerlof, who had just received the Nobel prize, Rosica Schwimmer of Hungary, Dr. Augsburg of Munich, and Mrs. Philip Snowden of England. Miss Schwimmer and Mrs. Snowden have since become familiar to American audiences, but until that time I had not heard either of them, and I was immensely impressed by their ability and their different methods—Miss Schwimmer being all force and fire, alive from her feet to her finger-tips, Mrs. Snowden all quiet reserve and dignity. Dr. Augsburg wore her hair short and dressed in a most eccentric manner; but we forgot her appearance as we listened to her, for she was an inspired speaker.

Selma Lagerlof's speech made the great audience weep. Men as well as women openly wiped their eyes as she described the sacrifice and suffering of Swedish women whose men had gone to America to make a home there, and who, when they were left behind, struggled alone, waiting and hoping for the message to join their husbands, which too often never came. The speech made so great an impression that we had it translated and distributed among the Swedes of the United States wherever we held meetings in Swedish localities.

Miss Lagerlof interested me extremely, and I was delighted by an invitation to breakfast with her one morning. At our first meeting she had seemed rather cold and shy—a little "difficult," as we say; but when we began to talk I found her frank, cordial, and full of magnetism. She is self-conscious about her English, but really speaks our language very well. Her great interest at the time was in improving the condition of the peasants near her home. She talked of this work and of her books and of the Council programme with such friendly intimacy that when we parted I felt that I had always known her.

At the Hague Council in 1913 I was the guest of Mrs. Richard Halter, to whom I am also indebted for a beautiful and wonderful motor journey from end to end of Holland, bringing up finally in Amsterdam at the home of Dr. Aletta Jacobs. Here we met two young Holland women, Miss Boissevain and Rosa Manus, both wealthy, both anxious to help their countrywomen, but still a little uncertain as to the direction of their efforts. They came to Mrs. Catt and me and asked our advice as to what they should do, with the result that later they organized and put through, largely unaided, a national exposition showing the development of women's work from 1813 to 1913. The suffrage-room at this exposition showed the progress of suffrage in all parts of the world; but when the Queen of Holland visited the building she expressed a wish not to be detained in this room, as she was not interested in suffrage. The Prince Consort, however, spent much time in it, and wanted the whole suffrage movement explained to him, which was done cheerfully and thoroughly by Miss Boissevain and Miss Manus. The following winter, when the Queen read her address from the throne, she expressed an interest in so changing the Constitution of Holland that suffrage might possibly be extended to women. We felt that this change of heart was due to the suffrage-room arranged by our two young friends—aided, probably, by a few words from the Prince Consort!

Immediately after these days at Amsterdam we started for Budapest to attend the International Alliance Convention there, and incidentally we indulged in a series of two-day conventions en route—one at Berlin, one at Dresden, one at Prague, and one at Vienna. At Prague I disgraced myself by being in my hotel room in a sleep of utter exhaustion at the hour when I was supposed to be responding to an address of welcome by the mayor; and the high-light of the evening session in that city falls on the intellectual brow of a Bohemian lady who insisted on making her address in the Czech language, which she poured forth for exactly one hour and fifteen minutes. I began my address at a quarter of twelve and left the hall at midnight. Later I learned that the last speaker began her remarks at a quarter past one in the morning.

It may be in order to add here that Vienna did for me what Berlin had done for Susan B. Anthony—it gave me the ovation of my life. At the conclusion of my speech the great audience rose and, still standing, cheered for many minutes. I was immensely surprised and deeply touched by the unexpected tribute; but any undue elation I might have experienced was checked by the memory of the skeptical snort with which one of my auditors had received me. He was very German, and very, very frank. After one pained look at me he rose to leave the hall. "THAT old woman!" he exclaimed. "She cannot make herself heard."

He was half-way down the aisle when the opening words of my address caught up with him and stopped him. Whatever their meaning may have been, it was at least carried to the far ends of that great hall, for the old fellow had piqued me a bit and I had given my voice its fullest volume. He crowded into an already over-occupied pew and stared at me with goggling eyes. "Mein Gott!" he gasped. "Mein Gott, she could be heard ANYWHERE." The meeting at Budapest was a great personal triumph for Mrs. Catt. No one, I am sure, but the almost adored president of the International Suffrage Alliance could have controlled a convention made up of women of so many different nationalities, with so many different viewpoints, while the confusion of languages made a general understanding seem almost hopeless. But it was a great success in every way—and a delightful feature of it was the hospitality of the city officials and, indeed, of the whole Hungarian people. After the convention I spent a week with the Contessa Iska Teleki in her chateau in the Tatra Mountains, and a friendship was there formed which ever since has been a joy to me. Together we walked miles over the mountains and along the banks of wonderful streams, while the countess, who knows all the folk-lore of her land, told me stories and answered my innumerable questions. When I left for Vienna I took with me a basket of tiny fir-trees from the tops of the Tatras; and after carrying the basket to and around Vienna, Florence, and Genoa, I finally got the trees home in good condition and proudly added them to the "Forest of Arden" on my place at Moylan.

XVII. VALE!

In looking back over the ten years of my administration as president of the National American Woman Suffrage Association, there can be no feeling but gratitude and elation over the growth of the work. Our membership has grown from 17,000 women to more than 200,000, and the number of auxiliary societies has increased in proportion.

Instead of the old-time experience of one campaign in ten years, we now have from five to ten campaigns each year. From an original yearly expenditure of $14,000 or $15,000 in our campaign work, we now expend from $40,000 to $50,000. In New York, in 1915, we have already received pledges of $150,000 for the New York State campaign alone, while Pennsylvania, Massachusetts, and New Jersey have made pledges in proportion.

In 1906 full suffrage prevailed in four states; we now have it in twelve. Our movement has advanced from its academic stage until it has become a vital political factor; no reform in the country is more heralded by the press or receives more attention from the public. It has become an issue which engages the attention of the entire nation—and toward this result every woman working for the Cause has contributed to an inspiring degree. Splendid team-work, and that alone, has made our present success possible and our eventual triumph in every state inevitable. Every officer in our organization, every leader in our campaigns, every speaker, every worker in the ranks, however humble, has done her share.

I do not claim anything so fantastic and Utopian as universal harmony among us. We have had our troubles and our differences. I have had mine. At every annual convention since the one at Washington in 1910 there has been an effort to depose me from the presidency. There have been some splendid fighters among my opponents—fine and high-minded women who sincerely believe that at sixty-eight I am getting too old for my big job. Possibly I am. Certainly I shall resign it with alacrity when the majority of women in the organization wish me to do so. At present a large majority proves annually that it still has faith in my leadership, and with this assurance I am content to work on.

Looking back over the period covered by these reminiscences, I realize that there is truth in the grave charge that I am no longer young; and this truth was once voiced by one of my little nieces in a way that brought it strongly home to me. She and her small sister of six had declared themselves suffragettes, and as the first result of their conversion to the Cause both had been laughed at by their schoolmates. The younger child came home after this tragic experience, weeping bitterly and declaring that she did not wish to be a suffragette any more—an exhibition of apostasy for which her wise sister of eight took her roundly to task.

"Aren't you ashamed of yourself," she demanded, "to stop just because you have been laughed at once? Look at Aunt Anna! SHE has been laughed at for hundreds of years!"

I sometimes feel that it has indeed been hundreds of years since my work began; and then again it seems so brief a time that, by listening for a moment, I fancy I can hear the echo of my childish-voice preaching to the trees in the Michigan woods.

But long or short, the one sure thing is that, taking it all in all, the struggles, the discouragements, the failures, and the little victories, the fight has been, as Susan B. Anthony said in her last hours, "worth while." Nothing bigger can come to a human being than to love a great Cause more than life itself, and to have the privilege throughout life of working for that Cause.

As for life's other gifts, I have had some of them, too. I have made many friendships; I have looked upon the beauty of many lands; I have the assurance of the respect and affection of thousands of men and women I have never even met. Though I have given all I had, I have received a thousand times more than I have given. Neither the world nor my Cause is indebted to me but from the depths of a full and very grateful heart I acknowledge my lasting indebtedness to them both.

THE END